Houses: Regional Practice and Local Character

**Twentieth Century
Architecture 12**

Regional Practice
and Local Character

Edited by Elain Harwood
and Alan Powers

Houses

Twentieth Century Architecture is published by the Twentieth Century Society,
70 Cowcross Street, London ECIM 6EJ

Number 12/2015. ISBN 978-0-9556687-4-6

Twentieth Century Architecture Editors: Elain Harwood and Alan Powers
Text Editor: Alison Boyd
Twentieth Century Society Publications Committee: Timothy Brittain-Catlin (chairman), Barnabas Calder, Susannah Charlton, Mark Eastment, Alistair Fair, Geraint Franklin, Fiona MacCarthy, Charlotte Newman, Otto Saumarez Smith, Simon Wartnaby and the Society's trustees

Designed and typeset by Esterson Associates
Printed by Deckers Snoeck, Gent, Belgium

The Twentieth Century Society gratefully acknowledges the generous support of Marc Fitch Fund, the Milton Grundy Foundation and the Paul Mellon Centre for Studies in British Art.

Individual authors have made their own acknowledgements in their articles. We would also like to thank Malcolm Airs, Holly Catford, James O. Davies, John Goodall, Elizabeth McKellar, Adam Menuge, Lucy Millson-Watkins, Phil Sayer, Nigel Wilkins and all those who refereed the articles for publication. We would specially like to thank John East for his help with three articles.

Cover: New House, Shipton-under-Wychwood, by Stout and Litchfield
(Historic England, James O. Davies)
Back cover: Linocut of Twitchells End, Buckinghamshire, under construction,
1934, by Betty Tuke Jenkins (private collection)
Frontispiece: Flax Bourton, houses by Artist Constructor
(Historic England, James O. Davies)

Contents

Biographies

Neil Bingham is an architectural historian and curator. His most recent books are *100 Years of Architectural Drawing: 1900 to 2000* (Lawrence King, 2013) and *Masterworks: Architecture at the Royal Academy of Arts* (RA, 2011); and exhibitions at the Royal Academy, 'Dream, Draw, Work: Architectural Drawings by Norman Shaw RA' (2014) and 'Sir Hugh Casson PRA: Making Friends' (2013).

Timothy Brittain-Catlin deputy chairman of the Twentieth Century Society, is the author of *Bleak Houses*, a study of failure, loss and disappointment in architecture. He trained as an architect and has been writing about architectural history for many years, specialising at first on the Gothic Revival and, later, on its many casualties. He is Reader in Architecture, Kent School of Architecture, University of Kent.

David M. Boswell spent thirty years teaching social sciences for the Open University and three in Malta, during which he began research into the activities of the Kitson family in the arts and architecture of Sicily and Leeds. He has published articles on Kitson's villa in Taormina and his commissions from Frank Brangwyn, and the Bedford and Kitson practice. In retirement he lectures at Oxford University's Department of Continuing Education. This article is based on an Open University project of 1983.

David Davidson is Architectural Adviser to the Hampstead Garden Suburb Trust, the estate management company which acts to protect the special character of the Suburb, its buildings and its landscapes. He was a Trustee of the Twentieth Century Society from 1999 to 2012 and has chaired the Society's Casework Committee. His study of the Birmingham Arts and Crafts architect Charles Edward Bateman was included in *Birmingham's Victorian and Edwardian Architects*, published in 2009 by the Birmingham Group of the Victorian Society.

Janet Douglas is a retired university lecturer, now able to devote herself to research on her adopted home town of Leeds. She is currently chairman of the West Yorkshire Group of the Victorian Society, as well as being a member of the Twentieth Century Society. Having concentrated previously on nineteenth-century studies, she is currently working on Leeds' inter-war architecture.

Fiona Fisher is a design historian in the Faculty of Art, Design and Architecture at Kingston University, London. She is co-author of *The Picker House and Collection: a late 1960s home for art and design* (Philip Wilson, 2012). Her book *Designing the British Post-War Home: Kenneth Wood, 1948-1968* will be published by Routledge in 2015.

Elain Harwood is a historian with English Heritage and a Trustee (co-opted) of the Twentieth Century Society. She is co-editor of the Twentieth Century Journal, with books forthcoming on post-war architecture, including *Space, Hope and Brutalism* to be published by Yale in 2015, a new edition of her book on post-war listed buildings and one on new towns.

Julian Holder is Lecturer in the History and Theory of Architecture at the University of Salford. He has previously worked for English Heritage, Edinburgh College of Art School of Architecture, the Polytechnic of North London and was the Society's first Casework Officer. He edited (with Steve Parissien) *The Architecture of British Transport in the Twentieth Century* (Yale, 2005), and is currently preparing (with Elizabeth McKellar) *Re-appraising Neo-Georgian architecture, 1880-1970* to be published by English Heritage in 2015.

Alan Powers has published widely on British architecture and art of the twentieth century, and teaches at NYU London. His most recent book is *Eric Ravilious, artist and designer* (2013).

Neil Swanson is a Chartered Landscape Architect. With his design practice, Landscape Projects, Neil has completed a range of award-winning landscapes and places, including the Cockpit Garden at Richmond Castle, New Road Public Realm in Brighton, Hulme Park in Manchester and the Cathedral Steps and Square in Liverpool. Neil teaches and writes about landscape and architecture.

Matthew Whitfield is an Investigator at English Heritage and is currently in the research phases of a monograph on the architectural history of English suburbs from 1850 onwards. He is a product of the Merseyside conurbation and a devotee of this peculiarly characterful corner of Britain.

Rachel Williams is a designation adviser with English Heritage and a long-standing member of the Twentieth Century Society.

Jon Wright works as a freelancer in the fields of architectural history and history buildings conservation. A former senior caseworker at the Twentieth Century Society and head of conservation at the Council for British Archaeology, he has written and lectured extensively on the conservation of twentieth-century buildings and is currently completing his first book, on the architecture of Mervyn Seal.

Alan Powers

Houses in History: Regional practice and local character

Two previous issues of Twentieth Century Architecture have been devoted to individually designed houses: *The Modern House Revisited*, 1996, and *Post-War Houses*, 1999, but these were very far from exhausting the potential of the theme for new discoveries and interpretations.

The Modern House Revisited was defined by style and period – the modern house between the wars, characterised primarily by its flat roof. Rather than focusing on individual architects or buildings, the articles mostly explored the identity of the modern house through general themes such as their motivation, mediation, use of decorative components, conservation and presentation as house museums, across a range of examples. The 1999 volume was its post-war counterpart, mainly filled with articles on groups of houses designed by individual practices, including the first published surveys of houses by architects such as Patrick Gwynne, Robert Harvey and John Penn, each a distinctive figure with a practice based outside London, who, while removed from the spotlight of fame, were able to develop their ideas through a sequence of house designs for individual clients.

Unlike the two previous journals, we have brought together here a range of houses that cover the whole span of the Twentieth Century Society's interests from 1914 to the present. The studies of two pre-modernist architects, Edgar Ranger and J. C. S. Soutar, come at the beginning of the story, each preferring a distinctive style – neo-Tudor and neo-Georgian respectively. Their spheres of operation make an interesting contrast, for Ranger served private clients, builders and developers, while Soutar operated in the housing and planning reform movement for organisations such as Hampstead Garden Suburb which had a social mission. John Procter is included as one of a small number of architects in the 1930s who used a regional client base to enter the Modern Movement at an early date. His houses may not have all the sophistication of the younger London figures who made up the MARS Group, but Procter's work predates theirs, and achieved prominence in publications. He is one of many significant architects of the period who has never been the subject of a publication before.

Then comes a study of a single building, Twitchells End, a Modern Movement house known through its publication in F. R. S. Yorke's *The Modern House in England*, 1937, a book which excluded all background information about the architect and client. This house was researched by David Boswell in the early 1980s and the stages by which Gilbert Jenkins and his wife chose their building site and their architect is now revealed in detail from documents and family history. The Open University course A305 for which this research was originally produced fostered many valuable building studies on similar lines, often just in time to collect oral history evidence that is no longer available.

We then move on to the post-war period in Britain, which can credibly be claimed to be one of the most active and original in terms of house design. More houses were designed by architects for themselves or their close family than at any other time, and they were often manifestos for new ideas of planning and construction, as the middle classes dispensed with live-in domestic servants for the first time and experienced the spatial freedom resulting from central heating. Once building licence restrictions had been lifted in 1954, a remarkable period opened for one-off house building, stimulated by the availability of building sites and loans, combined with a distribution of architectural talent around the country and a relative tolerance towards modern styles on the part of planners. This lasted into the 1970s, when rising costs and a more conservative attitude to style combined to restrict the flow. We are delighted to have the opportunity to bring to light a number of practitioners who contributed to the richness of house design within this period, most of whom are characterised by the location of their practices outside London.

Regionality and Regionalism

Regionality denotes a geographical condition, one that in British terms implies a distance from London. In addition, it can take the form of regionalism, a mode of practice in any area of culture that relates to the geographical and cultural character of an area. This usually also means an extension of design themes from the past, most often as manifested in vernacular architecture, both in its choice of materials and its responses to weather and site, and often borrowing typical forms of building grouping, profile and plan. From the late eighteenth century onwards, regionalism has often involved the literal borrowing of historic form to create an illusion of history, demonstrated at a highly accomplished level in the work of Edgar Ranger. Ranger built houses of Kentish derivation in Kent, although his practice was not always based there. Neo-Tudor was a popular style for many decades, and while regional in origin, was liable to occur anywhere in Britain or indeed across the world.

This has never been the only approach to regional character, however. 'Critical Regionalism' in architecture defines itself as a modification of 'International Modern' in favour of transmitting local character in less direct ways. While the term only came into common use in the 1980s, it can be recognised from a much earlier point as an approach to the past and to locality based on an attempt to capture essence rather than surface, to the point where such references may pass unnoticed. In fact a sensitivity to local character and building forms had been present in modernist work in Britain and elsewhere during the 1930s, although it was seldom remarked on. Regionalism can therefore mean several different things, which may represent opposing architectural philosophies.

There is a difference between regionalism and regionality of all kinds that several articles in this collection help to explain. The first is a property of the design itself, the second a property of its conditions of production. Regionality can be a fairly straightforward outcome of an architect building a group of works in a definable geographical area in which he or she would typically be based as a practitioner. It is likely to be the consequence of an interconnected network of clients whose buildings act as a spur for further commissions, possibly combined with a friendly relationship with local planners or councillors (another feature that changed drastically in the early 1970s with the reorganisation of local government). Individual commissions might in these conditions be combined with high quality speculative developments, as we find in the cases of Jo Parker, Keith Ingham and Mervyn Seal, since there was a strong urge during this period to show the public the benefits of a more considered approach to the design of private sector housing than that normally on offer from the house building industry, responding to the kind of criticisms raised by Ian Nairn's *Outrage* special issue of the *Architectural Review* in 1955 and its sequels.

Artist Constructor owed its origin to this desire, motivated also by the challenge to develop attractive rural sites in a more sensitive way than the conventional approach that would normally begin by removing all existing trees from a site. This could be considered a form of Critical Regionalism, although there was little conscious attempt in these buildings to capture an essential local style. Regionalism may coincide with regionality, but each may equally operate independently of the other.

Who, then, were these regional practitioners? Before the war, an architect with moderate financial means might look forward to a career rather similar to that of a country doctor or lawyer, living in agreeable circumstances as part of the community of a cathedral city or a small market town, and carrying out work in a range of building types. This type of practitioner did not disappear immediately after the war, but the conditions of practice changed so that larger practices needing to cover their higher overheads tended to avoid small domestic commissions because even the relatively generous fee scale of the RIBA at that time was seldom sufficient to cover the time spent in dealing personally with clients, planners and builders to produce a unique design of relatively low value. On occasion, an exception might be made for friends and family, but otherwise one-off houses were a commercial loss maker.

For a practitioner with a local patch, not only were the overheads and staff salaries lower, but the time and expense of site visits was also reduced, and relationships with local building firms could be cultivated, these being among the unseen factors liable to lead to better quality work even on a modest budget. The idea of introducing modern architecture at a local level, with small practices attending to local needs and sensitive to local character, was an ideal often outlined in literature of the interwar and post-war years, especially by J. M. Richards, the editor of the *Architectural Review*, who in his otherwise pessimistic valedictory speech at the RIBA in 1972 'The Hollow Victory', saw in this the main hope for public acceptance of modernism and the rescue of Britain from formulaic design of all kinds. There were never enough of them, nor did they achieve critical mass in relation to the competition, but some of the examples in this journal give a sense of what Richards meant.

The example of the *Women's Journal* House of the Year built in the prosperous Liverpool suburb of Woolton in 1959-60 by a collaboration of two architects based as teachers in the famous university school of architecture in Liverpool, shows how fifty years ago the dominance of London as the centre of design fashion, consumption and media attention was taken far less for granted than would be the case today. Indeed, the vigour of regional practice that we associate with the Victorians seems to have enjoyed a post-war resurgence that reflected a more even distribution of wealth and innovation in all areas of culture that has since become progressively centripetal.

It can be seen, then, that there is a distinct difference between regionality and regionalism. The second without the first can be seen in the work of Stout and Litchfield, a small London practice that found a range of clients in rural England, some of whom were building weekend or holiday houses. Starting with the New House at Shipton-under-Wychwood, their work displayed a sophisticated understanding of the potential of Critical Regionalism, while the only sort of regionality that they displayed was in their geographical spread of commissions. On the strength of their domestic commissions, we have included two practices, Kenneth Wood and the Bowyers, who contradict the idea that closeness to London is at odds with regionality. The description of their domestic work shows how within certain parts of London, especially in the prosperous suburbs where clients for modern houses were likely to gravitate, the pattern of clustering similar to that in a provincial city region could manifest itself without any conscious intention and can still be recognised as a geographical and cultural phenomenon.

The articles in this journal indicate how the work of regionally based architects both before and after the war often pushed at the boundaries of architectural decorum within modernism at a time when enjoyment of form for form's sake was frowned upon by critics. In other words, these architects and their clients, out of the circle of metropolitan criticism, were less afraid of vulgarity than their London counterparts, and this lack of inhibition liberated them to be more creative. The remarkable work of Artist Constructor not only offered an unusual model for speculative house development but also involved a form of practice in which qualified architects occupied a subsidiary position, the buildings being designed, as the practice title indicated, in a happy alliance of form making and practical building knowledge.

As his own house indicates, Jo Parker's designs became progressively less orthodox through the course of his career, becoming precursors of post-modernism without any obvious connection to the growth of an international movement. One might pick up an echo of John Vanbrugh's condemnation of the 'tame, small, sneaking South' in these examples, since the north nurtured the talents of other makers of enjoyable and sometimes outrageous shapes, such as Ryder and Yates in Newcastle and Sam Scorer in Lincoln. Not for them a sudden change of heart and rejection of a supposed false path, but rather a steady growth in confidence and freedom.

**Figure 2. 'A pity to cut down so many trees'
a cartoon by John Craig of Aldington Craig & Collinge, 1970s (John Craig)**

As a Yorkshireman, John Procter offered a similar challenge to the assumption that modernism radiated from London before the war. At a time when the development of modernism in the north seems to have been held back by cultural conservatism and economic crisis, Procter managed to build large flat-roofed houses that surpassed in scale if not in design sophistication the few early examples of modernism south of Watford. These examples make the case for seeing regional practice as more fundamentally different to that of London than is allowed on the relatively few occasions when this has been discussed.

Regionality and Reputation

This semi-obscurity of regionality, combined with its reluctance to abide by centralised canons of taste, might disparagingly be called provincialism, even though the work in question could be inventive and sophisticated. The prejudicial use of such categories is still a problem in architectural history and conservation, as we shall discuss later, a problem caused by the relatively elementary state of knowledge that exists about architecture in Britain in respect of the whole twentieth century.

Our knowledge of what exists, or existed in former times, is largely reliant on printed sources in books and magazines, or in rarer cases, the availability of archives, but these are far from objective or comprehensive. They may simply reflect back the desire on the part of architects, wherever they were located, to have their work published, combined with the willingness of the magazines to adopt them. From around 1900, Lutyens became known almost entirely through the advocacy of *Country Life*, which undoubtedly picked a winner and continued to back him. His contemporary Detmar Blow, by contrast, remains relatively obscure owing, at least in part, to the shortage of images of his work in circulation. The same sort of comparisons could be made for other magazines, which, because they supported the cost of taking photographs and converting them into 'process blocks' for printing, tended to dictate the content of the numerous survey books on houses published between the wars and after. In other cases, it appears that the architects themselves paid for photography and took an interest in styling the houses to their fancy, as was the case with Oliver Hill, one of whose clients, Lady Greene

Figure 3. No.1 Gaston Street Bergholt, Suffolk: by Peter Barefoot, 1965, with later additions when it became his own house. Turned down for listing and demolished (Elain Harwood)

at Joldwynds, complained that once the photo shoot was finished, Hill had no interest in returning to deal with building defects.

In the post-war period, magazines such as the *Architectural Review*, *Architectural Design*, *Country Life*, *House and Garden* and *Ideal Home* maintained the pre-war tradition of publishing private houses, often depending on the architects to commission and submit photographs. Stout and Litchfield became well known after their photogenic first house was widely published with photographs by Richard Einzig, who had been an architect at the LCC before becoming a full-time photographer and had a special insight into what his contemporaries were trying to achieve. Peter Aldington – whose early work was almost entirely domestic – also employed Einzig, whose quality of work ensured a high strike rate of publication, assisted by Renate Einzig who acted as her husband's agent and, by contacting magazines in her native Germany, gave it an international exposure uncommon for a village-based practice in the 1960s.

With a few notable exceptions such as these, architects working outside London tended to neglect publicity. Interesting figures as John Penn in Suffolk and Robert Harvey in Warwickshire virtually never published their work, leaving it to posterity to discover and protect where possible. In the current collection, Mervyn Seal and Jo Parker are similarly local practitioners who, while not confined to designing houses, found in this work (including houses for themselves) an outlet for their remarkable and still only partially recognised talents. Although their houses were sometimes published, it was not always in what are seen as the mainstream architectural magazines.

If we speak of the relative obscurity of these architects and their private houses, it is from a position of knowledge limited by factors that include the accidents of publication, among which is the willingness of clients to have their houses on the pages of magazines. It is often the non-professional lifestyle magazines that reveal the best houses, including the *Women's Journal* with its impressive sponsorship of Cedarwood by Dewi-Prys Thomas and Gerald Beech.

The thematic research work of the English Heritage Post-war Steering Group between 1992 and 2002 made a significant contribution to expanding knowledge of the period, with two rounds of systematic site inspection and report writing in 1994 and 2001 by myself and Bronwen Edwards to produce recommendations for listing. The provisions of the 'thirty year rule' meant that the 1950s and 1960s were covered in

Figure 4. House at East Grinstead by Katz and Vaughan, 1962, for Fred Kibler of Grand Metropolitan Hotels. Turned down for listing in 1994 as too eccentric but survives in total dereliction (author)

a preliminary manner. Some of these recommendations were lost for many years in thickets of bureaucracy but most have recently been confirmed at ministerial level. These were intended as 'exemplars' that would set the standard for future listings, and a number of cases were deferred or rejected owing to failure to sympathise with or understand the merits of particular examples. As yet, the threads have not been picked up for the extension of the work within this span of years or beyond into the 1970s, when many more important houses were built that have now become eligible.

It is worth noting that these discoveries are often the result of the visits organised by the Twentieth Century Society, resulting in the discovery of previously unknown or forgotten regional talent. Sometimes houses come to our attention through the Society's casework, its primary purpose as a statutory amenity society, monitoring proposals to alter or even demolish buildings of the period from 1914 onwards in the United Kingdom. This was the case when Jon Wright was working for the Society and began to investigate the work of Mervyn Seal, leading also to a South Devon tour featuring his work. Articles in the 1999 journal have helped to create wider understanding of previously little-known work, leading in some cases to listing. Such alerts have stimulated the task of recording a body of past work while the architects are still living and available for interview, a process that sometimes overlaps with more official university research projects, such as Fiona Fisher's work on Kenneth Wood at Kingston University, the owner of Wood's Stanley Picker house.

Academic research can, regrettably, encourage an entropic process of investigating the same canon of buildings again and again rather than branching out in new directions with primary investigation of buildings and documents. In the case of twentieth-century architecture, the field is broad and the need to record and evaluate is urgent, since the post-war generation of houses is increasingly coming under threat from densification of suburban areas and a sense of defeat in the face of construction methods devised for an age that cared little about energy conservation. A similar problem of relying on the authority of a limited body of knowledge occurs when buildings are proposed for listing. There is a tendency to reject those by architects whose names 'we don't know' – an irresponsible attitude given how little even the best-informed experts have so far discovered about this period, especially in relation to houses in the regions. It is surely better to find out and then to assess new discoveries on their merits.

David Davidson

Context, Texture and Restraint: John Carrick Stuart Soutar at Hampstead Garden Suburb

The design and planning of Hampstead Garden Suburb is usually seen as the achievement of Raymond Unwin, supported by a team containing the best domestic architects of the early twentieth century and with Edwin Lutyens contributing the formal centrepiece and the churches. But its evolution over a period of more than thirty years owes as much to John Carrick Stuart Soutar.

Soutar succeeded Unwin as consultant architect to the Hampstead Garden Suburb Trust in 1915 and continued until his death in 1951. It was the planning and design of the inter-war Suburb that occupied most of his career. Soutar can be credited with defining the style and texture of much of the place as we see it today, faithfully continuing Unwin's vision through difficult times and economic uncertainties. As the philanthropic ideals of the early experiment were compromised by war and changing economic circumstances, Soutar's architectural contribution consisted largely of houses for the middle classes. These are often groups of houses designed as street pictures, simplified in treatment, illustrating his awareness that individual statements must be drawn into a cohesive whole by a shared palette of materials and detailing.

Soutar's architectural practice was a particular and unusual type. At Hampstead he acted as architect, surveyor, town planner, letting agent and estate manager. This meant that, on behalf of the Trust, he maintained control over the architectural context in which his own house designs were inserted. In some cases, he was able to convince a plot purchaser to dispense with the services of their own architect and retain his to produce a suitable house. The inherent conflict between producing his own designs as well as vetting the designs of others did not appear to trouble him. Aesthetically, Soutar favoured a revival of Caroline, Queen Anne and early Georgian styles, following the tone established by Lutyens in his work for the Central Square. This style, with individual variations, runs through the extensive work which flowed from his office.

Because he ran a practice that did not need to strain for attention to attract work, he remains little known. Unlike many of his contemporaries, Soutar did not publish his work. His clients came to him because of his role, clients who wanted to commission a house which displayed good taste and sound judgement. The quality of work he achieved was high because of the standards he was able to set on behalf of the Trust and which reflected property values in this part of London.

Early Career

John Soutar was born on 25 January 1881 in Arbroath and studied architecture and building construction at Dundee University College. From 1897 to 1901 he was articled to Dundee architect Thomas Martin Cappon (1863-1939), FRIBA. His older brother, Archibald Stuart Soutar (1879-1951) also became an architect. On the completion of John's apprenticeship in September 1901, both brothers moved to London to take up positions with the London County Council. They worked as architectural assistants in the Housing Department under W. E. Riley, drawing up plans for the newly fashionable cottage estates on garden suburb lines. In his RIBA Licentiate application in 1911, Soutar states that he had prepared 'working drawings of large housing schemes etc for LCC'. In such a large office the work of individuals is subsumed into the mass but Archibald Soutar's initials appear on drawings prepared for cottages on the Old Oak Estate, Hammersmith, considered to be one of the most successful of the LCC cottage estates where, according to Susan Beattie, 'the influence of Hampstead Garden Suburb's pre-1911 development was completely assimilated and the Housing Branch brought LCC cottage architecture to splendid maturity'.[1] The estate contains architectural set pieces recognisably based on Unwin's work at Hampstead.

John Soutar's Licentiate application also mentions that the brothers had, by 1911, won several prizes in town-planning competitions submitted whilst employed by the LCC. Town planning was a growing area of interest for private landowners and numerous town planning competitions were organised. After the 1909 Housing, Town

Figure 2. Nos. 9, II and I5 Turner Close (Elain Harwood)

Figure 3. Barnett Homestead, Erskine Hill, 1915-16 (Elain Harwood)

Planning etc. Act, local authorities were also empowered to prepare plans. The brothers' major success in this area was the first prize in the Ruislip Manor town planning competition of 1910, for which Unwin was the assessor. This was organised by King's College, which owned 1,300 acres at Ruislip and Northwood that it was keen to develop along garden suburb lines, and the Soutars' design was one of the first master plans under the new legislation. The form of the plan is striking in its similarities with Unwin's work at Hampstead, mixing formal Beaux Arts elements with the picturesque, retaining existing landscape features where possible and knitting the houses into this setting. A. and J. Soutar were appointed as consultant architects to Ruislip Manor Ltd in order to take the plan forward.[2]

The winning scheme was a major achievement and brought them much attention. On the back of this success they commenced independent practice in 1912, taking an office at No. 8 King William Street, The Strand. The partnership would continue for the rest of their careers. Sir Lawrence Weaver's *Cottages: Their Planning, Design and Materials* illustrates A. and J. Soutar's work at Windmill Way and Manor Way, Ruislip.[3] As well as designing their own groups of houses the scheme attracted designs by Michael Bunney, Courtenay Crickmer, Herbert Welch and Cecil Hignett, all Unwin's men from his Letchworth days and prominent in the profession.

Soutar and the Hampstead Garden Suburb Trust

On 1 December 1914, the Board of the Hampstead Garden Suburb Trust met to appoint a successor to Raymond Unwin as consultant architect. Unwin, who had guided the development of the Suburb from 1905, was to join the Local Government Board as Senior Town Planning Inspector. He left Hampstead with a master plan, and much development had taken place since the first sod was cut in June 1907. The Artisans' Quarter was largely complete.[4] Many plots for middle-class houses had been let and

houses raised, while an additional 110 acres had recently been opened for development. And in 1909, Unwin had published *Town Planning in Practice*, a manual for planned settlements that was to set the tone for the rest of the Suburb's development.[5]

Of the candidates interviewed, the Trust Board, presumably advised by Unwin, chose A. and J. Soutar on condition that John alone would take up the post. The minute book records that he would receive a retaining fee of £250 per annum and set out a scale of fees for the letting of plots, for approving plans and for laying out the next 32 acres of development.

Soutar began work in early 1915. He continued to share the King William Street office with Archie and their joint practice carried on but, within a few weeks, he had also set himself up in the drawing office at Wyldes, the farm that Unwin had converted as his home and office in 1907. Unwin continued to live next door for the rest of his life and maintained a keen interest in the performance of his successor.

The early Suburb under Unwin's leadership had developed in a very particular way. Co-partnership companies built large groups of cottages and houses; they were good clients and let their architects (good ones) get on with it, with Unwin's guidance. Because they were building whole streets and groups, based on a master plan, Unwin was able to encourage streetscapes rather than just a series of houses. Unwin also formed the Garden Suburb Development Company in an attempt to provide coherent aesthetic treatments for one-off houses and small commercial developments. In this way he raised the standard of design. When Soutar arrived, his appointment included extensive estate management and planning control functions. The Development Company had been wound up by this time and the Trust wanted someone who would carry on Unwin's role of enforcing quality control. Yet there is no record of the criteria by which plans were to be vetted and approved or refused.

By 1915, the Trust had turned its mind to providing housing for victims of the war and asked Soutar to plan a small block of bedsit flats at the edge of Little Wood for war widows. The brief was specific: 'Each flat has a living room, a recess for the bed (separately ventilated), a scullery with a bath that can serve as a table, a sink, a gas cooker, a lavatory and a tiny plot of land, as well as the use of the wash house at pre-arranged times.'[6] Soutar designed a diminutive, simplified Elizabethan manor house with an H plan, horizontal casement windows and weatherboarded half dormers. The elevations were very carefully controlled, without an ounce of frivolity. Large, undecorated chimneys rise from the ridge, and oak balconies have a utilitarian robustness. Casement windows are made wide and shallow to light the modest spaces within without admitting excessive sunlight, while the cills are kept high for privacy. The building of the Homestead was funded by a generous gift from Sir Alfred Yarrow in commemoration of Canon Samuel Barnett and opened in 1916, continuing the philanthropic impulse on which the Suburb had been founded.

Soutar also worked from 1915 on a plan for a scheme of flats on land to the east of Central Square, Southwood and Bigwood Courts, following the formal axial layout inherited from Unwin. He planned two quadrangles of flats for servicemen's widows set in elaborate terraced gardens and gave them carefully organised elevations in a ripe Queen Anne style, using purple and red brick that reflected the eighteenth-century vernacular of Hampstead and Highgate. Casements were adopted rather than sashes, for ease of use, and leaded dormers followed Lutyens's work in North Square. When the flats were eventually built the proposed terraced gardens were replaced with a more pragmatic layout and part of the site carved up into plots for new houses, reflecting the changed economic realities of the inter-war world.

Soutar fell very much in thrall to Lutyens and pored over his drawings for Central Square, amending his own drafting style accordingly. He worked closely with Lutyens over many years, supervising and in some places redesigning his Institute building in Central Square and completing a corner of South Square in a sympathetic manner.

After the war the original aim of the Hampstead Garden Suburb Trust for
providing homes for all classes was compromised by events. Provision of housing for the
working classes was largely given over to local authorities under the 1919 Housing Act.
Money was tight. In 1920 Soutar drew up plans for Associated Housing Ltd for cottages
in Brookland Close that, like much inter-war cottage design, reflected the guidance
provided by the Tudor Walters committee in its report of 1918 which set standards for
working-class housing. The emphasis was on economy and simplification. Soutar was
listed in the report amongst those who provided 'expert information' to the committee.

Brookland Close has nothing of the picturesque qualities of Unwin's pre-war work,
with their riot of gables, half dormers and artful detailing. Soutar's cottages were semi-
detached pairs arranged symmetrically, finished externally in roughcast under a hipped
roof. However, at the road junction with Brookland Rise, Soutar persuaded his client to
produce an ensemble with a bit of vigour in the Unwin tradition, with a group of eight
paired cottages with L-shaped plans to define the corners of the space. These are tile
hung with steep roofs and tall gables, and much more complex in form as befits their
position as the gateway to the group. Each pair expresses a strong horizontality enhanced
by tile hanging, long, low windows tucked under the eaves and slightly jettied gables.
In contrast, a long ridge line is punctured by heavy, simple chimneys and the main first
floor rooms are given emphasis by taller windows, some breaking through the eaves as
half-dormers. Plans are practical, with a kitchen, parlour and 'living room' on the ground
floor and three bedrooms and a bathroom above.

There had been very little movement in the letting of plots for private houses during
the war.[7] By 1919 drawings were being prepared in Soutar's office for houses in
Rotherwick Road for W. S. Gibson, a local builder who was to commission many
more from Soutar in the 1920s. The design was adapted from pre-war houses in
Rotherwick Road by Barry Parker with leaded steel casements divided by brick mullions.

Figure 5. Nos. 5 and 7
Brookland Rise, 1922
(Elain Harwood)

Figure 6. No.1
Heathgate, 1920
(John East)

Figure 7. No.3
Turner Close, 1923
(Elain Harwood)

(Overleaf)
Figure 8. No.15 Turner
Close, for T. L. Fellowes,
1923 (Elain Harwood)

This vernacular revival style became something of a theme throughout much of Soutar's output. He soaked up the influences around him to contextualise his houses and built up a language of variable elements which he utilised throughout his work to bring a consistency to the townscape he created. The external treatment was varied, and included elements of Artisan Mannerism and brick textures for visual interest such as pilasters, floating pediments, stepped panels, primitive and stylised capitals. He favoured big roofs and simple gestures, relying on strong massing and powerful chimneys to create robust forms. He rarely 'decorated' a building, relying on careful use of good materials for effect – usually brown/purple brick and clay plain tiles. Texture came from the honest properties of his materials.

From 1920, commissions for large houses picked up and Soutar began letting some of the best plots on the land between Central Square and the Great Wall. These had always been intended for the most lavish homes and Soutar designed houses to fit in with the work begun before the war by Bunney and Makins, Deane and Bradell, C. H. B. Quennell and Herbert Welch. One of the first was a very prestigious plot on the Great Wall in Heathgate let to Frederick Story, overlooking the Heath Extension. Soutar's house had two main fronts, the entrance front to Heathgate and the garden front onto the heath. The house is essentially early Georgian in style. The heath elevation is simply treated with paired bay windows on the ground floor to address the view. The street elevation is more complex. A shell hooded doorcase sits under a sash window with its decorative brick surround set in a recessed panel between two projecting wings. The setback is achieved by returning the cornice and raising the eaves height in the centre of the elevation, so that the roof plane is continuous across the width of the house. Brick corner capitals suggest pilasters to the projecting wings. This is topped with huge chimneys with corner pilasters and recessed panels. Here Soutar is adopting elements from pre-war houses nearby.

23 Context, Texture and Restraint: John Carrick Stuart Soutar at Hampstead Garden Suburb

A series of other large houses followed, both one-off designs for specific clients and quality speculative houses for local builders. Soutar contributed to a particularly good group around Turner Close that shows his different approaches – muscular, restrained, self-effacing and showy, depending on the desires of the client, but always harmonious. No.3 Turner Close stands out as a very restrained effort relying on variation of fenestration for impact. The ground floor is divided by shallow pilasters under a stepped plat band to create a logic for the integral garage that had become a necessity for houses of this type. The roof is steep and straightforward, relieved by a central hipped dormer. A simple timber pedimented doorcase on scroll brackets and leaded casements suggests a bit of provincial early Georgian, but the playful arrangement of the windows offers a reading of the internal arrangement and enlivens the façade.

No.15 Turner Close is altogether more changeful. The big roof is pulled down over the ears for comfort, through which rises a canted bay with a parapet and ball finials. A tiny dormer peeps over the top. The door is protected by a low canopy stretched sideways over the adjoining window. The tension of vertical and horizontal elements is very pleasing and slightly comic, as if two very different houses have been stuck together. To add to the complexity, the right flank elevation facing Turner Drive is given a rather surprising jettied half-timbered first floor gable over a canted bay window which seems to respond to the Sussex vernacular of Ernest Turner Powell's wildly picturesque tile-hung concoction next door. As ever, Soutar is responding to his context. For a big house, it has a strangely miniature quality.

By this date, the motor house was becoming a necessity.[8] Soutar found himself frequently reporting to the Trustees that houses built before the war were difficult to let for want of a garage. He quickly had to adapt Unwin's layouts to accommodate the automobile, inserting new motor houses into spaces between houses and, in extreme cases, creating a garage out of a sitting room and redesigning the front elevation to accommodate a garage door. This pragmatism was a theme of Soutar's time in office, having to adapt the original plan to meet the challenges of technological changes such as electricity and the car, as well as the loss of servants, whilst managing to maintain the aesthetic and social principles of the early experiment. A more wilful and progressive designer might have tried to represent these changes by adopting an element of architectural modernism, but Soutar was perfectly content to see the thing

Figure 10. The lofty
interior of the studio
at No.4 Willifield Way,
1921, for the illustrator
W. Otway Cannell.
The sitting room can
be glimpsed through
the double doors
(courtesy Litchfields
Estate Agents)

through in a consistent and seamless style. This took a strength of character that is not
immediately obvious in his work.

He nevertheless popped in the odd Arts and Crafts design for a one-off client who
wanted something a bit picturesque for his money. A house in Constable Close is based
on pre-war designs by Michael Bunney and Baillie Scott, only tidied up to remove any
trace of the flippant or the pretty. Soutar could not help himself. Backing on to the Heath
Extension on a prestigious plot, the house is designed to face away from the road and
take in the view. Two double-height bay windows face the Heath. On the road elevation
the kitchen wing projects forward with the stair tower tucked into the return, with the
main roof brought low for contrast. The usual simple, big chimneys pin the composition
to the ground.

Occasionally a client appeared with an unusual brief and a site where Soutar could
spread his wings a bit. In 1921 the artist and illustrator of medieval stories William Otway
Cannell commissioned a studio house in Willifield Way where most of the space was to
be given over to a huge work room.[9] Soutar gave him a beamed baronial hall with walls of
painted brickwork, tall leaded casements in heavy timber frames and planked doors.
A sitting room-cum-hall opened off the studio through double doors, with a kitchen to
one side and a small bedroom to the other. The stair was tucked into a back lobby and
gave access to a further first floor bedroom. This was reached from a gallery, also
opening on to the hall, from which Errol Flynn might have launched himself on to the
iron chandelier. It was all terribly romantic. The detailing of the interior is robust but
exquisite. There is a fireplace in brick and tile creasing, gas fire surrounds in deep red
ceramic tiles, Art Nouveau iron door furniture and moulded handrails to the balustrade.

As flats became more popular in the mid 1920s, offering an easily maintained home
in a landscaped setting and making the occupation of a Suburb dwelling relatively
affordable, a number of small developments popped up amongst the large houses. No.30
Wildwood Road was built for Mr E. Schnattner in 1927. Named Edgehill, no doubt
reflecting its position at the base of a slope facing south over the Heath Extension,
the three large flats are designed to appear as a country house in extensive grounds.
The garden front is centred on a full height canted bay with decorative terracotta
balustrade. Under a steep tiled roof and heavy timber cornice the fenestration suggests
a seventeenth-century inspiration. Tightly spaced cruciform leaded casements light the

ground floor rooms with arched leaded casements above. The flats are entered from a door at the side into a staircase hall, pragmatically placed for ease of access. Above is a terrace to serve the first floor flat, protected by another terracotta balustrade. To the rear is the service court and garages. The publicity for the completed building was aimed at discerning purchasers. 'This delightful Block of Three Superb Flats was designed by an Eminent Architect for the Owner, who lives in one of them. The Flats provide distinctive and labour-saving accommodation. SET IN SURROUNDINGS AND ENVIRONMENT equivalent to a position in the HEART OF THE COUNTRY yet adjacent to all Conveniences.'

Soutar was commissioned to build more flats to complete the corner of South Square after Lutyens's plan for further houses had been abandoned. Two-inch grey bricks with red dressings were adopted to tie in with the rest of the Square. Soutar's instinct to play it safe served him well. Context is all. He borrows the two storey bay window and dormer-above-dormer side elevation from Sutcliffe's 1915 pair next door but the run of the elevation is well mannered and unspectacular. Polite pulvinated doorcases, arched upper windows and shaped casement dormers are stacked into a carefully controlled grid. The massive stone-capped brick chimneys with their raised panels are lifted straight from Lutyens. However, at the rear, it all gets a bit more vigorous, with bays, gables and changeful fenestration arranged to reflect the spaces within.

Later Works

From 1930, the final phase of Soutar's house building for the Trust took place on land acquired near Kenwood House, where it laid out plots for large villas for wealthy owners. The development was partly undertaken to fund the Trust after a number of lean years when dividends on investments had not been paid. However, Soutar was determined that this commercial development would have integrity, townscape interest and a distinctive architectural character of its own, and in this he was mainly successful. There was also the inconvenience of having wealthy clients. He was successful in reining in their greater excesses, but he had to refuse a number of the designs submitted to achieve it.

The large detached houses of Ingram Avenue, Winnington Road, Kenwood Close and Spaniards Close display a prevailing early-Georgian character. Ingram Avenue was cut through the huge oaks of Turners Wood and the houses were seen as villas in a woodland setting. Most of the houses constructed were by Soutar and appear more conservative than some of his earlier work. For the moneyed classes he offered good taste over individuality. Nicholas Taylor, in a historical analysis of the Suburb for Shankland Cox's conservation study of 1971, thought Kenwood Close and the top end of Winnington Road displayed an 'unusual faithfulness to Lutyens's values in their two-coloured brickwork and well-detailed white mouldings' but referred to the houses of Ingram Avenue as 'tired expositions of good taste'.[10] This is rather unfair. The achievement of this development is the integration of potentially conflicting elements into a coherent whole. Soutar's estate management role was as important as his architectural one.

Into this setting a couple of slightly surprising 'sports' were dropped. Adrian Gilbert Scott built a house for himself in Winnington Road in Lutyens's two inch grey brick, vaguely eighteenth-century in style but with touches of Frank Lloyd Wright in its horizontality. And a rather interesting house was designed by the modernist German architect Rudolf Frankel in 1938. Despite the designer's most ardently held modernist sensibilities, Soutar insisted that the frontage was given timber sash windows to conform with the rest of the road. The result was a fascinating hybrid, now sadly demolished. One house in Ingram Avenue stands apart – a sketch design by Lutyens for his patron and friend Reginald McKenna for his son as a wedding present. Soutar turned Lutyens's sketch into a fine house in grey brick with tall red brick chimneys rising from the cornice to frame the composition, flanking projecting pavilions to the forecourt and swan necked

doorcase. Lionel Brett used a photograph of one of Soutar's big Winnington Road houses in *Things We See: Houses* as an illustration of the attributes of various architectural styles.[11] Where the modernist house says 'I am happy', the Georgian design says 'I am correct'. Soutar would have concurred.

Soutar's estate management role was praised in a commemorative brochure issued in 1937 to mark the thirtieth anniversary of the Suburb.

> It is through the control thus provided that the Board and their architect have been able to secure harmony in the street architecture … This control, though it of course to some extent limits the freedom of the individual, has in fact benefited the community as a whole by securing the establishment and maintenance of those amenities which are the principal attraction of the Estate.[12]

Similarly, in his design work, Soutar was happy to subjugate his architectural vocabulary to an overall vision, aiming for the reduction of individualism in support of the co-operative, producing a series of houses which spoke of good taste and restraint over individuality. In October 1936, Christopher Hussey wrote of the Suburb in *Country Life*: 'Architecturally, the result is an outstanding success. For this much of the credit is due to Mr. John C. S. Soutar, who succeeded Sir Raymond Unwin as architect to the Garden Suburb in 1914. It is due to him that the original plan and standard of design have been so consistently maintained, in spite of many difficulties. Besides designing a large number of buildings himself, Mr Soutar has been responsible for the supervision – in many cases the considerable alteration – of all designs submitted.'[13]

Soutar's work at Hampstead has survived remarkably well because of the restrictive covenants imposed by the original Trust and the scheme of management administered by the new one, enabling it to manage the estate as a planned whole. A number of his buildings are statutorily listed.[14] His output contributes a valuable essay on a particular strand of domestic architecture of the early twentieth century.

1. Susan Beattie, *A Revolution in London Housing: LCC Housing Architects and Their Work 1893-1914*, London, Greater London Council / Architectural Press, 1980.

2. Unwin was retained as adviser to the college. The early development of the Ruislip-Northwood scheme is covered in Philip Booth, *Planning by Consent: The Origins and Nature of British Development Control*, London, Routledge, 2003, pp.66-74 and Mervyn Miller, *Raymond Unwin: Garden Cities and Town Planing*, Leicester, Leicester University Press, 1992, pp.141-7.

3. Sir Lawrence Weaver, *Cottages: Their Planning, Design and Materials*, London, Country Life, 1926, pp.304-8.

4. The Artisans' Quarter was the name given to the area of the Suburb set aside for workers cottages.

5. Raymond Unwin, *Town Planning in Practice*, London, T. Fisher Unwin, 1909.

6. Dame Henrietta Barnett, *The Story of the Growth of the Hampstead Garden Suburb 1907-1928*, London, HGS Trust, 1928, p.70.

7. It is reported in the Trust Board minute books that Soutar wrote to Henrietta Barnett on 7 June 1915 complaining of the expense of establishing a letting office in Rotherwick Road when business was so poor.

8. As well as building a great many motor houses around the Suburb, and a motor workshop in Corringway, in 1928 Soutar designed the Scandinavian style Austin House, Castle Street, Worcester, for the motor dealer H. A. Saunders. It contained a car showroom and workshops. The building was listed grade II in 2012. He also designed a house for Saunders in 1926, next to his own on Turner Drive, overlooking the Heath Extension.

9. The artist was sometimes known professionally as Otway McCannell. The house was later bought by the prolific maritime artist Kenneth Shoesmith, who provided a suite of murals for the Queen Mary in 1936. See the Shoesmith Society website: http://www.shoesmithsociety.org/s/Welcome.html. Artists were attracted to the Suburb from the outset and a number of studio houses were built.

10. Shankland Cox and Associates, *Hampstead Garden Suburb: A Conservation Study*, London, The New Hampstead Garden Suburb Trust Ltd, 1971.

11. Lionel Brett, *The Things We See – No. 2: Houses*, London, Penguin Books, 1947.

12. *Hampstead Garden Suburb: its Achievements and Significance*, London, HGS Trust Ltd, 1937, p.12.

13. Christopher Hussey, 'Hampstead Garden Suburb: Thirty Years of a Great Experiment', *Country Life*, vol.80, no.2074, 17 October 1936, pp.408-14.

14. There are 21 buildings on the Suburb by Soutar that have been included on the statutory list. The South Square flats are grade II*.

Timothy Brittain-Catlin

2

Picturesque, Modern, Tudor-Style: Edgar Ranger in Thanet

In this case it is the estate agents who have got it right. Advertisements for houses in Thanet at the easternmost tip of Kent designed by the interwar neo-Tudor architect Edgar Ranger proudly display his name – even describing him, in one recent case, as 'the nationally and internationally known architect'.[1] As early as the 1930s, when they were only a few years old, sales particulars recognised that these were well designed and detailed houses by an 'artistic' architect. But English Heritage, on the other hand, has rejected several applications for listing, and until the new edition of 2013, the Pevsner, John Newman's *North East and East Kent,* had failed to mention any of them.[2]

Yet these are fine buildings: even when glimpsed from the street they are notably superior to the large number of neo-Tudor villas in which Thanet excels. The high quality of their brickwork and detailing continues all the way around to the back, in contrast to the many where the best facing bricks stop just beyond the edges of the front elevation, and render and inferior ironmongery take over at the rear. Ranger's houses have a number of identifiable characteristics, and for those who enjoy inter-war neo-Tudor they provide plenty of reasons to defend the style against those critics who find it unimaginative and repetitive. Most significantly, perhaps, they show what happened to the legacy of mid-late nineteenth-century architects – the ones who might be called 'architects' architects' – when prolific provincial ones were inspired by them. A new story about how things worked out over the early decades of the last century starts to emerge. And yet as is so often the case, the range and the professional environment of localised architects such as Ranger – who chose an aesthetic ignored by mid-century critics and failed to present a useful set of ordered documentation – have conspired to ensure that their work has been all but forgotten.

Ranger built some forty houses in Broadstairs and Cliftonville, excluding various extensions and minor works, and about the same number of houses elsewhere. Some are large villas; many are middle-sized or small suburban houses. Nearly all of the Thanet buildings survive, but there has been at least one prominent casualty and several have been badly mutilated. Only Long Barn is listed. His largest work was the atypically Italianate Thanet Place, for Sir Edmund Vestey, designed in collaboration with Sir Charles Allom and which appears briefly in Clive Aslet's *The Last Country Houses.*[3] Thanet District Council has not retained records of any inter-war building applications, and nor has the Thanet contractor W. W. Martin, which built many of the houses, retained their copies of plans; those who know most about the houses are the residents themselves who, even if they are not descendants of Ranger's original clients, stay in touch with each other intermittently and exchange information and experiences.

One important single source of information, however, may yet prove to be the salvation of Ranger's reputation. In 1996 his son Anthony collated lists of his father's projects with dates, costs, and clients' names. He also compiled a separate list for the Thanet houses, giving street addresses for most of them. The main list is bound together with a collection of photocopies of the many articles published during his father's lifetime on his work: he was a particular favourite of *Ideal Home*, a monthly produced by the *Daily Mail* and linked to the annual Ideal Home Exhibition in London, and, apparently, of *Homes and Gardens*, but his houses also appeared in the German magazine *Innen-Dekoration*; some of his ideas for remodelling dilapidated London terraced houses, probably the result of his war work, appeared in *The Builder*. Ranger junior, who died in 2009, distributed the compilation amongst the present-day residents of his father's houses. He also gave one to the architectural historian Nick Dermott, who had recently joined the district council's planning department, and it is from that copy that much of this description of Ranger's life and career is based.

Ranger was not a Man of Kent. He was born on 8 September 1888 in East Peckham near Tonbridge on the far side of the county, and started his career in Gerrards Cross in Buckinghamshire, where he was articled from 1906-09 to Kerkham, Burgess & Myers. The practice, of two architects and a surveyor, was a new one, established following the

Figure 2. Poynings, on the North Foreland Estate to the north of Broadstairs, designed for William Morris in 1924. The half-timbered first-floor bathroom, left, was added four years later (Timothy Brittain-Catlin)

Figure 3. The porch bay on the north-west side of Poynings: the front door is hidden within the recess. Ranger occasionally designed half-timbered sections of wall that looked as if they reused old materials (Timothy Brittain-Catlin)

opening of the railway connection with London; Julian Gulson Burgess (1876-1933) was the nephew of the Leicester and London architect Edward Burgess.[4] Another young architect to join the practice that year was Walter Holden (1882-1953); in time Holden became a partner, changing the name of the practice to Burgess, Holden and Watson, although he soon achieved a reputation as the principal designer of branches of the National Provincial Bank.[5] The office that Ranger joined was kept busy designing neo-Tudor houses, mainly half-timbered and rendered, for the fast-growing estates that make up the Edwardian town; it also designed the prominent row of shops with oriel windows and rendered gables over jettied upper storeys close to the railway station on Packhorse Way.[6]

Ranger's own houses were neo-Tudor from the start; there are very few exceptions. He reused favourite ideas for new clients in different places with variations only in detailing. The first house in Anthony Ranger's compilation is Old Basing, of 1913, built by Edgar for himself in time for his marriage, followed by Cottered of 1919. The two houses are located in neighbouring plots, in Austenwood Lane, Gerrards Cross: both are vernacular late Tudor, with tile-hung upper storeys and tall chimneys; the small porch at the inner corner of Old Basing, at 45 degrees between the wings, was developed into a more significant bridging feature at Cottered, suggesting (not quite accurately) a butterfly plan. Ranger almost copied the Cottered plan and elevation for his Poynings of 1924, one of his first houses in Broadstairs. It is a plan that makes sense for villas set in relatively small square suburban plots, because the wings can enfold a private garden whilst keeping it quite separate from the entrance arrangements nearby. An article illustrating Old Basing in the *Studio Year Book of Decorative Art* for 1913 shows an 'old English' panelled dining room which was also repeated in style and character in countless houses to come. The design of the motor house – by the 1920s already called a 'garage' on Ranger's plans – was generally incorporated into that of the house, or otherwise formed part of the overall composition of the scheme.

But if Ranger used a relatively small range of architectural devices, and even reused house names including Old Basing, he compensated with originality of detail, particularly in its frank archaism. At Poynings an irregular timber frame, which looks (as does some of the interior carpentry) as if it might have been reused from an old building, as possibly it was, encases equally irregular herringbone brickwork nogging.

Figure 4. The south front of Barn Jet, the finest house in Ranger's first Broadstairs cluster, seen from Park Road. It was designed in 1927 for Archibald Martin, the proprietor of the local contractors who built most of his houses (Timothy Brittain-Catlin)

A jettied, hipped and oriented bathroom extension of 1928 to the same house is frankly quaint.[7] Ranger's wrought-iron ironmongery and fine leadwork are more substantial than they are in run-of-the-mill houses, with the decorative ornamentation of the lead rainwater hopper and downpipe different for each house. Ranger also liked stylish gimmicks such as a telephone niche or an en-suite cocktail cabinet big enough to stand in. Unlike the Gerrards Cross ones, the first Thanet buildings have corner windows. In several houses, including his own, there is a 'charming' studio (as described by a contemporary estate agent) over the garage, reached in at least three cases, again including his own, by a picturesque timber ladder.

Although Ranger's work at first glance may suggest Osbert Lancaster's 'Stockbrokers Tudor', his high quality archaisms pay tribute to George Devey, that architect's architect.[8] Some of Devey's best houses – constructionally, meatily 'real', gratifying, and aesthetically winsome – are located in both east and west Kent. Ranger spent the years 1909-11 sketching in Kent and Sussex, according to his son, and Devey's Leicester Square of 1848-51, at Penshurst, is but a young man's short bike ride from Ranger's Tonbridge.[9] Ranger's quaint timber ladder stairs surely owe their origins to Devey's home farm range at South Park nearby, built in 1850, and like Leicester Square easily visible from the public road. If nothing else buildings like these, whether Devey's or Ranger's, demonstrate John Ruskin's contrast between roughness and delicacy, and much else, changefulness included; it is odd how most interpretations of neo-Tudor fail to recognise that. One of Ranger's largest, but oddest, early schemes was for the remodelling of Stanmore Manor in Middlesex, which in 1926 he turned from a shapeless but inoffensive late-Victorian tile-hung 'Wimbledon Transitional' building called The Croft, vaguely Arts and Crafts, into something that looks a bit like a set design for a creepy, irregular, sprawling half-timbered olde-Englishe mansion.[10]

Anthony Ranger did not explain what brought his father to Broadstairs, the middle and most genteel of the three Thanet towns, but according to Anthony's son Simon he had regularly holidayed there before the First World War, in a flat above a shop facing onto the tiny square on Harbour Street which leads down to the jetty and the beach.[11] According to his nomination papers to join the RIBA as a Licentiate, he ran his own office in Gerrards Cross from 1911-15, and, after enlisting, ended the Great War as a lieutenant with the 7th Queen's Regiment in France.

The client of the first recorded executed house was a Mr Chapple, who commissioned Old Tolmers in 1923. Ranger houses seem to have been built in clusters, one happy customer perhaps recommending his architect to the purchasers of neighbouring plots, and Old Tolmers now sits at the centre of an impressive Ranger group. It is located at what was then the end of the built-up part of Stone Road, which leads north from the centre of Broadstairs towards the North Foreland lighthouse and the strange collection of mid-eighteenth-century follies at Lord Holland's estate at Kingsgate. In 1923 he designed Chaileys, next door to Old Tolmers, for Archibald Martin, the second-generation proprietor of W. W. Martin who erected most of Ranger's houses; then came Noran Cottage behind them to the west at No.42 Castle Avenue, one of a recent estate of streets named after chess pieces and which provides ample opportunity to compare Ranger with contemporary Rangeresque.[12] A fourth house dated by Anthony Ranger to 1923 is Little Campden at No.2 Park Road almost directly opposite Chaileys; the client was a Rev. W. Ranger, and Simon Ranger says that this was probably Edgar's uncle William, a vicar in Kensington. The finest house of this group is the slightly later Barn Jet (1927) at No.3 Park Road, the second house built for Martin. According to one Ranger family connection, the architect himself lived here briefly at some point, suggesting that he was managing to circumvent the prohibition on RIBA members acting as property developers.[13] It was also the only one of this cluster to have been published, and deservedly so. Although rendered on the upper floor, unusually for Ranger, it was picturesquely and stoutly framed of oak. It has a sleeping balcony on the easternmost corner, and is set in a dell behind what is still a pretty although much reduced garden on the road side.[14]

These clusters of Ranger houses are mostly built in the estates which had been first laid out in the early years of the century around the pleasant beaches outside Broadstairs town centre: on or by the North Foreland estate just beyond Stone Road to the north; and Dumpton Gap, to the south west, off the new Ramsgate Road. During the inter-war years empty sites there filled up fast. The most delightful of all of the clusters is, however, the one which sits around Callis Court Road, the old route from St Peter's, the inland medieval core of modern Broadstairs, out to Joss Bay at the easternmost tip of Thanet. It was the extension northwards of a stretch of road nestling below the railway track called Beards Hill, now Bairds Hill, which is noted for the fact that the architect M. H. Baillie Scott was born in one of its five houses in 1865. It is not known which of these, nearly all nineteenth-century, Scott emerged from – but it is tempting to imagine that it was the fine sixteenth-century half-timbered one that has survived in the shadow of what was then the new railway line, making him the product of an agreeable melding between the ancient and modern.

Ranger's own first Broadstairs house, Long Barn, was completed in 1925 about 450 yards north of this poignant location. Did he know who had been born there? Anthony Ranger mentions Scott as the first of his father's two declared influences, alongside Edwin Lutyens, so very possibly he did. As Alan Crawford has put it, Baillie Scott's houses 'say "Home sweet home" so sweetly', and so do Ranger's; as *Ideal Home* put it, his work showed 'a fine geniality of atmosphere'.[15] It is fair to surmise that Ranger was

Figure 5. Ranger's own house, Long Barn, was originally completed on a small scale in 1925 but he continued to extend it in a similar style as late as the 1950s (John East)

Figure 6. Long Barn's staff cottages and garage on Callis Court Road (1932), opposite the main house (John East)

positioning himself in the same field as his hero. Long Barn has a long south elevation divided into three gabled bays, but the ground floor originally contained only a single large reception room and a separate dining room in addition to the kitchen and offices. The living room was dividable by curtains, an economical homage to Baillie Scott's ideas about versatile planning. In the entrance forecourt and attached to the dining room Ranger built a garage, with a timber ladder leading to his picturesque studio above; this was heated by a characteristic archaism, a Tudor-Gothic corner fireplace in rough brick. Here he worked alone but for a typist and, at busy times, a copyist for drawings; he also maintained an office at No.9 Gray's Inn Square in London. The architectural editor of what appears to be *Homes and Gardens* – it is not possible to identify the publication title and its date from Anthony Ranger's compilation – managed to fill two pages of text with a description of the house – stretched out somewhat to include glib poetic references to Thanet's sands and breezes – and this no doubt served as a useful advertisement. The house, now listed, also appeared in *Architecture*, in January 1926, and in *Country Life*.[16]

The cluster around Long Barn came a little while afterwards: in 1932-33, as he was leaving Broadstairs, Ranger enlarged the house for Joshua Levitt by building out the central bay on the garden side and extending the house to the west; he also built a large staff house with garages on the other side of Callis Court Road.[17] Just beforehand he designed Oak Cottage for another Levitt, perhaps a brother, immediately to the south of the staff house. Oak Cottage has a prominent decorative, pargetted gable to the roadside, by then another Ranger feature, and a fine fireplace. In 1932 he designed a small master's house for St Peter's Court boys' preparatory school at what is now No.29 Sowell Street, just a hundred yards to the south of Baillie Scott's birthplace.[18]

The two other clusters are less concentrated but contain between them many houses of interest. One is to the north of the Stone Road / Park Road cluster and includes several houses on the North Foreland Estate, and the other is to the south of Broadstairs inland from Dumpton Gap. The worst loss to Ranger's work in Thanet was the demolition in 2007 of Edgecliff, later Sheridans, on the southernmost edge of the North Foreland group. This was a long narrow house like Long Barn, although larger, and was designed in the same year; as before, the lower storey was brick, and the upper one tile hung, with a single half-timbered bay at one end, the structure of which projected slightly outwards from base to eaves. Built for Arnold Leiner, Edgecliff was published in 1928, together with a short article by Ranger and views of two other of his houses, in the German journal *Innen-Dekoration*, a considerable tribute to the architect considering that only four other non-German-speaking architects were illustrated in the magazine that year, all world famous: Barry Parker, Henry van der Velde, Jin Watanabe from Japan, and Frank Lloyd Wright.[19]

Poynings, mentioned above, was just to the north of Edgecliff, and a cottage called The Little House, now subsumed into a much larger building, was close to the end of its drive. To the west of Edgecliff a large house on Stone Road itself originally named Pines Hurst, now North Foreland Manor, appears more or less intact from a distance but was partly altered and rebuilt following bomb damage. It was built for W. H. Thompson, the Ramsgate brewer, who required balconies with sea breezes for his disabled son.[20] A fine survivor with something of the quality and character, if not the scale, of these two is Windy Ridge, at the northern end of the estate just below the North Foreland lighthouse.[21] It was built in 1926 for A. P. Cork and has survived unchanged, complete with a 'charming study or boudoir' with an eyebrow window above the garage at the narrow north end as admired by the estate agents. In their sale particulars, printed for its only subsequent resale in 1936, they described the house as a 'Picturesque Modern Tudor-Style Residence' and drew attention not only to its 'grand sea views' but also to the fact that it had been designed by 'the artistic architect, Mr Edgar Ranger'.

Much the most unusual building of this cluster, however, is the large Italianate

Figure 7. Oak Cottage, designed for Percy Levitt (1933) and located a few yards south of the staff building on Callis Court Road, features a prominent gable with fine ornamental plasterwork. The north wing, just visible on the left, is a recent extension (John East)

mansion called Thanet Place designed and built by Ranger in 1926-28 in collaboration with Sir Charles Allom for Sir Edmund Vestey, the beef magnate. Vestey had returned to Britain in 1919 from business operations in Argentina, where he and the family firm had based themselves to avoid the high rates of British taxation; according to a biographer, he failed to convince a royal commission to change the law in his favour, but in 1921 he both acquired a baronetcy and devised a complex scheme that reduced his tax bill to his satisfaction.[22] He also remarried, and decided to build a house on a site that would allow him to watch his ships passing through the English Channel. This is the only building designed by Ranger in an Italianate style, and it seems likely that the idea for it came from Allom, grandson of the architect of many of the houses on the Ladbroke Estate in Notting Hill and himself a high-class decorator: his firm, White Allom, had worked at Buckingham Palace and St James's Palace for Edward VII, at the Frick mansion in Manhattan during the First World War and for Queen Mary.[23] A reasonable assumption is that Allom, having sketched out his idea, referred Vestey to a local architect who could complete the design and supervise the project.

Thanet Place is a curiously unsatisfactory building. Its site was always relatively small, about seven acres, so it feels as if it is crammed onto it, especially since the house faces south-west rather than east towards the sea. There is something spindly about the colonnade that runs around it, and the detailing seems crude: it is tempting to condemn it as the product of a tax avoider who preferred a decorator to an architect. Yet Anthony Ranger's list includes building costs and this one is given as £100,000 – a colossal sum. It is hard to see what it was spent on: surely even the interior decorating, carried out by Allom's own firm and which included an Aeolian organ and an innovative window detail that drew the attention of *The Builder*, did not soak up so huge an amount?[24] Was the house expensively equipped with up-to-date technology within? Did the evasive Vestey build large, secret, underground chambers, as many in Thanet have historically done? For the chalk beneath is soft and as, for example, a Victorian view of the West Cliff in

Figure 8. The entrance
hall of Edgecliff, as
seen by readers of
the German journal
Innen-Dekoration
(1928). The house
was demolished
a few years ago
(Architectural
Association Library)

nearby Ramsgate will demonstrate, it was once fashionable to build rooms with impressive sea views into the cliffs. *The Builder* published a photograph of Thanet Place's only large room, the oak-panelled but sparse central lounge hall and staircase; as these have recently been subdivided out of existence it is difficult to assess what merit they might have had as spaces.[25]

Allom's interest does not seem to have extended as far as the lodge, or the coach house, modestly called the 'garage building'. These are clearly Ranger's work, designed in his usual style: Anthony Ranger's compilation includes a cutting from the *Daily Express* of 1927 pointing out that these, being in the 'Queen Anne style', will provide 'a contrast' to the main house. Ranger may at least have charmed Hannah Vestey, his client's daughter, because he completed a large residence for her in Dixwell Road, at the western end of The Leas, in Folkestone, in 1930. This is more akin to his usual style, a sort of regularised Tudor – inter-war Jacobean, perhaps.[26] In the Thanet Place cluster Ranger also designed a small master's house for Stone House School, one of the many 'high-class' boys schools in the area referred to by the vendors of Windy Ridge, and located opposite Pines Hurst.

The new estate around Dumpton Gap at the other, southern, end of Broadstairs was more modest than North Foreland, with smaller plots. Ranger designed three houses in Waldron Road, one street back from the sea front: one large one of 1926, Corner House, at the junction with Leyborne Road at the northern end, and two smaller ones, Three Gables (No.32, 1924) and Clanna (No.18, 1934).[27] On Park Avenue, to the west beyond the Ramsgate Road, the plots were bigger: he designed Ladram at No.38 with picturesque, irregular half-timbering and brick nogging in 1924 and, five years later, Walcheren, at No.52. This latter house attracted the attention of a writer of an article for another unidentified magazine – perhaps *Homes and Gardens* again – included in Anthony Ranger's compilation. This article too has an overstated feel to it – the house, in reality a small suburban villa recessed slightly from the building line, is described here

Figure 9. Windy Ridge
(1926) was the smaller
forerunner of Edgecliff
at the opposite,
northernmost tip of
the North Foreland
estate, and is seen here
from the south east.
The house has not
been altered since it
was built in 1926
(Timothy Brittain-
Catlin)

as a 'delightful country house stand[ing] well back from the road' – but the three pages of text and illustrations show a pleasant home with 'silvery toned oak' features in the stair hall and an ornamental fireplace wall. A close look at the house today reveals some very pretty ornamental plasterwork – this is, unusually for Ranger, a mostly rendered building – including pargeting around the front door and a fine band of foliage above the upper-storey windows. A little later, in 1934, Ranger added the small Dove Cottage at No.40.[28]

Ranger's pre-war work in Broadstairs also included two fine pairs of semi-detached houses on Crow Hill and King's Avenue: they form a mini-cluster with Bradstow Lodge, a cottage on the former. There is also a charming, tiny flower shop of 1925 near the railway station with a Deveyesque combination of stone and brick on its street front, which has survived (with rear additions) as a Quaker meeting house, and there are various other cottages, garages, extensions, alterations and outbuildings.[29] The great advantage of the Tudor style is that additions can be added subtly and graciously: even a practised eye would be unlikely to be able to distinguish, at Ranger's own Long Barn for example, the parts of the house that were added later, and whether they date from the 1930s or even the 1950s. In Cliftonville, the easternmost part of Margate to the north-west of Broadstairs, Ranger built houses either side of Rutland Avenue: the picturesque, oak-lined Five Ways of 1924 at No.44 Devonshire Gardens; and Bretaye at No.36 Princes Gardens the following year, with a large budget the size of that of Edgecliff. He also designed a much smaller house at No.6 Avenue Gardens nearby.[30]

During this period Ranger occasionally built elsewhere: the remodelling of Stanmore Manor has been mentioned, and this project included a large gatehouse. Anthony Ranger's compilation includes a substantial house in Wimbledon of 1926 based around an uncharacteristic large staircase hall – 'Aldwych Farcical' in style, if one may return to Osbert Lancaster for a moment – called Old Court, with a canted bay like that at Edgecliff, pointed timber windows and more brick nogging. He designed another house called Long Barn, also with a den reached by a timber ladder, this time at

Figure 10. Thanet
Place, a large house
on a relatively small
site designed in
collaboration with Sir
Charles Allom. This view
from the west shows
part of the garden front
just before the recent
conversion of the
building into flats
(John East)

Portsdown Hill in Hampshire, in 1931. The following year he built a somewhat functionalist restaurant not far away at the Clarence Pier at Southsea: 'a dream café come true' according to the local paper, but if so it was one which was short lived.[31] He also designed an exhibition pavilion for display at the London Olympia in 1934 for Thomas Lawrence and Sons, the well known Bracknell brickworks.[32] In fact from the late 1920s onwards he was carrying out plenty of work in Hampshire and the Home Counties.

In 1934 Ranger moved from Broadstairs to Marlow in Buckinghamshire, where two years beforehand he had built himself a house: again, Anthony Ranger did not explain why. Broadstairs is at the far end of a peninsular, and possibly his father had felt that it was too inconvenient to spend so much time travelling to visit sites, especially if the estates where he had done his most rewarding work were now almost fully developed. In 1936 he designed Spinfield, a large house in Marlow that at £8,500 was bigger than any of his projects beyond those for the Vestey family; possibly this was the commission that caused him to leave the town. He came back to Broadstairs after the war mainly for old clients, it seems. He added a further building at St Peter's Court boys' preparatory school, designed a small cottage adjacent to one of his earlier houses in Luton Avenue, and made further additions – a flat over the garage – to Long Barn for its new owner. Ranger also built three pairs of semi-detached houses for W. W. Martin on the corner of Bromstone Road and Ramsgate Road, and in 1962-63 designed a final house for Archibald Martin: Woodside, behind Long Barn, thus augmenting his Callis Court Road cluster.[33] The style of these late houses is still neo-Tudor, if it is anything, although now they are simply designed in brick alone. But for the most part, the productive Thanet chapter of his career was over.

From Anthony Ranger's compilation one can see examples of the many houses that Ranger went on to build. Some are large and impressive, such as Arran Court in Purley, Surrey, with its decorative pargetted gable reminiscent of that at Oak Cottage in Broadstairs; several reuse or readapt a few major features such as the timber steps to up the den. The houses are spread all around villages on the outskirts of London: the cluster phenomenon of a small town at a time of rapid development was a thing of the past, and Ranger's work now joined that of many others building at the time. Thus the Thanet period of his life is a story in its own right.

There are other reasons, too, why this is the case. Look at the photographs of his houses in Marlow, Bray, Purley, Arkley, and the others, and you will see them sitting in lush gardens or well-tended suburban settings. Those at the easternmost point of Thanet are, on the other hand, for the most part located on sites that were then – and still are – unremittingly bleak, the best efforts at gardening scarcely coaxing recalcitrant shrubs to rise more than a metre or so. *Country Life*'s correspondent when reviewing Long Barn in 1925 observed that the house's site had 'no trees and not a single feature of natural beauty', and furthermore thought that Ranger's tall narrow chimneys made the scene look even bleaker.[34] It seems part of the overlooked history of neo-Tudor building in the 1920s and 1930s that these were houses that tried to create not only pleasant, reassuring elevations and interiors, but also a kind of broad ambience that extended from building to building, and across the gardens between them: Joan Hunter Dunn might be found at tennis there. Ranger's clusters of houses are almost big enough to have that effect, but the harshness of the local landscape has largely defeated them. They want to be optimistic, ambitious buildings trying to bestow, retrospectively, a sunny attitude onto the most humble Elizabethan domestic architecture that no doubt the original only very rarely possessed. They are trying then, like much architecture, to 'recreate' a non-existent romantic past. It was a guess that Baillie Scott was born in the pretty half-timbered house by the railway bridge; perhaps, in fact, he was born in one of the plain Victorian villas and longed for the whole of his life to recreate the dream world of the Tudor one next door.

Acknowledgements: I would like to thank Nick Dermott, Lianne Clark, Eleanor Gawne at the Architectural Association Library, Mr and Mrs John Icke, John Martin, Chris Meredith, John Newman, Simon Ranger, Mr and Mrs Stephen Samuels, Irénée Scalbert, Karen Severns, Mosette Broderick, Ross Finocchio, John East and Robert Owen for his contribution to the photographic editing. This article is for Keith Diplock

1. This is from the recent sales particulars for Five Ways, Cliftonville (1924): http://www.zoopla.co.uk/ for-sale/details/15913662, accessed 1 December 2013.

2. An application to list Pines Hurst, by Ranger (see below), was rejected on 10 August 2004 because of post-Ranger alterations to the house, some of them following bomb damage, but some recent: case note 156822. But of course houses are altered when they are not listed, and they are not listed because they are altered. The most recent *Buckinghamshire* Pevsner (1994) is a little better, including two houses out of the many that Ranger designed in the county.

3. Clive Aslet, *The Last Country Houses*, New Haven and London, Yale, 1982, p.329.

4. Obituary: *RIBA Journal*, vol.40, no.17, 22 July 1933, p. 743.

5. According to his obituary, *RIBA Journal*, vol.60, no.7, May 1953, p. 297, Holden joined the National Provincial Bank as the assistant to the bank's architect F. C. R. Palmer in 1920: this was only a year after the Burgess practice had been relaunched under its new name. It is unclear whether he maintained any practical connection with Burgess, Holden and Watson thereafter; Ranger's nomination papers to become a Licentiate of the RIBA in 1930 mentioned that Holden 'was with this firm'.

6. Some research into Kerkham, Burgess, and Myers was published on the internet at the time of the Gerrards Cross Centenary Exhibition in 1906: http://www.gx2006.co.uk/pages/ burgess.html, accessed 2 December 2013. The estates where the practice built a large number of houses were designated a conservation area in 2009.

7. Poynings is now Dean Park, and is located at the junction of North Foreland Avenue and Cliff Road. It is largely unchanged but for a recent rear extension and some alterations to the garage and kitchen.

8. Ranger's mentors Kerkham, Burgess and Myers worked in Osbert Lancaster's 'Wimbledon Transitional' – that is, their houses displayed a 'plentiful use of pebbledash ... [a] giddy treatment of gables and [a] general air of self-conscious cosiness'; and Burgess's uncle Edward had designed simultaneously in various historical styles, for example a neo-mid-Georgian reference library in Bishop Street, Leicester (1904-05) and a Free Gothic St Edward's House in Great College Street, London (1903-05). Thus the story of Ranger and the context he sprang from elegantly demonstrates the unfolding styles of the period between the 1900s and the 1930s and the generational distinctions between them. For more on Wimbledon Transitional and Stockbrokers Tudor, see Osbert Lancaster, *Pillar to Post*, London, John Murray, 1963 edition, pp.74, 76.

9. Biographical information, unless noted otherwise, is from the introduction preceding p.1 of Anthony Ranger's, 'A Selection of Houses designed by Edgar Ranger, R.I.B.A', unpublished typescript, 1996.

10. With Burgess, Holden and Watson: see ibid, pp.13-19. The house survives with a fine gatehouse by Ranger and is mentioned in Bridget Cherry and Nikolaus Pevsner, The Buildings of England, *London NorthWest*, London, Penguin, 1991, p.292, but without an architect's name.

11. Author's telephone conversation with Simon Ranger, 14 April 2013.

12. Old Tolmers, at No.101 Stone Road, and Noran Cottage survive apparently intact from the outside; Chaileys, No.99 Stone Road, soon became Stepping Stone Cottage, and has been recently very much enlarged.

13. Message from Chris Meredith, Anthony Ranger's nephew, to Elain Harwood, 11 October 2011. According to Anthony Ranger's list, his father built four houses for himself in Gerrards Cross, as well as several others, which reinforces this impression.

14. Barn Jet, now Middlemarch, seems largely intact, although the sleeping balcony has been enclosed. See *Ideal Home*, April 1929, p. 350.

15. "Home sweet home": *Oxford Dictionary of National Biography*, 'Mackay Hugh Baillie Scott', online; 'Fine geniality': *Ideal Home*, ibid.

16. *Architecture* (published by *The Builder*), vol.4, no.9, June 1926, p. 299; *Country Life*, vol.58, no.1488, 11 July 1925, pp. 77-78. The house was listed grade II on 7 February 2007.

17. He made a further extension to Long Barn in 1955 when he added a flat over the easternmost garage (Ranger 1996, op.cit., p.94).

18. Extant. The rest of St Peter's Court, the prep school attended in 1910 by the future Duke of Gloucester, has been demolished, including (presumably) its choir house, a late Ranger building of 1960, leaving behind merely Ranger's cottage and a poignant pair of gothic gate posts.

19. 'Englische Landhäuser von Architekt Edgar Ranger', *Innen-Dekoration*, 1928, pp. 214-28. The other two houses illustrated are Ranger's own Long Barn, and a 'Landhaus in Cliftonville' that appears to be Bretaye (see below).

20. See note 2 above. The brewery is in fact called Tomson and Wooton: 'Thompson' is from the local *Kelly's* directory for 1929 and Anthony Ranger's list.

21. Edgecliff, Ranger's most expensive neo-Tudor building in Broadstairs, cost £6,500, and Pines Hurst £6,000; Windy Ridge was a modest £3,300.

22. *Oxford Dictionary of National Biography*, 'Sir Edmund Hoyle Vestey', online (entry by Richard Perren).

23. My thanks to Ross Finocchio of New York University for information regarding the Frick house.

24. *The Builder*, vol.136, no.4484, 11 January 1929, p.107. There is also a plan of the house on p.105, and a view of the garage building on p.98.

25. The house is accessible from Stone Road just south of the turning into Cliff Road. After a long period in use as an old people's home, the house was converted into flats in 2012-13. Ranger 1996 includes photocopies of a series of views, including the entry hall, which appear to have come from *The Builder* but if so they are unindexed and untraced.

26. Hannah was a recurring name in the Vestey family, but daughter seems the most likely.

27. All extant.

28. All these houses in the Dumpton Park cluster have survived, apparently intact at least from the outside. Almost directly opposite the junction of Park Avenue with the Ramsgate Road are located yet more of Thanet's many architectural surprises: two pairs of semi-detached houses by Ernö Goldfinger at Nos.167-73 (odd), of 1952-53.

29. No.42 Crow Hill / Nos.2-6 (even) King's Avenue and No.19 Crow Hill. The former flower shop is on the corner of Fordoun Road and St Peter Park Road. At St Alban's Court, Nonnington, in east Kent (1875), Devey designed a large mansion in red brick set over irregular courses of stone to give the impression that the house was built over the remains of a much older building.

30. All three houses are extant; Bretaye has been subdivided.

31. Long Barn survives, on Portsdown Hill Road north of Cosham. The 'dream café' at Southsea is referred to in an undated, untitled local newspaper cutting in Ranger, 1996, and was also illustrated and described in *The Builder*, vol. 141, no.4638, 25 December 1931, pp.1036 (text), 1039 (view).

32. *The Builder*, vol. 147, no. 4779, 7 September 1934, pp.376-7.

33. Nos.116-20 Ramsgate Road / Nos.3-7 Bromstone Road; No.4 Fig Tree Road: all extant.

34. *Country Life*, vol. 58, no. 1488, 11 July 1925, p.77.

Janet Douglas

3

Modernism in Yorkshire: The work of John Procter

Over fifty years ago Nikolaus Pevsner noted that John Procter's Kirkby House at Kirkby Overblow was 'quite a historic monument now, in that it is among the early houses in England to adopt the new style of France and Germany'.[1] Including Kirkby House in his survey of the Modern Movement in Britain, Alan Powers reiterated these comments on Procter's precocity, writing that he was 'one of several regional architects … who seem to be "ahead" of their London contemporaries'.[2] Yet what both Pevsner and Powers overlooked was that Kirkby House was not Procter's first engagement with modernism, for three years earlier he had designed Five Oaks in Ben Rhydding; three other modernist houses were to follow, two in Yorkshire and one outside Dorchester.[3]

Procter was more than a domestic architect, and amongst his other work were buildings for the University of Leeds that included his Dudok-inspired Algernon Firth Institute of Pathology (1932-3) and BBC Studios in Leeds and Bristol (both built in 1933). Two years before the outbreak of the Second World War he designed a huge civic centre for Leeds City Council which was eventually abandoned, though the director of the City Art Gallery, Philip Hendy, kept a model of the complex in his office hoping the scheme would be resurrected after the war. It never was, and by 1946 Hendy had moved on to the National Gallery. Although much of Procter's work of the 1930s was published in the architectural press, today he is largely forgotten even in his home city of Leeds. He left no professional archive or personal papers.

John Clifford Procter was born in 1882 in Great Ouseburn, a village outside York, though his Quaker family originated in the Newcastle area where they had long been associated with the tanning business. Ten years later his father, Henry Richardson Procter (1848-1927), was appointed as a lecturer in the newly established Leather Sciences Department at the Yorkshire College (from 1904 the University of Leeds), and the family came to live in Leeds. Educated at the Friends' Bootham School in York, Procter began his architectural studies at the Leeds School of Art in 1899 and joined the office of W. H. Thorp (1852-1944), one of the best-known architects in the North of England. In 1903 he passed the intermediate examinations of the Royal Institute of British Architects, and from 1904 worked for two years as an assistant to Paul Waterhouse (1861-1924). Since 1891 Paul Waterhouse had been in partnership with his father, Alfred Waterhouse, architect to the Yorkshire College, and together in 1905 they designed the somewhat austere Leather Industries Building where John Procter's father became the professor. This connection and the fact that Paul Waterhouse was about to embark on a series of buildings for the new university probably explains Procter's appointment.

Having passed his final RIBA examinations in 1907, winning the prestigious Ashpitel prize, Procter established his own practice. This was in Leeds, with an office in Basinghall Street in the city centre, although he still lived at the family home, Rowangarth, in Ben Rhydding outside Ilkley. His early work was domestic, mostly small in scale and Arts and Crafts in style with the exception of Hoyle Court (1912), a large Wrenaissance house in Baildon designed for Sam Ambler, a member of a wealthy family of Bradford industrialists.

During the First World War, Procter served with the Gloucestershire Regiment and was awarded the Military Cross – neither he nor his father was a practising Quaker. He moved to Leeds on his marriage in 1918, combining his office and private residence firstly at No.62 Woodhouse Lane, and from the mid-1920s in a detached Victorian villa at No.40 Clarendon Road. For most of the decade his practice relied on small houses, or alterations and extensions to larger houses, though in 1924 he was responsible for a detached country house, Southburn Close near Driffield, which was illustrated in Roger Smithells's *Modern Small Country Houses*.[4] Having been elected a committee member of the Leeds and West Yorkshire Architectural Society just before the war, in 1920 Procter became its youngest president and he was to remain active in its affairs until his death. In 1930 he was elected a fellow of the RIBA, proposed by Joseph Addison, head of the school of architecture at Leeds College of Art. Unlike other Leeds architects,

Figure 2. John Procter,
Five Oaks, Ben Rhydding
Drive, Ben Rhydding,
1929-30, garden elevation
(John East)

he eschewed professional partnerships, preferring to work with other architects only on specific projects. In a letter to Sir Ian MacAlister of the RIBA, William Ledgard, a fellow architect and one of his executors, considered that Procter 'was not a business man in the accepted sense, and was far more concerned with doing and obtaining satisfactory work for his clients, than with the amount of fees he was entitled to charge'.[5]

Procter was never a member of any avant-garde crusade, for like so many provincial architects he worked in a variety of architectural styles, sometimes ones not of his own choosing. At Devonshire Hall (1927-8), where he worked with another Leeds architect, F. Charlton (1889-1961), the University Sites Committee held long and sometimes fraught debates about whether their first purpose-built hall of residence should be Tudoresque or neo-Georgian before settling on the former. One can only speculate about what attracted Procter to international modernism. He came from a cultured background: his father was a distinguished scientist and a fellow of the Royal Society, while his brother Ernest Procter (1886-1935) was a relatively successful artist associated with the Newlyn School, who a year before his death was appointed Director of Studies in Design and Crafts at the University of Glasgow. Perhaps the cult of simplicity that characterised modernism chimed with Procter's Quaker background.[6] We also know that he was a pioneering car owner at a time when, from William Ledgard's testimony, 'to be a motorist was also to be an adventurer'. Foreign travel might also have exposed Procter to new architectural idioms, but except for rock climbing trips to Norway we know of no visits abroad.

Procter must have read the same professional journals as architects in the rest of the country, for the architectural press played a crucial role in nurturing modernist ideas.[7] More specifically the annual journals of the Leeds and West Yorkshire Architectural Society underline the fact that local architects were not all cautious conservatives, for half of the ten presidents who served in the inter-war years were noted modernists.[8] As early as 1924, Eric Morley referred in his presidential address to the need for buildings to become taller, and that steel frames, reinforced concrete and electricity were all leading to new architectural possibilities. Two years later William Alban Jones in his address emphasised 'the restless spirit of the age' and, in the context of the critical responses to the work of Reginald Blomfield, noted that 'this appearance of antagonism between age and youth are in the nature of things more than a thing of yesteryear and long may the vigour of the game continue.'[9] Noted advocates of modernism visited the LWYAS: in 1927 Howard Robertson of the Architectural Association gave a talk on 'Current Modern Work in Europe and the USA', and in the following year members debated whether 'the architect should endeavour to create new forms and not accept the traditions of a previous age'. Two years later the Society held an exhibition of photographs of modern buildings by Francis Yerbury that had been shown at the RIBA in the previous year. In 1930 G. S. Francis gave a talk on 'Modern Tendencies in Architecture, Furnishing and Light Design', while the next year there was a talk on concrete buildings by Grey Wornum and Joseph Emberton spoke on 'Rational Architecture'.

G. H. Foggitt's presidential address of 1932 is quoted at some length because it aptly illustrates the local awareness of modernist ideas and practice:

> Today there is a growing interest in the public mind on matters architectural … A good deal of prominence was given recently to an English translation of M. Le Corbusier's book, *Towards a New Architecture*. In it he indicates his dissatisfaction with things as they are, and arouses our interest, even if he does not entirely convince us, by his forcefulness. He speaks of one profession, and one only, namely architecture, in which progress is not considered a necessity – where laziness is enthroned and in which the reference is always to yesterday. He speaks of our houses as machines for living in, as tools to be used … In spite of his sweeping criticisms, the spirit of progress is manifesting itself on all sides. Our professional press is giving more and more attention to the work of modern schools in Sweden, Denmark, Austria, France, Germany, Holland and America, and we are receiving inspiration which is bringing a fresh breath of life into our art.[10]

If many Leeds architects were open-minded about modernism, the same could not be said for local clients. In 1933 the president of what had now become the West Yorkshire Society of Architects, B. R. Gibbon, speaking albeit of local authorities, noted that 'we are trying to get back to essentials, to evolve an architecture based on modern needs expressed in modern materials. Yet it too often happens that we are told modernism is taboo'.[11]

Yet modernism was not taboo for everyone. When Procter designed his first modern house, Five Oaks, he presented his client, Edward W. Chary, with two designs, one in a traditional Yorkshire vernacular style and the other the modern house we see today. Situated about a mile from the centre of Ilkley in Ben Rhydding Drive, Five Oaks replaced a house of 1902 that had been destroyed by fire in 1927.[12] The new house sits on a sloping site with panoramic views over Wharfedale to the north. Categorising the architectural style of Five Oaks is problematic; for example, a recent estate agent's leaflet described it as a superb example of 'Bauhaus architecture', which it certainly is not, whilst an article in the *Architects' Journal* of 1930 thought the house 'transitional and perhaps too timorous'.[13] Describing Five Oaks as 'first rate in design', Raymond McGrath in his *Twentieth Century Houses* referred to its style as 'Regency mixed with a touch of Bruno Taut and Lurçat'.[14]

In planning Five Oaks, Procter had to prioritise between panoramic views to the north or maximising sunlight, and in keeping with the spirit of the times he choose sunshine over vista. The result is that the two main facades are treated very differently: the south-facing garden façade is sleek, rectilinear and largely symmetrical, whilst from

the north the house appears as a series of adjoining cubes, with the central projecting cube containing the main entrance set slightly to the right and five arched windows above. The windows, McGrath felt, were the only errors in a design that ought to 'have no business with arches'.[15] Although largely constructed of brick and white stucco, the house stands on a stone plinth that receives greater exposure at the rear of the house where it extends through the lower ground floor. Concrete is used for the floors and for balconies that can be found on both the front and rear elevations. The only embellishments are bands of exposed grey concrete at roof level, below the windows and topping the balconies. The main feature of the garden elevation are two curved bay windows with, springing between them, a long curved balcony supported by two slim pillars that frame the garden entrance to the house. To the west are double-door French windows to a sitting room that runs the entire width of the building. Originally the eastern section of the façade consisted of a large blank wall at ground floor level; behind was the maids' sitting room, and the absence of windows was intended to prevent the domestic staff from disturbing the privacy of the garden.

The front entrance gave access to the lower ground floor, where various service rooms were located, and a short staircase led through a semi-elliptical arch to a large hall that linked the front and rear of the house. To the west were the sitting room and the quaintly named 'men's room' whilst the eastern section, with the exception of the dining room, was given over to service rooms. Bisecting the first floor was a long corridor that gave access to five bedrooms plus two for the maids, who had their own staircase from the kitchen area below. Both bedrooms at the front of Five Oaks had doors to the balcony that looked over the garden, whilst at the rear with its scenic views the bedroom over the entrance block had its own small balcony flanked by two larger balconies accessed from the central corridor.

Procter was also responsible for the interior fittings, which included a decorative

wrought-iron screen at the head of the entrance staircase, a main staircase in Austrian oak with a black ebony cap to the polygonal newel post, a magnificent set of ground floor walnut doors banded in ebony, and plain grey marble fireplaces. Five Oaks has been subdivided into two separate dwellings, when a window was inserted into a blank wall, two small porthole windows on the first floor were replaced by larger openings and the metal frames to some windows disappeared. The concrete screen that once shielded the garden from views of the kitchen courtyard has also been demolished. Despite these changes, however, Five Oaks remains, as the *Architects' Journal* noted in 1930, 'a house full of light, with a feeling of spaciousness for its size, and one voted very easy to run'.[16]

Five Oaks provided the exemplar for further houses, including Kirkby House (1930-1), White Lodge (1932-3) at Adel in Leeds, and Shenley (1936-7) in Burn Bridge outside Harrogate.[17] Like Five Oaks, these houses are basically rectilinear in plan, but the monotony of large areas of flat walling is relieved by projecting bays, curving balconies and wrap-round windows. Main entrances were placed to the rear, leaving a garden façade devoted to windows, French doors, loggias and terraces. At Kirkby House – as at Five Oaks – the entrance was insignificant, in this instance placed next to the garage, while at Shenley the door was set in a turquoise mosaic surround and sheltered by a wooden canopy supported by two stainless steel columns that are no longer visible. The entrance door at White Lodge was given greater prominence by being set in a projecting semi-circular turret, and has an Art Deco motif above, the one exception to the suppression of ornament in Procter's modern houses. To the right of the entrance turret, a bold curving chimney flue adds an abstract sculptural dimension to the rear of the house that was perhaps unintended. In keeping with the contemporary passion for fresh air and sunshine, windows tend to be large and rectilinear, though again White Lodge is an exception – where, replicating the arches that McGrath so deplored at Five Oaks, tall arched sitting room windows (one a French door) face south over the terrace, and are complimented by four arched windows with louvered shutters placed centrally at first floor level. The original fenestration of Procter's designs has largely disappeared, but original photographs show small-paned metal windows save at White Lodge, where the dining room window has opening lights at the side and top, with a large sheet of plain glass in the centre to give an unobstructed view of the garden.[18]

The division between the house and the garden is diminished by features such as French windows, loggias for sunbathing and dining (which are therefore often located close to dining rooms and kitchens), and – except at White Lodge – curving balconies that sweep around the garden facades. Accessible from bedrooms, dressing rooms and first floor landings, these afford views over lavish gardens and the countryside beyond as well as providing additional spaces for sunbathing and open-air exercising. One of the balconies at Kirkby House has a glazed roof supported by slim columns; light and air were clearly important requirements for this client as in addition a roof-level sun room glazed from floor to ceiling and with folding doors is set between the two chimney stacks.

According to the *Architects' Journal*, 'as with the design of the exterior, the aim internally has been to eliminate "nonsense" as much as possible'.[19] Although none of Procter's houses were open plan, there were surprisingly few rooms on the ground floor. Gone were the separate sitting rooms for ladies, morning rooms, libraries and billiard rooms; instead family life was concentrated into the sitting room and the dining room. Halls, however, remained large; at White Lodge and Shenley they ran from the rear to the front of the house and accommodated washrooms, lavatories and such new-fangled features as telephone cubicles. The customary division between family rooms and the kitchen quarters was strictly maintained, with large and airy sitting rooms the full width of the house placed to one side of the hall, well away from the kitchen areas. Dining rooms occupied a more central position on the garden frontage linked to kitchens and loggias for al fresco dining. One of the innovations found at White Lodge was a separate small cocktail bar in a curved room accessible from the dining room. Unlike the living

Figure 5. John Procter,
White Lodge, Adel,
Leeds, 1932-3
(John East)

Figure 6. John Procter,
White Lodge,
Adel, Leeds, 1932-3,
the entrance
(John East)

accommodation, service rooms retained their traditional complexity, with kitchens for cooking, larders, sculleries, pantries and sometimes a maids' sitting room. At Five Oaks there was a separate garage house for four cars with a chauffeur's flat above (now demolished), but in Procter's later designs there were integrated garage wings located either close to the front entrance of the house or within the kitchen courtyard.

First floors were given over to sleeping accommodation, including separate bedrooms for maids. Bisected by a corridor running the length of the house, major bedrooms usually overlooked the garden whilst servant rooms were placed to the rear. The master bedroom was often situated above the dining room, with its own adjoining dressing room and bathroom, while the remaining two or three bedrooms shared bathroom facilities. Despite the so-called servant problem of the inter-war years, Procter's houses had two or three maids' bedrooms with a shared bathroom.

Architectural reviews of the period rarely provide details of the internal fittings and furnishings, though we know from accounts of Procter's BBC studios in Leeds of his interest in contemporary interior design.[20] Staircases in his houses often had stainless steel handrails and painted tubular steel balustrades. Fireplaces were equally spare, in stone or unpolished marble, though the dining room fireplace at White Lodge had a hidden surprise: the stone mantle supported on wrought-iron shafts had an open top covered in glass, within which were concealed strip lights. 'Built-in furniture', according to Roger Smithells, had become 'an important factor from the inception of the architect's plan', and extant plans for Procter's houses indicate plentiful hall cupboards, corridor linen cupboards and fitted bedroom furniture.[21] An image of the interior of the

Figure 7. John Procter,
Shenley, Burn Bridge,
near Harrogate, 1936-7
(John East)

Figure 8. John Procter,
Shenley, Burn Bridge,
near Harrogate,
1936-7, detail
(John East)

principal bedroom at Shenley shows a double bed set in a complex of open shelves, bookshelves and two tall wardrobes, with smaller cupboards running across the entire length of the wall.

The design of Hyde Crook, built at Frampton near Dorchester in 1936, differs from Procter's other modernist houses. Perhaps the drama of the near-white house in a green setting did not appeal to the refined taste of its patrons, the siblings Norman and Agnes Lupton. This sombre house was constructed of greyish brick and its severe geometry was unrelieved by the fripperies of curving bays and balconies, or any ornamentation except for patterned brickwork.[22] Robert Rowe, later Director of Leeds City Art Gallery, remembered seeing this 'large, unlikely house with a flat roof' whilst travelling on the Great Western Railway, and was intrigued.[23] Procter's clients were ardent collectors of antiques, textiles and etchings, and owned an extensive collection of watercolour paintings. Both brother and sister were talented amateur artists and needed studio space. 'Hyde Crook' was, according to Rowe, 'very much a purpose-built affair, a machine for living in perhaps, but for a very special way of life'. The flat roof allowed for top lighting wherever it was needed, ceilings were high and windows were carefully situated to protect the collections from excessive sunlight. In the corridors were ingenious display cabinets designed by Procter after those found in Sir John Soane's Museum, which accommodated as many drawings or prints as possible in such a way that they were not damaged by excessive light.[24]

Agnes and Norman Lupton were members of a wealthy and well-established Leeds family who came to prominence as woollen merchants in the late eighteenth century. Norman was a friend of John Procter's brother Ernest and owned a number of the artist's paintings, and as a member of the board of Leeds Infirmary he would have known John's extensions to the School of Medicine and the Algernon Firth Institute of

59 Modernism in Yorkshire: The work of John Procter

Pathology, another modernist building constructed in brick. Like Procter's other houses, Hyde Crook is rectilinear in plan with cubic projections. The main entrance on the north side opens into a vast hall with a long window that extends through to the landing above. A huge drawing room to the right projects westwards from the main body of the house, its north wall devoid of window openings. The main features of the south elevation are the projecting morning room and dining room linked by a covered loggia. The setback eastern service wing reveals the complexity of Hyde Crook's ample domestic arrangements, which include a strong room and flower room. At first-floor level, over the service wing and overlooking the garden, are four maids' bedrooms; beyond is Miss Lupton's bed sitting room with its accompanying dressing room and bathroom, and Mr Lupton's bedroom and bathroom. Facing north is a large studio, a spacious landing and three additional bedrooms.

As aesthetically discerning clients the Luptons differed from Procter's Yorkshire patrons. The client for Five Oaks, Edward W. Chary (1878-1953), was the son of German immigrant Emile Chary, who had come to Huddersfield some time before 1871 but later found employment with N. Heydemann, a member of the large community of German stuff merchants (dealers in worsted woollen cloth) based in Bradford. Following Heydemann's retirement at the end of the century ownership of his firm was passed to the Chary family. Edward Chary was an extremely wealthy man who spoke fluent German and frequently travelled on business to Berlin and other German cities. With this background and, according to his grandson, an extrovert and self-indulgent personality, we can speculate that Chary was drawn to architectural adventurism in a search for cultural distinction.[25] According to family legend, Five Oaks was known locally as 'Chary's Folly'; revelling in its notoriety, Edward Chary loved the house, but it proved an embarrassment to his upright English wife who hated it. Why he selected

61 Modernism in Yorkshire: The work of John Procter

Procter as his architect remains something of a mystery as Chary appears to have had no Leeds connections and there were plenty of talented architects in Bradford, but it seems to be too much of a coincidence that Procter's original family home was situated a few hundred yards from Five Oaks for it not to be of relevance.

Two of Procter's other houses, Kirkby House and Shenley, were also built for Bradford businessmen. The former was commissioned by John Malcolm McLaren (1895-1966), a worsted spinner whose maternal uncle, Sam Ambler, had earlier employed Procter to design Hoyle Court in Baildon. The patron for Shenley was Walter H. Rhodes (1888-1962), whose father established a cleaning cloth company in Bradford, which later became Allied Industrial Services with branches in London, Glasgow and Birmingham. The sons of self-made men, both McLaren and Rhodes were born in Bradford and, like Chary, became extremely wealthy. We know that Kirkby House cost £6458, whilst Rhodes was described as a millionaire.[26] All three men lived in Heaton, a prestigious Bradford suburb, before their exodus to the Yorkshire countryside, and it is highly likely that they knew each other, meeting at the Wool Exchange and the Bradford Club.

Such local networks however do not apply in the case of Adel Lodge, where the client was Gordon McLean May (1901-68), a third generation wholesale clothing manufacturer who traded as Joseph May and Sons and later used the trademark 'Maenson'. Just before the First World War Samuel May, Gordon's father, had constructed a substantial Queen Anne house, Athill Court in Adel, designed by the Leeds architect G. W. Atkinson; Adel Lodge, built in its extensive grounds, was possibly a wedding present to his son who married in 1933. It has not proved possible to trace any connections between the May family and John Procter, or with his other patrons. In the 1920s Gordon May regularly travelled to the USA, Canada and South Africa on behalf of the family business, which had developed an extensive export trade based on stylish, high-quality men's clothing frequently advertised in the press and magazines, and in 1936 the firm opened a London showroom on Regent Street. This forward-looking approach to business perhaps extended to a taste for modern architecture. There are hints that he enjoyed a chic and elegant life style, for a year after their marriage May and his wife travelled to Bermuda (perhaps on a belated honeymoon) at a time when the island was becoming a holiday playground for rich Americans and a few wealthy British tourists. In none of Procter's other house plans is a space designated for a cocktail bar.

The caution and conservatism of British taste has meant that until a few years ago it was believed that only a handful of English architects were enthusiastic about 'the new architecture', but recent research is uncovering an increasing number of provincial practitioners who designed buildings in a modernist idiom. Why, after twenty years designing buildings in a variety of conventional styles, there was a sudden shift in Procter's work remains something of a puzzle, for we know of no eureka moment. Modernist houses did not usually endear themselves to the middle classes, so the change may be due to the sympathies of Edward Chary; thereafter much of Procter's work, both domestic and otherwise, was informed by modernist precepts. All five of Procter's domestic patrons were involved in industry – even Norman Lupton, before his retirement, was the managing director of an engineering company – but the vast majority of businessmen remained chained to cultural conformity. Although they lend support to Louise Campbell's proposition that 'personal and professional networks emerge as the most significant factor in patronage', lack of personal information means that such relationships can be difficult to substantiate.[27] Perhaps the most that can be said is that individual desire and ambition is the result of a melange of internal and external factors, which in the interwar years meant that for architects like Procter there were opportunities to develop their practice in new directions.

1. Nikolaus Pevsner, The Buildings of England: *Yorkshire, the West Riding*, Harmondsworth, Penguin, 1959, p.288.

2. Alan Powers, *Modern: the Modern Movement in Britain*, London, Merrell, 2005, pp.204-5.

3. In the latest edition of The Buildings of England, *Yorkshire West Riding: Leeds, Bradford and the North* (Peter Leach and Nikolaus Pevsner, Yale University Press, 2009, p.349), the White House, Ilkley, is attributed to Procter but this designation now seems doubtful and the house is possibly the work of Leslie Taylor Appleyard or Arthur Sykes of Baildon.

4. Roger Smithells, ed., *Modern Small Country Houses*, London, Country Life, 1936, pp.10-11.

5. Biographical Files, British Architectural Library, RIBA.

6. Timothy Mowl in his *Stylistic Cold Wars*, London, John Murray, 2000, p.17, suggests a connection between John Betjeman's 'fling' with modernism and his membership of the Society of Friends in the early 1930s.

7. Elizabeth Darling, *Reforming Britain: Narratives of Modernity before Reconstruction*, London, Routledge, 2007, pp.27-31.

8. The Leeds and West Yorkshire Architectural Society Annual Journal ('the Green Books') can be found in the Family and Local Studies Library, Leeds City Library, The Headrow, Leeds

9. LWYAS Green Book, 1926.

10. LWYAS Green Book, 1929.

11. LWYAS Green Book, 1934.

12. The lodge to the original house is still standing.

13. *Architects' Journal*, vol.72, 5 November 1930, pp.684-8.

14. Raymond McGrath, *Twentieth Century Houses*, London, Faber and Faber, 1934, p.95.

15. ibid.

16. *Architects' Journal*, vol.72, 5 November 1930, pp.684-8.

17. 'Kirkby House, Kirkby Overblow', *Architects' Journal*, vol.74, 14 October 1931, pp.500-1; 'A Modern House in Yorkshire: White Lodge, Adel', *Homes and Gardens*, vol.16, no.10, March 1935, pp.45-6; 'House at Burn Bridge, Harrogate', *RIBA Journal*, vol.45, no.18, 15 August 1938, pp.923-5.

18. Although these resemble the frames designed by Crittall, they may have been manufactured by Hope's of Manchester, who certainly provided the windows for Procter's Gipton Wood Inn of 1937.

19. *Architects' Journal*, vol.74, 14 October 1931, pp.500-1.

20. 'Broadcasting House, Leeds', *Architecture and Building News*, vol.134, 9 June 1933, pp.276-7; *Architectural Review*, vol.73, June 1933, pp.231-4.

21. 'Foreword', in Smithells, op.cit., pp.vii-viii.

22. Despite the common adjective 'white' in the names of modernist houses, colours varied, and two of Procter's houses were described as 'pale cream' and 'buff'. Procter had earlier designed the much-admired Algernon Firth Institute of Pathology at Leeds University (1933) in brick.

23. Foreword to *The Lupton Collection*, Leeds City Art Gallery, 1972.

24. When the Luptons left their collections to Leeds City Art Gallery in 1952, the display cabinets came to Leeds and are now in the offices of the Art Gallery staff.

25. Author's interview with Edward Chary's grandson, David Chary, 5 March 2013.

26. Details of the cost of Kirkby House are in McGrath, op.cit, p.95; for Rhodes's fortune, see the *Children's Newspaper*, no.1066, 26 August 1939, p.11.

27. Louise Campbell, 'Patrons of the Modern House', in Twentieth Century Architecture 2, *The Modern House Revisited*, Twentieth Century Society, 1996, p.44.

David M. Boswell

4

Designing Twitchells End at Jordans, Buckinghamshire

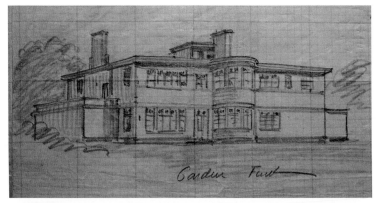

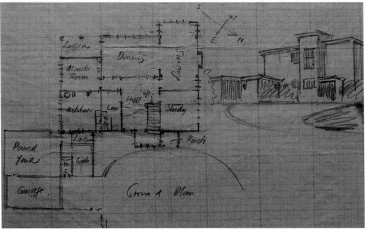

Figure 2. Alternative
plans and perspectives
suggested by
C. H. B. Quennell,
6 February 1933
(private collection)

C. R. Crickmay's Twitchells End was designed by a young architect embarking
on his first private commission for John Gilbert (known as 'Gib' or 'Jenks') Jenkins
(1896-1972), the eldest son of the Canon and Rural Dean of St Mary's, Bangor.[1]
After reading history and law at Jesus College, Oxford, Jenkins joined the Inland
Revenue, later becoming Secretary to the Entrance and Examinations Council of
London University in the new Senate House.[2] In 1930 he married Elizabeth (Betty)
Tuke (1907-68), daughter of an East Anglian rector, James Sant, but adopted after her
mother's death by her maternal aunt Eva, whose husband William Favell Tuke was to
become chairman of Barclay's Bank. From a fine Georgian town house, which became
the civic offices of Saffron Walden council, they removed to Berkhamsted where Mrs
Tuke died in the 1919 influenza epidemic. Betty's nanny, Kate Louis Witham, assumed
great importance and became a resident family member until her death in 1966 aged 94.

After their daughter Gwynnedd's birth in 1931, and with a second child, Elizabeth
Ann, expected in 1933, the Jenkins needed more space. Having lost interest in a Georgian
house in Penn because of its institutional neighbours, Gib Jenkins asked a Berkhamsted
friend, the architect C. H. B. Quennell (1872-1935), for some ideas for a new house for a
site on the edge of Jordans, the Buckinghamshire village recently developed by the
Quaker Frederick Rowntree.[3] Quennell warned 'Jenks' of Bernard Ashmole's lack of
water pressure at High and Over above Amersham, which had required Connell and
Ward to add a separate water tower. He made three sketch designs, one with a
Regency style central bow, whose flat roof and horizontal banding bear some
resemblance to his 1919 designs for workmen's houses at Braintree for the Crittall
family. Less ambitious in scale and more modernist in appearance was Quennell's
second scheme, which paid closer attention to the clients' specific spatial requirements.
Even this was probably too expensive, hence Jenkins's search for another architect.[4]

By 1933, Gib and Betty also had more radical ideas about design. Gib's brother

Figure 3. Perspective
sketch of Twitchells End
from below by C. R.
Crickmay, mid-1933
(private collection)

Cyril, a freelance film maker, introduced Betty to the famous modernist print maker,
Claude Flight, with whom she studied at the Grosvenor School of Art, becoming a
proficient linocutter after joining the school's visit to France.[5] In 1933 the couple went
for a walking holiday in the Black Forest during which they visited modern buildings
in Stuttgart, presumably the Weissenhof Siedlung and Erich Mendelsohn's Schocken
department store. These probably encouraged Betty to seek a more modern design for
their new house. The Jenkins may also have listened to the radio talks on modern design
or attended the popular *Exhibition of British Industrial Art in Relation to the Home* at the
Dorland Hall in July 1933.[6] Quennell's sketched elevations must have looked 'old hat'
compared with what they had seen in Germany, but Colin Crickmay recalled that when
they first interviewed him in 1933 'they were not quite sure and Gib wouldn't have come
on his own. He very much hung on what she wanted.'[7]

Colin R. Crickmay (1904-99) was acquainted with Gib and Betty through his
friends the Hardings, and was conveniently living in Jordans by 1933. His grandfather,
G. R. Crickmay, was the successful Dorset architect in whose London office the young
Thomas Hardy worked while embarking on his literary career. Of G. R.'s sons only
Colin's father was dissuaded from taking up architecture, and became a reluctant
stockbroker. From Marlborough College, Colin, aged eighteen, went to the Architectural
Association where Robert Atkinson was the Principal, followed by Howard Robertson.
The country houses of Edwin Lutyens, E. Guy Dawber and C. F. A. Voysey were
influences, he recalled, as was the work of the Dutch architect W. M. Dudok and several
Scandinavians whose designs were reflected in town halls designed by Atkinson and his
final year master at the AA, Stephen Rowland Pierce.

In contrast to the emphasis on drawing in the school curriculum, Crickmay
considered that architecture was 'very much a practical thing. You've got to start by
knowing your materials, the proper way of putting them together, how they behave under

weathering conditions – all that sort of thing. You can only know that by going continually onto building sites with someone who is very knowledgeable … By then architectural development had passed to the engineers and only these Northern Continentals had taken this up in building.' In 1927 Crickmay and his friend Ian Forbes went to see modern buildings in Frankfurt, presumably including the new housing by Ernst May and his colleagues, but what particularly impressed these young men was the functionality of 'very good swimming baths that also looked nice. This sort of thing was not being done over here.'

The depression after 1929 had a crippling effect on the architectural profession. Crickmay was laid off from his first job in a suburban London practice just after getting married but found a cheap cottage for his expected family in Jordans, an area where he already had friends. Crickmay lunched with Robertson at the AA, who suggested he should apply to Serge Chermayeff for a job. As he recalled, 'I think I went down that afternoon. That changed my life!'[8]

Chermayeff had no formal training and Crickmay was his first assistant with architectural qualifications. As he recounted, 'he probably took me on to deal with the practical side of working drawings, saying that he needed someone who knew about drains and that sort of thing'. Several leading Modern Movement architects, engineers and artists visited Chermayeff's offices on the top floor of James Wyatt's former Pantheon in Oxford Street, including Amyas Connell and Basil Ward, Joseph Emberton, Ove Arup, Eric Gill and Wells Coates, for whom Crickmay was to make drawings for an airport project in 1932.[9] To mark his transition from interior design to architecture, Chermayeff developed an eye-catching project for a large country house in reinforced concrete, intended for his own family, published in 1932. Crickmay recalled the hours they spent on the model, which featured in the *Architectural Review* with plans and a full-page axonometric drawing by Crickmay, printed in colour.[10]

On a visit to Germany in 1931 Chermayeff met Erich Mendelsohn, becoming associated with him the following year in the abortive project for an Académie

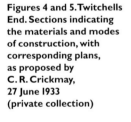

Figures 4 and 5. Twitchells End. Sections indicating the materials and modes of construction, with corresponding plans, as proposed by C. R. Crickmay, 27 June 1933 (private collection)

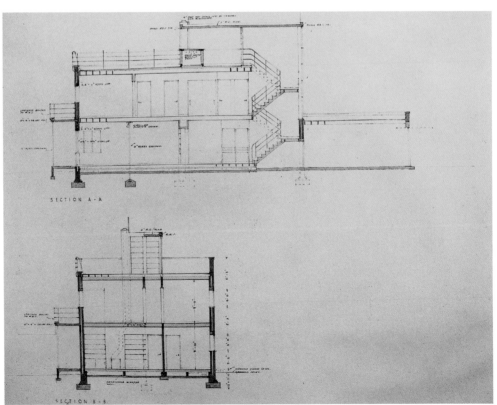

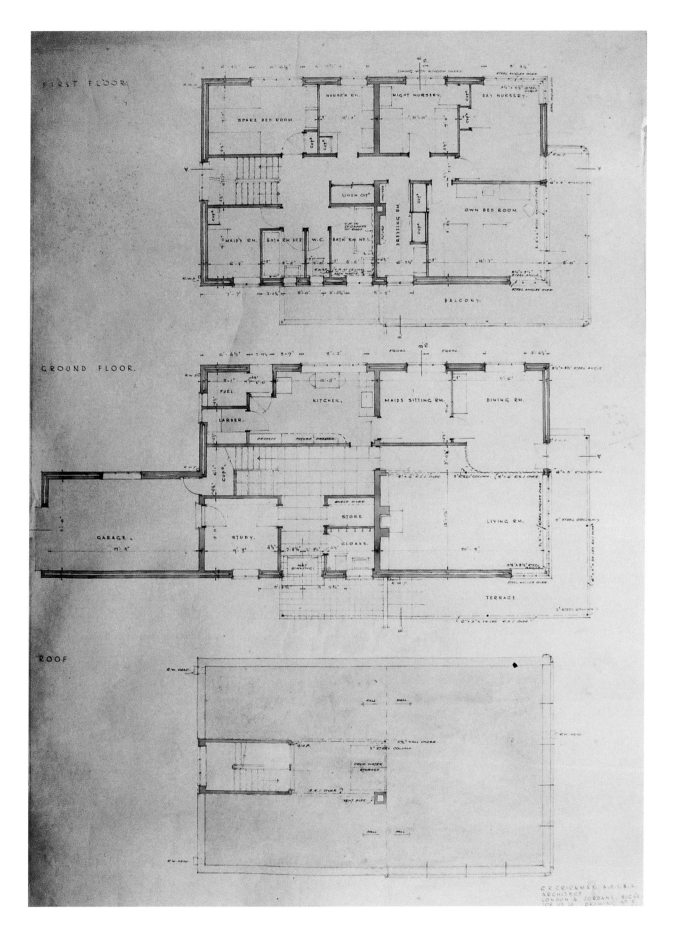

69 Designing Twitchells End at Jordans, Buckinghamshire

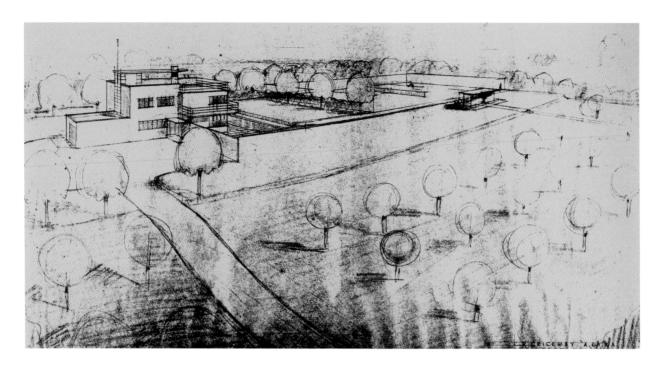

Européenne Méditerranée. When the Nazis took power in 1933, Mendelsohn was forced to flee and formed a partnership with Chermayeff. Crickmay recalled how the pace of activity in the practice quickened, while he appreciated how much he learned from working with him. As he recalled, 'Mendelsohn had simply walked out of Germany with nothing, leaving the beautiful house he had just designed for himself on the Rupenhorn in Berlin. The only thing he brought with him was F. M. J. (Hannes) Schreiner who was his chief assistant. ... Almost immediately the designs for the Bexhill Pavilion (competition) began. At the same time the designs for Shrub's Wood started.' This was a substantial new house to be built at Chalfont St Giles in Buckinghamshire using slender reinforced concrete walls that quivered as the upper storey was being constructed. Crickmay, who lived nearby, was appointed site architect and more architectural staff were taken on for these two jobs.[11]

'Mendelsohn's own style of work', as Crickmay described it, 'was to concentrate on the general design himself and then leave it to his principal assistant. Schreiner would start the whole thing off and then he would distribute it through the staff and [he] did most of the supervision as well. It was rather a second-hand sort of relationship through Schreiner from Mendelsohn, although I got to know [Mendelsohn] quite well. At one time I shared a room with him. Sometimes he used to reminisce for half an hour and then he would say, "What are we doing? We must do some work!"' Crickmay appreciated the meticulous detail of Schreiner's working drawings and got to know him well enough to collaborate on an independent competition design outside the practice in 1935 for Croydon town centre, which won second prize.[12] Crickmay was pleased that Mendelsohn commended his drawing style, 'It was really the practical side coming out ... the main object of drawing was to tell people as clearly as possible what you wanted them to do. Your drawings had to be neat and tidy and economic in giving the information. Schreiner did most of the small-scale working drawings and a very good draughtsman he was. They were of a Continental type. I don't think that sort of thing came out of English offices at that time.' He recalled how Mendelsohn admired the quality of English metal fittings and their provision by the suppliers in packets separately labelled for their precise use that had been ascertained from site visits by their staff.

Crickmay was influenced by Mendelsohn's way of drawing perspectives, describing how he 'held his pen upright and flourished it from the shoulder to produce the sharp angles of his dynamic drawings … He was more like a sculptor than an architect and he didn't like perspectives done by anyone else but Schreiner to whom he had taught his technique.' In his worm's eye view of Shrub's Wood Mendelsohn even conveyed an upland setting to its flat terrain for dramatic effect. At Twitchells End, Crickmay drew his first scheme in a similar style, with greater justification given the steep slope leading up to the house. See figure 3.

Crickmay's first large perspective for Twitchells End is dated 17 May 1933 when Chermayeff had already accepted the Shrub's Wood commission, taken over by Mendelsohn as soon as he arrived in June. Twitchells End was deemed too small for the practice and Crickmay was allowed to accept it as his first private commission. He worked on both jobs in tandem and benefitted from contact with Ove Arup on Shrub's Wood and Felix Samuely, the engineer for the De La Warr Pavilion, from whom he learned about steel structures.

Twitchells End was to be built on a plateau above steeply rising ground on the edge of a narrow valley of the Grove estate outside the zone of Jordans protected by a restrictive covenant. Quennell had envisaged the drive curving up and around to an entrance on the north-eastern side, which would have entailed costly levelling across the slope. The essentials of the brief, discussed at length between architects and clients, remained similar to the one given to Quennell, but the design was technically more innovative and cheaper. Siting the house 'four-square to the sun', as Betty Jenkins

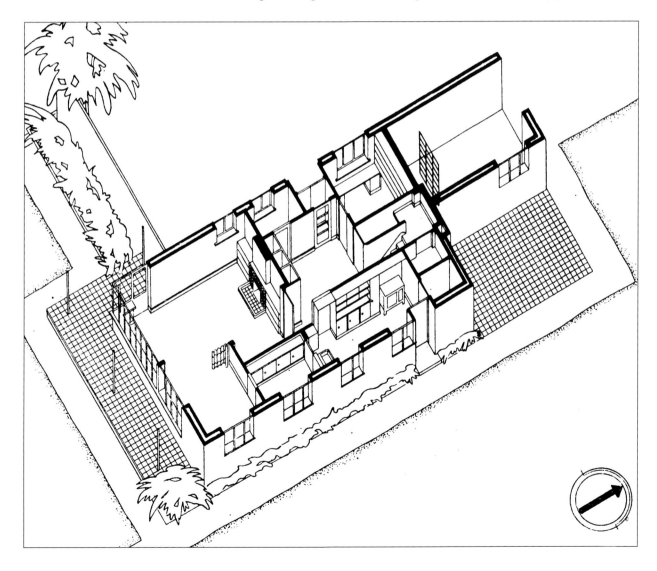

described it in an article to the *Evening Standard*, fitted the site's contours. It was also consistent with good country house design. Her text listed some of the features, including 'the garden screen wall, the use of concrete, the desire to see out from the flat roof, the position of the central heating, the ingenious access to the backroom services, the hall, the open planned living room, the insulation of sound from the kitchen and servants' room, the numerous smaller rooms upstairs, two bathrooms and painted exterior as a background for flowers'.[13]

Crickmay's plans and drawings, retained at the house along with other documents, demonstrate his modifications between May and July 1933, when he produced revised perspectives, elevations and sections, with a list of potential omissions to reduce costs. The watercolour perspective of 19 May 1933 depicts the narrow south-facing garden front with a terrace, swimming pool and lightweight railings to the flat roof, evoking the spacious elegance of a Riviera villa transplanted to the Chilterns. In this design the wide first-floor balcony is cantilevered, unsupported by columns, and wrapped around the south-western corner to catch the sun and shade the rooms below. The rounded corner is further emphasised by the bull-nosed canopy above the flat roof terrace. This and the first birds-eye perspective of 17 May, with the undated drawing of the house from below, all reflect Chermayeff's decorative approach and even Mendelsohn's dynamic panache. From the beginning, Crickmay proposed a garden wall projecting from the west elevation to screen the entrance door from the more private area of the garden. Although its size was progressively reduced, it remains as a significant feature of the house.

The body of the house was a rectangle with the staircase in a projecting tower to the north, and a balcony wrapping round the south-western corner. The living room and dining room made an L-shape at this corner, but apart from this the plan consisted of smaller rooms in accordance with the brief. Extensive use of fitted furniture was proposed on both floors.

When the cantilevered balcony proved too costly and complicated, thin steel columns were introduced to hold it up, combined with concealed steel and concrete projecting from the walls. The western corner windows of the living and main bedrooms gave access to the balcony, and the screen wall was repositioned further south to support it. The nursery now had balcony access but Gib's dressing room was moved to the western entrance front above the corresponding living-room window.

Figure 10. The house
on its ridge as seen by
an approaching car.
Photograph by Cyril
Jenkins, 1935
(private collection)

In its original position the screen wall came midway along the elevation marking the
centre line of the double-square plan, so Crickmay redesigned the entrance front, placing
the doorway centrally in the northern portion with its porch inset and double doors
opening inwards to a glazed door beyond similar to Shrub's Wood. Internally he
rearranged the plan to provide more usable space, reducing the separation between the
service and nursery suites, enlarging the kitchen by incorporating several smaller
compartments and creating a more spacious hall flanked by Gib's study and a
cloakroom.[14]

The areas either side of the screen wall each have their own focus of interest,
one from the verandah into the garden and the other the more theatrical sweep of the
gravel drive to the front door, captured by Cyril Jenkins's pre-war colour photograph.
Crickmay considered this wall's final position 'went rather nicely with [it] rising up into
the balcony and [was] reflected by the staircase and roof over the other end'. North of
the main house, the wall is balanced by the line of the single-storied garage, plain and of
equal height, which in plan forms a third square with the adjacent backyard. Reviewing
the design in the *Architectural Review*, F. R. S. Yorke considered the composition was
marred by the resulting imbalance between the two halves and this was probably one
reason why the Jenkinses subsequently planted a line of trees to continue the line of the
wall and conceal this effect.[15] The most significant change was the adoption of standard
square and rectangular windows instead of ribbon and hoppered ones. Set almost flush
with the wall plane there are parallels with Chermayeff's concrete house at Rugby,
completed in 1933.[16] Ribbon windows were retained along the garden frontage, however,
and the expensive VITA glass for the nursery.[17]

The folding and sliding strip windows meeting at the corner were standard units
made by Crittall and fitted with bronze handles, similar to those used at Lubetkin and
Tecton's Highpoint I in Highgate and Wells Coates's Embassy Court in Brighton, both
completed in 1935. Despite exposure to the weather, these have remained unchanged.
At the northern end the tall glazed staircase window provides a dramatic vertical feature
rising into a tower with the kitchen chimney to support the concrete sun roof canopy.
Although the tower's central flagstaff was omitted and the canopy scaled back and
trimmed square at its southern end for economy, the conjunction of these features
resembles some of Connell, Ward and Lucas's subsequent houses.[18]

Figure 11. Living room.
Early perspective
by Colin Crickmay
(private collection)

Internally, the swirling balustrade of open metalwork seen in an early perspective was replaced by a polished timber handrail over a boarded and panelled base, changing to chunky wooden banisters for the flight leading to the roof. Crickmay was impressed by the master-joiner A. J. Axe's skill in setting out the curvaceous handrail, but the light transparent drama of the first staircase design was lost.

The flat roof was of Ragusa asphalt with chicken wire over wooden boarding, with the sun roof canopy cast in concrete and supported between the chimney stack, the stair tower and a single steel column. The angles of the ribbon windows were supported by Z-shaped angle-irons masked by external brickwork and inside by plaster. The main walls were of brick, washed with cream distemper, so that their texture stood out in a raking light.

On the ground floor the main space in the combined living and dining room was L-shaped without a partition, so beige curtains from Heals were hung across to screen off the table. See Figure 14. Fitted furniture, much favoured by modernists, was included in most of Crickmay's revised plans. 'His and hers' bookshelves flank the living-room fireplace. In Gib's study, the desktop was one of Cripps's flush doors that had been installed throughout the house.[19] The kitchen cupboards had sliding glazed doors and draining shelves. Upstairs the partition walls between the bedrooms are interlocking wardrobes and a special locker and cupboard fitment with shelves for toys and books lines the day nursery wall. In common with many English Modern Movement buildings, all the light fittings were supplied by White, Bays and White – multi-bulb translucent discs in the living room, chrome-mounted globes in the kitchen and landing, and chrome-fitted naked bulbs in the smaller service rooms.

In the main bedroom and dressing room, the furniture was not fitted, but ordered from Ambrose Heal's limed oak range, indicating a more traditional but still contemporary Arts and Crafts taste, at least on the part of Gib Jenkins. See Figure 16. Nanny brought some of her own furniture for what she termed 'the servants' 'all'.[20]

Figure 12. The staircase hall. Early perspective by Colin Crickmay showing a lighter staircase design than was realized (private collection)

Figure 13. Staircase at first floor landing, showing the two different forms of banister (author)

Savings in laying out the garden reduced the Riviera look of Crickmay's first proposals. The wide tiled terrace fronting the verandah under the balcony was abandoned with the swimming pool, while a shallow-tiled paddling pool was dug further from the house, but soon became a lily pond as the children objected to the insects in its murky water. Even in its less ambitious form, the simple modernist structure of the garden design is still apparent. A low box hedge flanks the lawn from the south-eastern corner of the house, zigzagging around the rectangular pond, and follows the way to the tennis court. The slopes down to Twitchells Lane were planted as a cherry and apple orchard. All round the house, mature trees planted in the 1930s have changed the initial openness into a sense of enclosure.

Crickmay looked back philosophically on the results of designing on a tight budget. 'I think I would have preferred a lot of money and I think I would have preferred bigger rooms – also more space. Because this is one of the things I found so attractive about Shrub's Wood … It wasn't cramped anywhere. It had a big hall. There was room to put a gracious staircase in it. And when you look at Twitchells End it's like trying to put a quart into a pint pot. … That's not unusual for architects starting off. People who had pots of money wouldn't have come to me at all.'

Twitchells End never set out to be a grand exemplar of the Modern Movement but demonstrates how several of its key features could be incorporated into an otherwise traditional brick structure. It has a carefully considered geometry, but this inevitably became less elegant after the position and heavier structure of the balcony had to be altered from the first cantilevered design, although Crickmay was able to juggle with the balcony, screen wall and fenestration to give the house an individual site-specific character.

The roof was a real terrace with its own reinforced concrete canopy and the balcony was wide enough to sleep or exercise on with access from the nursery and main bedroom. Ann Lenox recalls that, after the first children's party on the roof, her mother

Figure 14. The dining and living rooms dividing curtain from Heals. Seen in the far window is the other new house across the valley, later screened by trees. Photograph by Cyril Jenkins, as published in *Architect & Building News*, December 1934

Figure 15. Kitchen with fitted cupboards etc. by C. R. Crickmay, with open doors to the 'servants' hall' and dining room, photographed by Cyril Jenkins, 1935 (private collection)

Figure 16. Dressing table and chair from Heal's limed oak range bought for the main bedroom c.1933 (author, 2013)

had never again risked any of them falling through the railings. Apart from a visiting uncle, nobody slept on the open balcony on summer nights – the exposed site and changeable weather discouraged them all.

In an anonymous article in 1935 on 'Home Planning and Design', Crickmay described how he adapted his design to the personality of his clients: 'It was my interpretation of what the clients wanted … They must have been used to modern houses, so I knew I was free to do it in a contemporary style. But I did not have to try and make it in any particular style.'[21] He and his wife enjoyed their time in Jordans and he was touched when the Jenkins called to present him with a wireless set as an expression of their appreciation. After her mother's death, the younger daughter, Ann, moved back with her husband Donald Lenox, so the house has served two generations over eighty years with remarkably little alteration. Betty Jenkins replaced most of the basic living room furniture with more antique pieces and Ann Lenox, an artist who found some of her parents' original decorations drab, has introduced much more colourful curtains and covers.

In 1981 Crickmay was pleased to learn that the roof had only just needed relaying and this is again now necessary. At that time, all the Crittall windows and doors were in good working order, but by 2013 the most exposed south-western door on to the balcony showed severe corrosion and some settlement of the support for the top of the staircase window looked more serious. Externally, the main difference is the growth of the trees, including tall evergreens planted by Gib Jenkins to screen out a house on the opposite slope. Deciduous trees were planted along the eastern boundary after a further strip of land was acquired, but the main lines of the garden remain as originally laid out.

One can clearly see how the 'new architecture' had impressed the clients, by way of High and Over and the Weissenhof Siedlung, and the impact on their architect of his experience with Chermayeff and especially Mendelsohn at Shrub's Wood. When Crickmay brought him to see Twitchells End, Mendelsohn 'exclaimed as they turned up the drive, "My word, that's nice you know". … He was used to something much more

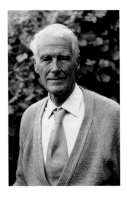

Figure 17. Linocut by Betty Tuke Jenkins, including the lily pond and line of the box hedge (private collection)

Figure 18. Colin Crickmay (1904-99) in retirement at Dorchester in Dorset, 1981 (author)

Figure 19. Twitchells End in its mature landscape setting, July 2013 (Alan Powers)

affluent and grander, but he wasn't stuck up about it. He just said, "Yes, I think it works."' Gib Jenkins recalled him sitting down and asking 'But where do you put the cigars?'– perhaps a joke shared with Crickmay alluding to Chermayeff's elegant, rotund furniture for Waring and Gillow illustrated in their catalogue with captions indicating the concealed site for cigar boxes. 'Mendelsohn used to laugh at himself, saying "My English is very bad but it is very descriptive".'

Crickmay took full advantage of his first completed private commission. In 1934 it featured in the *Architect and Building News* with Cyril Jenkins's photographs. On a visit to Chermayeff's offices, J. M. Richards had seen the drawings Crickmay was preparing and invited him to put it in the *Architectural Review*, for which fresh photographs of the exterior were taken by John, son of Frank Yerbury, then secretary of the AA and director of the Building Centre who was himself an accomplished architectural photographer. More important for posterity, the house has featured in successive editions of Yorke's *The Modern House in England* since 1937. In the combination of materials used to achieve the internal plan and different frontages it represents a forerunner to Jeremy Gould's third phase of a more pragmatic and economical approach to modernist domestic design.[22] Two houses of this period seem to share some features but have no known direct link with Twitchells End. Clifford Culpin's house at Cuffley, Potters Bar, has an inset porch like Shrub's Wood and Twitchells End, and Eugen C. Kaufmann's own house of 1934-5 in Wimbledon adopted a similar ground-floor plan and balconied verandah.[23]

On the strength of this successful publicity and the prominence of Twitchells End, Colin Crickmay set up in practice on his own with a room hired in the Gordon Square offices of Cyril Sweett, the gifted quantity surveyor for Chermayeff and Mendelsohn. His cousin, Hugh W. Crickmay (1908-78), had studied at the Bartlett School of Architecture and became an associate of the RIBA in 1931, four years after Colin, and began his practice in Slough. Hugh was a son of G. L. Crickmay who had been the senior partner of the family practice based in London and Weymouth, which was continued by both his brothers F. A. and Henry Crickmay, but it was not until Henry died in 1937 that Colin and Hugh acquired the Weymouth practice where they practiced until Colin

retired in 1972 and Hugh in 1977. The London office in Victoria Street was bombed out in the Second World War but they had never practiced there.[24]

Colin probably worked on several project drawings, such as those for Wells Coates and Schreiner, but by the time his next executed house was published in 1937, it is apparent that his cousin had joined him in partnership. During these years before the war, Colin Crickmay designed half a dozen more houses, mostly in the same area, and the Mayfair Cinema, Stamford Hill, which replaced the Roxy there in 1939.[25] On the strength of his experience, he considered launching his own modular furniture business from Jordans and produced a brochure illustrating the plywood pieces designed for his own home and their changing uses by a young and active family. But the economic climate was too bleak and he subsequently discovered that the organic glues then in use attracted woodworm.[26] After the major interruption of war service, both Colin and Hugh returned to Weymouth to rebuild their practice. As a result of building Twitchells End, Betty Jenkins's adoptive father, W. F. Tuke, had commissioned some work for Barclay's Bank before the war, which encouraged a successful application to become the Bank's architects in Dorset and this regular work helped to re-establish what became a thriving local practice.[27]

Twitchells End was both a first and last for Colin Crickmay who concluded his discussion by explaining why his subsequent houses were less expressive of the Modern Movement. The next house, for Miss Ellershaw at Jordans, had a pronounced pitched and catslide roof. Hobble Barn at Beaconsfield, published in 1938, is a larger variation on this theme.[28] 'I came to the conclusion quite early on that a flat roof was not really suitable for this country. That was one of the reasons. Clients were not receptive to this type of design and it was not until well after the war that it was generally accepted. Local authorities were not in favour of modern design. The other was that I could not see any excuse for building that sort of house unless it was in reinforced concrete. (A): you would want an engineer, which clients would not necessarily be prepared to pay for; (B): there were all sorts of technical problems that the builders weren't very good at. So I went right off it.'[29] 'I suppose my own houses were influenced by the simplicity that one gained from another. I always used to say to people "Why have a flat roof at all?" Mendelsohn used to say that if you didn't have to design the plan to have a pitched roof, you could have any shape you like. I suppose … that's true of Twitchells End, because that plan with a pitched roof would have looked terribly clumsy. It's wide for its length and you couldn't do that. I think that a pitched roof for this country is right. You don't see many houses being designed now with flat roofs.' At Twitchells End, however, this was what the clients wanted and their young architect had the fortunate experience of working with architects and engineers who understood the technical requirements for achieving not only this but the type of steel balcony and sun roof required to accompany it. They collaborated to make this house their contribution to the Modern Movement in England.

Figures 20 and 21.
C. R. Crickmay,
'Birchwood', house
for Miss Ellershaw
at Jordans, c.1936
(from H. Myles Wright,
Small Houses £500–£2,500,
London, Architectural
Press, 1937)

1. This research originated in 1971 when R. E. C. Swann, a friend of Colin Crickmay in the 1930s, introduced me to Gilbert Jenkins. It developed in 1981 as a project for Tim Benton's Open University Course: History of Architecture and Design 1890-1939. I am grateful to the late Gilbert Jenkins, his daughter and son-in-law Ann and Donald Lenox, the late Colin Crickmay and his daughter Jo, and the Open University's cartographer John Hunt. Copies of all the original course dissertations were presented to the RIBA Library Archive by the Open University.

2. Gilbert Jenkins retired to work on the *Victorian County History of Staffordshire* and was a founder of the Buckinghamshire Record Society. He wrote books on Jordans, and *Chequers: a history of the Prime Minister's Buckinghamshire House*, Oxford, Pergamon Press, 1967. See also Elizabeth Tuke Jenkins, *Happy Childhood Memories*, High Wycombe, Precision Press, 1970.

3. See Arthur L. Hayward, *Jordans: the making of a community*, London, Friends Home Service Committee, 1969.

4. Elizabeth McKellar, 'C. H. B. Quennell (1872-1935) Architecture, History and the Quest for the Modern', *Architectural History*, vol.50, 2007, pp.211-45. Land's End House Charvil, Twyford, by Guy Morgan of 1934-5, *Architectural Review*, vol.78, July 1935, pp.33-6, resembles Quennell's 'A' scheme, with a central bay in a ribbon-windowed front and a rotund cornice and flat roof.

5. Interview with Cyril Jenkins in 1981. Cyril is noted for his collaboration with Lázló Moholy-Nagy, whom he first found poaching time in his Wardour Street cutting room while working on *The Life of the Lobster*. They became friends and colleagues, working together on *The New Architecture at the London Zoo*, shot in 1936 for the exhibition *Modern Architecture in England* at MOMA in New York in 1937.

6. The Dorland Hall exhibition from 20 June – 12 July 1933, supervised by Oliver Hill, and the BBC talks on Design in Modern Life between 18 April and 27 June were in response to the Gorell Report of the Board of Trade Committee on Art and Education in 1932.

7. Interview with Colin Crickmay, 1981, and further correspondence. Subsequent quotations from Crickmay are from these sources and are not individually referenced.

8. See Alan Powers, *Serge Chermayeff, Designer, Architect, Teacher*, London, RIBA Publications, 2001.

9. Wells Coates and David Pleydell-Bouverie, 'Design for an Airport', *Architectural Review*, vol.72, November 1932, p.116.

10. Serge Chermayeff, 'An English Country House', *Architectural Review*, vol.72, November 1932, pp.213-14.

11. See Bruno Zevi, Erich Mendelsohn: *Opera Completa*, Milan, Etas Kompass, 1970, pp.83, 188-95; Charlotte Benton, *A Different World: Émigré Architects in England*, London, Heinz Gallery, 1995, pp.187-90; Charlotte Benton, '"Enough Mistakes and Experience Behind Me": Buildings in England and the Partnership with Chermayeff, 1933-1941', in Regina Stephan, ed., *Erich Mendelsohn: Architect 1887-1953*, New York, Monacelli Press, 1999, pp.190-203, 271; Powers, op.cit., pp.64-7.

12. *Architect and Building News*, vol.142, 21 June 1935, pp.337-40. Schreiner subsequently left to join Mendelsohn in the USA.

13. C. H. B. Quennell, letter, 6 February 1933; Elizabeth Jenkins, 'Four-Square to the Sun', *Evening Standard*, 21 February 1935.

14. 'House at Jordans, Bucks, 1935', *Architectural Review*, vol.78, August 1935, pp.53-4; 'House at Chalfont St Giles', ibid, November 1935, pp.174-8.

15. 'House at Jordans, Bucks, 1935', ibid.

16. F. R. S. Yorke, *The Modern House*, London, Architectural Press, 1934, pp.164-5.

17. Elizabeth Jenkins, op.cit. 'VITA' glass was advertised for its positive effect on the transmissibility of ultra-violet rays. Crickmay observed that 'Betty Jenkins sought to do the best for her children'.

18. See Yorke, op.cit.; Connell, Ward and Lucas, 'Semi-Detached House at Ruislip', 1935', p.121; 'House at Wentworth', 1937', pp.101-3; 'House at Moor Park, Rickmansworth', 1937', pp.138-42.

19. For a similar use by Wells Coates, see Dennis Sharp, ed., *The Rationalists: Theory and Design in the Modern Movement*, London, Architectural Press, 1978, p.98, fig.6.

20. Although acquired at this time, the first models for the Heals bedroom furniture had been introduced between 1906-33. See Oliver S. Heal, *Sir Ambrose Heal and the Heal Cabinet Factory, 1897-1933*, Wetherby, Oblong, 2014, and the illustrated catalogues of the Millinery Works Ltd, London, 2003, 2006, 2010 and 2014.

21. *Modern Building Practice*, vol.1, no.15, 1935, pp.225-30.

22. Jeremy Gould, *Modern Houses in Britain, 1939*, London, SAHGB, Architectural History Monographs, 1977.

23. *Architects' Journal*, vol.85, 1 April 1937, pp.576-7; Kaufmann and Benjamin's 'House at Wimbledon 1935', in Yorke, op. cit., note 1, pp.36-7; Lynne Walker, 'Interview with Elizabeth Benjamin', in Neil Bingham and Alan Powers, eds., Twentieth Century Architecture no.2, *The Modern House Revisited*, London, Twentieth Century Society, 1996, pp.73-84, in which Benjamin describes the difficulty of working with this experienced refugee architect who kept changing his mind as he picked up new ideas for his house at 55 Victoria Road, Wimbledon. Although forming a single square, both the ground-floor plan and the balconied verandah are broadly similar in design and structure although the latter was itself glazed in.

24. Information in a letter from Colin Crickmay to Kevin Wheelan, 8 February 1984. Crickmay and his cousin resented having to buy their deceased uncle's practice. The website of John Stark and Crickmay, Weymouth, and Hugh Crickmay's obituary of 1978 suggest variant dates.

25. 'The Mayfair Cinema, Tottenham, N, by Crickmay and Sons with L. O. Eccleshall', *Architects' Journal*, vol.89, 16 March 1939, pp.464-5.

26. In 1933, Chermayeff had launched the Plan range of chairs and unit furniture, but it was not a commercial success. See Powers, op.cit., pp.50-8.

27. Crickmay and Ann Jenkins assumed that Mr Tuke had provided financial support to realise the Jenkins' final design and, tellingly, his photograph is the first in their album on the building and life in the house.

28. 'Jordans, Bucks, by Crickmay and Crickmay', in H. M. Wright, ed., *Small Houses: £500-£2,500*, London, Architectural Press, 1937, p.100; 'House at Beaconsfield by C. R. Crickmay', *Architects' Journal*, vol.87, 3 February 1938, p.206.

29. Crickmay recalled attendance with one of Ove Arup's assistants at a research trial of different concrete mixtures, 'after which one of the builders remarked that he wished they'd just let them get on with it their own way'.

Twitchells End was published in architectural periodicals as follows: 'A House in Jordans, Buckinghamshire', *Architect and Building News*, vol.140, 14 December 1934, pp.336-7, with photos by Cyril Jenkins; 'House at Jordans, Bucks, 1935', *Architectural Review*, vol.78, August 1935, pp.53-4, with photos by John Yerbury; 'House at Jordans, Bucks', *Architectural Review*, vol.80, December 1936, pp.243-4. The last includes the same images as the August 1935 article, minus two interiors, adding technical information. The two pages from the December 1936 issue were reproduced at reduced size in F. R. S. Yorke, *The Modern House in England*, London, Architectural Press, 1937 and 1944 editions.

Neil Bingham

5

A Second Skin: Houses and Housing by Gordon and Ursula Bowyer

In 1965, a year after her husband James Callaghan became Chancellor of the Exchequer, Audrey Callaghan wrote an article for *House and Garden* magazine lamenting having to leave the family home in Blackheath, south London, to live in the Chancellor's official residence, No.11 Downing Street:

> But I do miss the house that was so expertly tailor-made – or perhaps I ought to say architect-designed – to the requirements of the Callaghan family by our friends Gordon and Ursula Bowyer. The rare kind of house that exactly suits one's way of life is like a second skin. It was a wrench to leave.[1]

Photographs of the entrances of each house illustrated the article: the elegant modern and the historic Georgian. The article was a follow-up; the Blackheath house had already featured in the pages of *House and Garden* when the Callaghan family had moved in when it was new in 1958.[2] Designed by husband and wife architects Gordon and Ursula Bowyer, the future Labour Prime Minister and his family had been their neighbours for most of the previous decade, living just north of the heath down Maze Hill where the Bowyers still live today in a large mid-eighteenth century house overlooking Greenwich Park.

The Callaghan house was one of a mirrored pair in a terrace of houses facing the heath, Nos.17 and 17a Montpelier Row, on the site of a war-damaged gap between a Georgian and a Victorian residence.[3] Set back from the road, the houses are modest and discreet yet distinctive.[4] Today, they are little changed, although the windows of No.17a have been replaced by uPVC units. Restricted by post-war building regulations to a maximum of 1500 square feet per unit, the structure is three storeys, each house with a garage, cloakroom and study on the ground floor – the Callaghans requested a smaller study in order to accommodate a utility room – with a living room, dining room and kitchen on the first floor and four bedrooms on the second. The garden may be accessed at ground level as well as by a door and external stairs from the first storey. The Bowyers designed built-in furniture and large glazed sliding doors, with hidden tracks in the ceiling, which the Callaghans found useful when entertaining, and Ursula designed bespoke kitchens of beech-faced blockboard with a natural polish and worktops of oiled teak.[5]

The Montpelier Row pair are Gordon and Ursula Bowyer's most noted houses, although their architectural career included many designs for houses and housing scattered amongst the more prestigious projects that made them highly respected post-war British architects. Coming first to prominence in 1951 when they were in their mid-twenties – Gordon was born in 1923 and Ursula in 1925 – they were part of the Festival of Britain team under Hugh Casson and created the space-framed Sport Pavilion. During the 1950s, their fine understanding of contemporary styling and exacting standards of detailing and execution were evident in such designs as the up-market home furnishing shops of 1958 for Primavera in Sloane Street, London, and Kings Parade, Cambridge. By the early 1970s, they were creating stylish salons around Europe and the USA for the fashion hair stylist Vidal Sassoon and undertaking many design jobs for the international technology giant IBM. In 1990, having spent a career that included much exhibition work, the Bowyers undertook the new Japanese Gallery and re-designed the Prints and Drawings and the Oriental Antiquities galleries at the British Museum.

With all these larger projects on the books, and with houses never greatly profitable, Gordon says that he and Ursula did not go out of their way to seek domestic commissions. The majority of their private houses were designed in the 1950s and early 1960s. During the 1970s, the Bowyers shifted their focus in residential work to terraced housing and flats for independent housing associations, and to council blocks mainly for the London Borough of Southwark. However, for much of her career, well into the 1980s, Ursula focussed upon house and flat conversions, undertaking as many as three

Figure 2.17 and 17a
Montpelier Row,
Blackheath, London,
a pair of houses
completed 1958. Future
Prime Minister James
Callaghan and his family,
friends of the Bowyers,
were the first occupants
of No.17, on the left

or four a year. Kitchens were her speciality. 'Those were the times', she recalls with disparaging resignation, 'that the little woman architect was expected to do such things'.[6] She was called upon to design ideal kitchens for magazines, and in 1957 created an exhibition kitchen for the Council of Industrial Design in their new London showroom at the Design Centre in Haymarket. Audrey Callaghan even asked Ursula to No.11 to redesign the kitchen of the Chancellor's house.

When in 1954 the commercial artist Ronald Waddams approached the Bowyers for a house in Chalfont St Giles, Buckinghamshire, they had to turn many of the working drawings over to an assistant, Michael Le Pelley, because they were busy designing the Max Factor cosmetics shop in the Royal Arcade in London's Old Bond Street. The house, built within the restriction of 1500 square feet and for less than £4000 (not a great deal of money for such a project), concentrated on a long, low horizontal form split between two levels. Highly influential on the design was Harbour Meadow, the house in Birdham, West Sussex, designed by Peter Moro in 1938-40, which the Bowyers knew well. Both Gordon and Ursula had been Moro's students at Regent Street Polytechnic, where the couple had met. They were to remain lifelong friends with Moro,[7] and at the time of the Waddams House, they were sharing offices with a group of architectural colleagues at No.71 Blandford Street near Baker Street, including Moro.[8] Gordon was even commissioned by the client of Birdham, Mrs Tawse, to paint a mural for the house in 1947, which she eventually installed instead in her Regent's Park flat. The Birdham house, says Gordon, was 'our goal, we admired it enormously'.[9]

Also in 1954 while doing the Foster house, the Bowyers designed another under-1500 square foot house near Tunbridge Wells for John Raven, a director of the

British Coal Exporters Federation who worked as a writer at Crawford's Advertising
Agency where Gordon had spent a year or so from 1945, training for a job in industrial
design while attending evening classes on plastics.

In 1956, the Bowyers built their most substantial private house: Greenacres, Belton
Lane, in Grantham, Lincolnshire. The clients, Ralph and Kate Foster, had billeted
Ursula and her sister Anna during the war. Ralph Foster was a building contractor who
had spent that period making camouflaged ammunition warehouses. The new single-
storey, four-bedroom house with a flat roof was distinguished by its courtyard plan of
three blocks arranged in an H-form.[10] Large windows afforded views across terraces
that incorporated a sunken pool and wooden platform bridge. The living spaces were
open plan, a fireplace creating a wall reaching to the height of the transom clerestory
between the living space and the dining area with its weathered sycamore finish and
rosewood dining table. Ursula designed another of her signature kitchens. As a building
contractor, Ralph Foster asked the Bowyers to draw up a design at one-quarter inch to
a foot, with no details, for a pair of semi-detached houses, which he then had worked
up and built 'in the hundreds' in the Grantham area; Gordon thought them 'of good
quality and modern in style'.[11] At the time, the Bowyers were actively involved in the
high profile debate led by critic Ian Nairn on Subtopia, 'the insidiousness … national
disease' of poorly designed new housing developments in suburban areas. With
sponsorship from the Royal Institute of British Architects, the Bowyers worked with
Nairn to design a thirty-panel Subtopia travelling exhibition.[12]

Two houses followed over the next few years. The Curtis House in Peterborough,
of about 1958, was for a manager of Combex, the plastic manufacturing company for
whom the Bowyers had designed a showroom in London's West End, on Ganton Street
near Carnaby Street. And similar to the Curtis House was the residence that the

Bowyers designed in the peaceful Buckinghamshire town of Newport Pagnell,
Buckinghamshire, on a site that proved the client's undoing. This was a Mr Shearer,
a director with Sogenique (Service) Limited, introduced through Colonel Brian
Rowe, theme convener for the Bowyers' Sport Pavilion at the 1951 Festival of Britain.
In 1957-8 the Bowyers had built an elegant two-story office and workshop for Shearer's
company which serviced precision scientific and mathematical instruments made by
the Swiss parent company Société Genevoise; the entrance lobby to the offices featured
furniture by the Bowyers' friend Robin Day, and a mural by Henry and Joyce Collins
showing draughtsmen at their drawing boards and machinists servicing precision
machines just as they did in the rear factory building. The house commission thus
came from an interested client. But Shearer and his wife had little time to enjoy the
modern one-storey brick house, for within a short time of moving in, the M1 motorway
opened in 1959 just a few hundred feet away from them, over an artificial embankment.
The noise, believes Gordon, contributed to their early deaths.

Gordon and Ursula Bowyer's modern house designs culminated in their most
experimental work, and one of Britain's finest original and sophisticated investigations
into the possibilities of change and flexibility within domestic living, when at the 1961
Furniture Show held at the Earls Court Exhibition Centre, London, they presented
'The Growing Home'. It was a feature display of the show. Under the auspices of the
Design Research Unit, the highly influential government-backed consortium that
had contributed greatly to the 1951 Festival of Britain, the Bowyers created a very
large exhibit showing how a home for a family of four could develop over 23 years as
conceived in four full house interiors of no less than eighteen display rooms. In the first
stage, for example, the children, a boy and a girl, are born and given a common nursery
which in the next stage is divided into separate bedrooms, and then returned in the

Figure 5. Burnt House Cottage, Alfriston, East Sussex, 1962. Alterations and additions to an old farmhouse and brewhouse included this snug modern inglenook fireplace (Edgar Hyman / G. & U. Bowyer)

Figure 6. 2 Langton Way, Blackheath, London, 1965. The conversion of the coach house included a new kitchen, dining and living space by Ursula (G. & U. Bowyer)

Figure 7. Detail of double-height glazed entrance linking the converted garage and main house, 19 Morden Road Mews, Blackheath, London, by Ursula Bowyer, 1970 (Edgar Hyman / RIBAPC35622/4)

final stage to a single room for guests after the children had grown and departed. The showing of two of the staged interiors by day and two by night created a sense of time and atmosphere. The specialist critic in exhibition design, Robert Gutmann, writing in the international magazine *Moebel Interior Design*, called the Bowyers' work 'not only the best of this large exhibition, but as an arrangement it belongs to the most impressive things ever seen here for a long time', while praising the 'very cultured colouring'.[13]

In the 1960s the Bowyers extended and converted several houses and cottages. They included a picturesque nineteenth-century coach house, complete with a few Gothic revival windows, at No. 2 Langton Way, Blackheath for George and Ann Dannatt. Much of the new work consisted of a kitchen, dining area and living space by Ursula. They also designed a holiday home, Burnt House Cottage, in Alfriston, East Sussex, for Serena and Graham Hughes. The traditional flint-built farmhouse consisted of attached brew-houses with a large brick fireplace, copper and baking oven, which they retained while adding an annex wing with a kitchen, bedrooms and a new entrance porch in glass and timber, a careful balance of old and new.[14] This was one of the first jobs where the Bowyers were assisted by Iain Langlands, who joined the office as an assistant in 1960, undertaking the working drawings and site supervision. He became a partner in 1966.[15]

As the practice grew, Gordon tended to concentrate on the large commercial jobs, and while Ursula often assisted, she found it more convenient to work from home as she undertook the many kitchen, flat and house conversions that came to dominate her side of the practice. Of the many dozen such conversions, one in particular can stand as an excellent example, No. 19 Morden Road Mews, Blackheath. Ursula transformed a two-storey garage, situated on a muddy lane backing the big houses on Morden Road, into a home for an art collector. The upper floor, which had been a billiard room, was converted to a picture gallery for the client's watercolour collection. A new wing for living accommodation was added with a link block for the principal entrance, staircase and fine glazed wall.

Ursula's long and strong involvement with her local heritage group, the Greenwich Society – which gained her life presidency of the society and an Honorary Doctorate of Design from the University of Greenwich in 2010 – gave both her and Gordon a greater appreciation of conservation issues. So they were greatly prepared and highly sensitive when it came to their largest conversion, Vanbrugh Castle just a few minutes stroll up Maze Hill from their home. Designed and built by the Baroque architect and playwright Sir John Vanbrugh in 1718 for his own use, the picturesque brick pile was in a very poor state having served as a school for more than fifty years before standing empty for a further two years, when the Bowyers faced the challenge of converting it to residential houses and flats in the late 1970s. Little rooms, passages, pipe work and external fire escapes were stripped away; window openings were re-instated, two sets of internal stairs created and the rooms converted into dwellings.[16]

The Bowyers also worked with independent housing associations and in social housing. Most of these projects were in southeast London, with their first undertaking a private development, in 1963, a terrace of five houses, Lydale Close, off Foyle Road, Greenwich. The two-storey brick houses had compact plans and a modern appearance similar to the Span estates in nearby Blackheath that the Bowyers admired. However, the Bowyers' terrace exhibited a greater articulation of the façade at a time when terrace elevations, including those of Span, were mainly flat and linear.

In the early 1970s the Bowyers built four developments for housing associations. These were undertaken during the associations' infancy, when local authorities still provided the great majority of social housing. Completed in 1972, the Greenwich Housing Association sponsored Hatfield Court, Heathway in Greenwich, a ten-unit block of flats for the elderly set around a pleasant communal

Figure 9. Lydale Close, Foyle Road, Greenwich, London, 1963. A terrace of five houses (Edgar Hyman / RIBAPC35580/1)

Figure 10. Hatfield Court, Heathway, Greenwich, London, 1972. View around communal garden (Chorley Hyman & Rose Ltd / RIBAPC35598/4)

garden. For the Family Housing Association, the Bowyers designed two blocks of flats in 1974: one at No.41 Gloucester Drive in Finsbury Park, North London, and the other on a picturesque site facing the old parish church in Mossfield Green, Barkingside, Ilford, which included the early provision of handicapped access to the ground floor flats. The following year, for Quadrant Housing Association, the Bowyers designed a substantial four-storey brick block of flats at the corner of St Margaret's Road and Adelaide Avenue in Brockley, Lewisham, London.

Gordon and Ursula Bowyer's three social housing projects were all carried out for the London Borough of Southwark. By now the office had grown, and these developments were largely the responsibility of Iain Langlands and Stephen Batchelor, who joined the practice in 1970.[17] The practice's first two social housing schemes were done concurrently, commissioned in 1970. Thornton House at Nos.16-31 Townsend Street, on the corner of Congreve Street off the Old Kent Road, was designed to compensate for the lack of 2-person and 6-person dwellings in the borough, with a projected figure of eighty inhabitants.[18] The larger maisonettes at ground and first floor have gardens, while the smaller flats on the top two stories are entered along the street side via continuous open covered balconies. A unique feature is the V-shaped roof, shaped for easier drainage. Also built of brick, but more finely textured in varying russet tones, No.72 Grove Lane consists of two three-storey blocks of flats for 114 tenants sharing two- and five-person flats.

The Bowyers also carried out two further accommodation projects in Southwark. For the Borough, they designed a hostel for children with special needs, then referred to as 'mentally handicapped children'. The Lordship Lane Hostel at Nos.269-81 Lordship Lane, Dulwich, was opened in 1975 and had a combination of short-term and long-stay accommodation with bedroom and living facilities.[19] The hostel was carried out in tandem with their creation of a nearby school for children with special needs, Cherry Garden School.

Also within Southwark, between 1972 and 1974, the Bowyers built a four-storey block of flats, Cherry Tree Court, at the corner of Queen's Road and Woods Road. The housing was part of the redevelopment of a site in the possession of the Peckham Methodist congregation. With the demolition of a large Victorian church – described by Bridget Cherry and Nikolaus Pevsner in the Buildings of England as 'a monstrously ugly building of 1864 by Hoole' – the site was freed up for the Bowyers to create both a smaller church building and flats.[20] As the principal frontage of Cherry Tree Court runs along the busy Queen's Road, the architects gave it a monolithic elevation at ground floor level, almost solid brick wall, and on the upper two levels used the continuous open covered access balconies thus placing the large windows of the principal living accommodation on the quiet south side facing overlooking the church.

Housing is the intimate world of the personal, family and friends. For Gordon and Ursula Bowyer, their own home has long been their most cherished design. They first leased the house at Maze Hill in 1950, purchasing it not long after. Three stories and five bays wide, mid-eighteenth century with a core of about 1690, the brick house is the northern and lower side of a paired terrace on the steeply inclined road bordering the east side of Greenwich Park. Gordon calls it 'a six-hearth central stack house, related to the houses of Deptford ship captains and shipwrights'. In the 65 years they have lived there, Gordon and Ursula have restored and, gently, changed the house. Partitions have been removed, and a large picture window and door inserted on the garden side first floor living room with outside access via a Victorian spiral cast iron staircase. The panelled walls are hung with fine prints and drawings, and tables dotted with sculpture, many by friends like Victor Pasmore and Robert Adams. And, of course, the house boasts one of Ursula's fine kitchens.

Figure II. Thornton House, Townsend Street, housing for the London Borough of Southwark, London, 1970 (Chorley, Hyman & Rose Ltd / RIBAPC35592/3)

Figure 12. Living-dining space and kitchen, stage 4 of 'The Growing Home' feature at the Furniture Show 1961, Earls Court, London. The Bowyers created 18 display rooms showing how a home for a family of four could develop over 23 years (RIBA, Maltby Collection [no. 45714] John Maltby, photographer)

Figure 13. Garden elevation of Gordon and Ursula Bowyer's home, Maze Hill, Greenwich, London, where they inserted a large picture window and door with a Victorian spiral staircase into the mid-18th century façade (Historic England, Lucy Millson-Watkins)

Acknowledgments: My warmest appreciation to Gordon and Ursula, as well as thanks to Iain Langlands, Michael Mellish, Suzi Freeman, Justine Sambrook and Valeria Carullo

1. 'Mrs James Callaghan on her new life in No 11', *House and Garden*, vol.20, no.2, February 1965, pp.21-23. Labour politician James Callaghan was Chancellor of the Exchequer from 1964 to 1967, and subsequently Home Secretary from 1967 to 1970, Foreign Secretary from 1974 to 1976, and Prime Minister from 1976 to 1979.

2. 'Uncommon neighbourliness: An architect and an MP build two houses and cultivate one garden in Blackheath', *House and Garden*, vol.15, no.6, June 1960, pp.58-59. The Bowyers had planned on moving into No.17a Montpelier Row upon completion, but instead remained in their Greenwich home; the Callaghans purchased No.17.

3. 'Two Houses at Montpelier Row, Blackheath, London', *Architectural Design*, vol.29, no.11, November 1959, pp.447-48. No.17a was photographed for this article.

4. Blackheath grew as a hotbed of Modern Movement architecture from the mid-1950s with major houses by Peter Moro, Patrick Gywnne, and 22 housing schemes by Eric Lyons for Span built between 1956 and 1984.

5. Interview with Gordon and Ursula Bowyer, 10 February 2013.

6. Interview with Gordon and Ursula Bowyer, 2 November 2013.

7. Peter Moro, 'Harbour Meadow, Birdham', in Twentieth Century Architecture, no.2, *The Modern House Revisited*, London, Twentieth Century Society, 1996, pp.8-14. Gordon Bowyer moved in with Peter and Anne Moro in 1947 when they bought No.32 Crooms Hill, Greenwich that year. Moro built his own family house, No.20 Blackheath Park, in 1957.

8. Peter Moro had been on the design team of the recently completed Royal Festival Hall. Also sharing office space were Richard Finch, Walter Greaves, Georgio Subiotto and Trevor Dannatt, who had been best man at the Bowyers' wedding.

9. Gordon Bowyer, 10 February 2013.

10. 'House at Grantham, Yorkshire', *Architectural Design*, vol.27, no.1, January 1957, pp.10-11; 'House at Grantham, Lincs', *Architectural Review*, vol.121, no.721, February 1957, pp.119-120; 'H for Sunshine', *Ideal Home*, vol.77, no.6, June 1958, pp.37-40.

11. Gordon Bowyer, 10 February 2013.

12. *Architects' Journal*, vol.125, no.3250, 13 June 1957, p.868.

13. Furniture Show in London', *Moebel Interior Design*, vol.1, no.5, 1961, pp.220-2.

14. *Architectural Design*, vol.35, no.8, August 1965, p.417.

15. Interview with Iain Langlands, 20 May 2013. Langlands graduated from the Northern Polytechnic, London, in 1953.

16. Peter Weatherhead, 'An Englishman's Home: Vanbrugh's picturesque castle is rescued from rot', *Building Design*, No.441, 20 April 1979, p.36.

17. Stephen Batchelor became a partner in 1982, when the practice became known as Bowyer Langlands Batchelor (BLB). A few years later, John Coleman was also created a partner and today Batchelor and Coleman run BLB Architects Limited.

18. 'Townsend Street, Congreve Development Area, London Borough of Southwark', October 1970, architects' brochure in Robert Elwall Photographs Collection, Ref. 35592, RIBA.

19. A. Ivan Nellist, 'Help for the handicapped: Cherry Garden School, London borough of Southwark, and hostel for mentally handicapped children on Lordship Lane, Southwark', *Architects' Journal*, vol.162, no.37, 10 Sept 1975, pp.508-11.

20. Bridget Cherry and Nikolaus Pevsner, The Buildings of England: *London 2: South*, Harmondsworth: Penguin Books, 1983, p.618.

Julian Holder

6 Busman's holiday: Houses in Lancashire by Keith Ingham

Keith Ingham (1932-95) is today remembered as the architect of Preston Bus Station, but in his lifetime his reputation rested on a passion for housing.[1] As both the son and grandson of building contractors in Lytham St. Annes, he was well placed to observe that 'there seems to be a barrier which deters the builder from approaching the Architect. He does not realise the wide implications and responsibilities of design: he is often looking for someone to draw up some plans as cheaply as possible to hoodwink local councils'.[2] With a personal motto of 'design excellence in everything', Ingham's work was a life-long battle to break down such barriers. This is reflected not only in his work as an architect but across a breadth of professional interests that included industrial design, furniture, interiors, graphics, landscaping, and urban design. In this respect he was an ideal employee of Building Design Partnership (BDP) where he stayed for much of his working life. Established by George Grenfell Baines (1908-2003) – usually referred to as 'GG' and one of the key figures in the architectural culture of the region – BDP was one of the first multi-disciplinary practices in the United Kingdom and aimed to establish the modernist ideals of Walter Gropius and the Bauhaus here. As his widow Milena recalled, 'his ideal was the Bauhaus – the different professions under one roof'.[3] GG finally met an elderly Gropius on a visit to Harvard, and reported being told that 'you have done what I would like to have done in Dessau'.[4]

Although it is now best known for a succession of dramatic brutalist buildings, in its early days BDP was known for housing design by a talented group of young architects GG attracted to his practice, including John Ashworth, Brian Cobb, Ervin Marek, Tom Mellor, David Rock, Keith Scott, S. H. Tasker and Keith Ingham. The later successes of BDP have tended to obscure these early years when Ingham was one of its rising stars.[5] The ethos established by Grenfell Baines was one of a socialist-informed anonymity to ensure that the principal architect alone did not receive the credit for work which he had not designed and, more significantly perhaps, profits were shared.[6] Whilst Ingham shared his principal's politics his desire for individual recognition was a recurring tension. Fortunately this was offset by the individuality of expression afforded teams within the practice and the strong regional character favoured by BDP that respected the *genius loci* of the firm's roots in Preston and the north-west of England.

This regionalism suited Ingham well as West Lancashire generally, and the Fylde and Lytham St. Annes more specifically, remained his heartland and with few exceptions his best work is centred on this quiet low-lying corner of the country.[7] He was already designing houses for his father, Arnold Ingham, whilst studying at Preston Art School between 1950 and 1953, a practice which continued after he went on to the Bartlett School of Architecture at University College London.[8] The School was then under the direction of Hector Corfiato, a Beaux-Arts classicist and colleague of Albert Richardson. Ingham did not find Corfiato's teaching conducive and recalled learning more from the Professor of Planning, William Holford, who 'gave from the outset a broader context to all my design work. Any building whilst excellent in itself must be part of a place.'[9]

With Mondrian in mind: early housing and Greystones

Many of Ingham's early houses for the family firm are still readily identifiable in parts of Lytham and are typical examples of the then fashionable New Empiricism with its strong Scandinavian influence. However, there was already something different about his designs, such as a delight in a very formal pattern language – most usually seen in the fenestration – that looks to the abstract modernism of De Stijl. This is overtly seen in his so-called 'Mondrian House' on Blackpool Road, Lytham St. Annes, but appears in other house designs of the late 1950s.[10]

These early incursions into speculative housing were also informed by his work and subsequent friendship with fellow local architect Tom Mellor (1914-94), who had worked for Holford before joining Grenfell Baines and later formed his own practice.[11] Ingham spent his student year out in 1954 working for Mellor, who had just completed his own

Figure 2. An example of the type of house designed by Ingham for his father's building company in the 1950s. The clean sharp lines look to Scandinavia, the large sweeping roof to Dior's 'New Look'

Figure 3. Greystones, St. Annes, rear elevation with link to garage, completed in 1956. Ingham continued to play with the 'Contemporary style' in his own house but brought in historicist details and a nod to the local vernacular in the chimney stack clad in local beach pebbles

Figure 4a. Part of the entry of Grenfell-Baines & Hargreaves to the 1958 *Ideal Home*/RIBA Small Houses competition. Ingham's winning design created a varied public face whilst retaining privacy for owners and unity of design by the use of the linking wall. Built throughout the country, but particularly in the north-west

house in Lytham, Churchwood, which was clearly modelled on Sven Markelius's house in Kevinge, Stockholm, of 1945, one of the touchstones of New Empiricism.[12] Mellor became a formative influence on Ingham's future career, not only as an architect but as an interior designer. In 1952, in succession to John Murray, he was appointed design consultant to the progressive Lancashire textile firm of David Whitehead, at a time when Lancashire and West Yorkshire were still the centre of a textile industry made vibrant by the quality of local design companies. Under Mellor's guidance, Whitehead brought affordable modern art to the masses in the shape of well-designed 'contemporary' furnishing fabrics, an example Ingham looked to when he was briefly responsible for running the family's own shop, which sold modern Scandinavian household design in Lytham.[13]

The architectural world Ingham joined was ably described by Mellor when in 1953 he wrote that 'since 1945 enforced austerity and architectural propaganda of the "building for the people" variety have made modern architecture respectable and commonplace…[but] in the process of assimilation something has gone wrong'.[14] This was the growing perception that modern architecture had too narrowly copied a set of ideas from Gropius and Le Corbusier that concentrated on a formalist agenda at the expense of human values. No less rooted in Lancashire than Ingham, Mellor saw the need for regionalism in modern architecture, urging architects to:

> without any loss of efficiency or contemporary character, aim at regional differences in our buildings. Variations in landscape, climate and local materials and in the character of the local people and their daily lives should be reflected in contemporary architecture. Surely it is wrong that the same pattern of local authority house in the same pebble dash or rustic brick, appears on the Lancashire Plain and along the steep sides of the Rossendale Valley in the Pennines 1,000 feet above sea-level, where the climate is as different as that of Central Norway or the Shetlands. [15]

Given the later trajectory of his housing design, Ingham may also have been influenced by examples of regionalism coming out of Italy, France and, most notably, works by Harwell Hamilton Harris and William Wurster in the Bay Region Style then being illustrated in magazines such as the Californian *Arts and Architecture*. In the same article

Mellor also argued for a commitment to craftsmanship: 'If we cannot build the glittering towers of the city of to-morrow, at least we can try and get a good mortar joint, and a neat finish to our flashings.'

Greystones, completed in 1956, the year of his marriage to Margaret Dearden, was the first of two houses Ingham designed for himself and his family. It embodies many of the ideas found in Mellor's work, especially in its design details and setting. A dormer bungalow, with a second floor concealed in the very large and steeply pitched roof designed to counter exposure to the Irish Sea, its load-bearing brick construction is rendered in particularly thick pebbledash suggestive of the Greystones of its name and the local geology. The extruded section of heavily framed windows, then much favoured, puncture the ground-floor gable end walls whilst a ribbon of almost continuous glazing to the rear elevation suggests the semi-open plan of the ground floor with its feature open-tread stair. The extrusions continue with a lightweight floating covered walkway connecting the rear door to the garage. Two eyebrow dormers, part anthropomorphic, part Regency, are separated at the ridge by a chimney stack clad in beach pebbles – the same pebbles used extensively in both polite and vernacular architecture locally, especially in the nearby Lytham Hall estate and Mellor's war memorial in Smithy Lane.[16] The details of well-designed doors and windows, and the importance of setting, were a recurrent interest of Ingham's, at times bordering on a personal crusade. In 1987, from his position as a member of the Housing Design Award's panel, he wrote that, 'Windows and doors have somehow become the primary character in the look of British houses, compared with Continental houses, where they seem to be hardly noticed. In spite of great improvements in new house designs, Britain must seem aggressively ugly with its chaotic rash of prominent windows.'[17]

A keen photographer, Ingham took pictures of Greystones from low angles and locations to portray it largely enveloped by trees and vegetation, with only the roof and dormers visible above it. The architect clearly wanted privacy (a leitmotif of all his domestic designs) but also for the building to have a 'natural' presence in its setting. A large antique lamp to light the rear entrance at first appears as an afterthought to strengthen the slight historicism of the dormer windows – their rakish angles borrowed from Mellor and the New Empiricism – but drawings show it to have been a deliberate and original conceit of the design.

The *Ideal Home* / RIBA 'Designs for Small Houses' competition, 1958

Two years after completing Greystones the *Ideal Home* magazine and the Royal Institute of British Architects announced a joint 'Designs for Small Houses' competition.[18] The RIBA hoped the competition, for houses costing 'up to £4,500 and with a maximum floor area of 1,100 square feet', would demonstrate the advantages of architect-designed houses and combat what it saw as the 'continued erection of badly designed houses and badly designed estates'.[19] As the *Architects' Journal* acerbically noted in an editorial on speculative housing, 'The demand for houses is so great that the spec. builder can sell almost anything if he gets his prices low enough'.[20] It is a comment that could have as readily been written by Ingham, such was his low estimation of the building industry.

The competition proved to be an attractive but controversial affair for many of its members. Its 1,523 entries were the most that the RIBA has on record for an architectural competition in Britain; however, in place of premiums, fees were to be paid to the thirty winners.[21] This was controversial because the fee was to be a cash payment of £75 plus a low royalty of £10 for each set of prints of working drawings sold, with copyright retained by *Ideal Home*.

On completing his qualifications Keith Ingham joined Grenfell Baines & Hargreaves, who won a commendation and one of the thirty prizes. The commendation was for a design by the practice in association with Thomas Hargreaves and John Wilkinson (soon to establish a Manchester office for GG). However, the prize was for a scheme where Ingham was the only named member of the design team and it bears much of his imprint. This winning entry, design no. 517, became known as the Link House for its approach to creating a co-ordinated estate. Following the example again of Markelius, Arne Jacobsen and other Scandinavian architects, the Link House was be a continuous development of houses and garages each linked to its neighbour by screen walls.[22]

Basically the house was designed as an open-plan bungalow – but with the capacity to extend into the loft to become a six-person house – and provided 925 square feet at an anticipated cost of £3,350-£3,355. Its steeply pitched roof (45 degrees) and linking walls gave uniformity to an exterior that was thereby capable of an individual expression in layout and materials not usually found in contemporary estates. In certain respects 'the Link' was to re-establish the virtues of the row or terrace house re-evaluated in Steen Eiler Rasmussen's influential *London: the unique city*, and recently applauded in Powell and Moya's council housing at Highworth, Hampshire, of 1953.[23] 'It is a pity', Grenfell Baines wrote, '…that we haven't been able generally to find a solution to terrace designing that really appeals to the public. It is the key to a dignified, coherent grouping – and it adds to and maintains property values!'[24]

The interior of the Link, reflecting the Festival style Ingham had used in shop interiors in Lytham, was a flexible space with dining, living and kitchen areas flowing into each other and opening onto a garden terrace. A large central cupboard allowed the insertion of a staircase at a later date. Stylistically the house still bears many of the hallmarks of the New Empiricism and Scandinavian design in its clean lines and use of materials. The winning designs were exhibited at the Building Centre, London, in September 1959, where 1,500 copies of *The Book of Small House Plans* were sold to an eager public.[25] By April 1960 show houses had been built in Bromley, Maghull near Liverpool, Stockport, and at Highgate Park, Preston – an estate of 175 houses. Most of the show house interiors were overseen by a team of designers with Margaret Casson, architect wife of Sir Hugh, acting as consultant for the Council for Industrial Design.[26] Nonetheless three winners chose to do the interiors themselves, including the Grenfell Baines team, who employed interior designer Raymond Ashley with furnishings supplied by Swedish Modern Ltd, a well-established store in Preston set up by brothers William and Peter Howarth.

Before publication in *Ideal Home*, proofs were sent through to the architects for comment. Ingham altered his set in two significant ways. Firstly, he amended the title to

Figure 5. So-called 'Rat-Trad' housing by Ingham for BDP designed in 1961 consolidated a reputation for housing and won him the RIBA's 'Good design in housing' medal in 1964. These examples are in Norris Hill Park, Stockport

reduce a slight directed towards Northern England and, secondly, he expanded the design credits to give prominence to his own name. As submitted the title of the article read 'A Link Home for the Neighbourly North'; Ingham amended this to read 'A Link Home for Neighbourly Living'.[27] This title was subsequently used, though with the concession to regionalism that 'although designed for country-wide application, its general character makes this design particularly suitable for building in the North of England'.[28] 'Northernness' was even ascribed to the choice of heating by electric sub-floor coils ('Northern emphasis – *and* thrift – typifies heating plans'), the steeply pitched roof and 'smaller, weather-wise windows, and the tightly designed interior'.[29]

Grenfell Baines may have been less precious about the regional slight, arguing that its 'snuggery' area reflected the fact that 'We northerners like to get a crowd in a small place – like a pub bar – for warmth and sociability'.[30] It is noticeable that 'northerners' are being promoted as models of neighbourliness at a time when the government was worrying about issues of social cohesion in the wake of sociological studies such as Young and Willmott's *Family and Kinship in East London*.[31] It is also noticeable that the then Minister of Housing and Local Government, Henry Brooke, welcomed the 'Small Houses' competition in the hope that it had roused 'the public's interest, not only in good design but in good neighbourliness.'[32] Noticeable too that 'Northernness', as a model of 'neighbourliness' was being promoted at the same time as Granada T.V.'s *Coronation Street* was first broadcast in December 1960.[33]

Mellor's earlier argument for a more nuanced modernism had argued for regional variation, not merely for reasons of performance but also culture, when he wrote that 'if we are to consider our clients as human beings, we shall have to stop being self-conscious about the styles of the past. If someone wants an ingle nook with a dog grate, it is a mistake to give him a lecture on the economics of space heating, or try to force him to have a radiator.'[34]

The Small House competition was as much about trying to improve estate layout as it was about the standard of speculative house design – overcoming 'the barrier which deters the builder from approaching the Architect'. Writing on 'Tomorrow's Estates', Grenfell Baines, along with fellow travellers Geoffrey McLean and Eric Lyons, stated that 'the gap-tooth grin of modern semi-detached estates is about their most objectionable characteristic'.[35] The Grenfell Baines approach was 'the cluster', eight to ten houses arranged to form a large irregular court with houses linked together to create enclosure. With illustrations by a young David Rock, who had recently joined Grenfell Baines and Hargreaves's new London office, the article also showed a model of their Highgate Park estate in Preston then being built and an estate in Heaton Mersey, both of which included the competition winning designs. As the *Architects' Journal* observed:

> The critical planning difference which distinguishes the new style of suburban living from the old is the use of enclosed outdoor space. The use of this space recognises that the idea of indoor/outdoor living has come to stay and that sufficient privacy is not to be got by facing all rooms on to adjoining property.[36]

One of the earliest groups of the Link to be built was constructed by the family firm on a road almost opposite Greystones. Here a row of six linked houses were built, some with the gable end facing the road, others laid out laterally but all linked to create continuity of elevation and avoid the 'gap-toothed grin'. Continuity was also created by steeply pitched roofs clad with clay pantiles, whilst individuality was expressed with each house being given a different texture by a variety of facing materials and a De Stijl inflection once again.

At the end of the competition an editorial in *Ideal Home* expressed mock surprise that 'In talking to the winning architects we have found no remnant of the hoity-toity attitude for which clients and builders have often criticised architects in the past.'[37] Only months earlier the magazine was asking its readers 'When architects build for themselves do they try out pet theories? Or do they, when faced with the most forthright critics of all – their own families – play safe and merely rearrange proven ideas?'[38] Looking to both Greystones and the Link, there was little by way of an experimental 'pet theory' being tried out and more of an attempt to import contemporary Scandinavian practice and lifestyle. In doing so an architecture of social welfare was adapted to private enterprise under the influence of an expanding consumer society.[39]

Large numbers of the Link were built throughout the country and Ingham, now well established within the expanding Building Design Partnership in Preston, continued developing its principles. In 1964 he was awarded the medal and diploma for Good Design in Housing of the Ministry of Housing and Local Government for an estate at Norris Hill Park, Stockport. This more organic design, complete with exposed cedar clad porch and with terraced and flatted options available, was built by (amongst others) Hampson and Kemp and Arnold Ingham and Son from 1961 and marketed as the 'Panorama' range. A show house, built on Sark Road, Chorlton-cum-Hardy, Manchester, was open for six weeks from 30 March 1961 with an official opening ceremony performed by stars from *Rose Marie*, a play then on at the Palace Theatre, Manchester. As a local paper reported, 'If you are about to buy a house, can afford a moderate price, and want one of top design this is one site you *must* visit.'[40]

Growing in confidence and enhancing BDP's reputation for housing design, and with his medal win following a series of Civic Trust awards, Ingham increasingly proselytised on behalf of the profession. In an editorial on housing ('Those Designed and Those that Just Happen') for *Architecture North West*, the regional magazine he helped establish and for which he was a regular editor, he lamented the poor quality of private housing:

Figure 6. Set amidst
nineteenth century
terraces and inter-war
semi-detached housing
in Wigan, Ingham's
house for Reece
Edwards shows his
love of the Modern
Movement, a love he
displayed earlier in
his industrial and
maritime buildings

However lively the individual houses, collectively they mean nothing. They have
none of the vitality of folk art, no true vernacular, no evidence of the slightest
skill or forethought; just an incoherent assembly of gimmicks and 'non-ideas',
each cocking two fingers at the skilled architectural advice so readily at hand.[41]

Ingham's solution, as seen in the Link and its later derivatives, was increasingly to
advance the idea of a pattern-book. This was perhaps not so dissimilar from the idea
behind *The Book of Small House Plans*, where the RIBA – through its president and
mouthpiece Basil Spence – had urged 'using local Architects as agents and for layout and
supervision – all at a reasonable fee, but applied with some compulsion'.[42] He recognised
that 'This may strike horror in those who strive for total freedom of expression but the
national design situation is desperate and extreme measures are required to rescue the
nation from finally sinking under a morass of mediocrity.' The basic unit he continued to
see as exemplified in the so-called rationalised traditional ('rat-trad') houses of Powell
and Moya, which clearly informed his designs for Hampson and Kemp.[43]

It fell to a client for a one-off house in 1967, Reece Edwards, to give Ingham the
opportunity to strip away the humane modernism of the New Empiricism in favour of
the modernism it had sought to soften through regional inflection.[44] Set on a busy road
on a sloping corner site in Wigan, and sandwiched between nineteenth-century terraces
and inter-war suburban housing, it is an important bridgehead to his most remarkable
and well-known house at Lytham St. Annes. At Wigan a flat-roofed, low-slung design
of sheer white walls acts as a cradle in which Ingham placed the accommodation.
This is then punctured by a brick stack which ties the house to a brick podium
when seen from the front elevation. In reality the podium is another screen wall
(on which the accommodation balances) punctuated by a series of five sleek slit
windows concealing the garage and giving privacy to the garden. Its geometry is thus a
series of interlocking squares with living accommodation hovering above the wall which
acts as a baffle to the noise and intrusiveness of the road. Regionally it took its place
alongside similar works such as Anthony J. Grimshaw's house at Parbold of 1963, and
later Brian Dockray's house at Kendal of 1967. An exercise in modernism it nonetheless
held few of the 'pet-theories' feared by the *Daily Mail*. That fell to No.10, Regent Avenue,
Lytham St Annes which, whilst it shared the formal language of the house in Wigan,

represented the ultimate realisation of Ingham's radical approach to addressing post-war housing problems.

No.10 Regent Avenue, Lytham St. Annes

Ingham's best known house design, described by the local Civic Trust as 'giving its surroundings a much needed jolt', was the second he designed for his family.[45] No. 10 Regent Avenue was completed in January 1968 and is a remarkable concept, its significance belied by the architect always humorously referring to it as 'Number 10'.

Designed as a large family house, it also embodied ideas that addressed the needs of first-time buyers during the housing crisis of the late 1960s. Strikingly photogenic, it was well-illustrated in the professional press of the day and was reviewed in the *Architects' Journal*, *House and Garden*, and *Building Trades Journal*.[46] It was also included in a wide-ranging survey of contemporary housing by June Park, where it took its place alongside houses by Patrick Gwynne, Nelson & Parker, Aldington & Craig, and Richard & Su Rogers.[47] The title of the article in *House and Garden* summed up its essential characteristics well – 'Architect's Own House built within a Series of Courtyards'.

Planned within a private walled compound of one hundred by seventy feet, *House and Garden* reported that 'the site gave Mr. Ingham an opportunity to put into practice ideas which had been concerning him during the decade or so since he had built his first family house'.[48] These ideas, still developing the sense of privacy and enclosure of the Link, were to make maximum use of the land allocated to any given house by placing accommodation in the centre and creating a series of courts around it including a drive-in car port for three cars. 'In principle', *House and Garden* continued, 'he feels that the plot should be walled-in, with only access openings and the odd filtered view, in and out'.[49] As Ingham himself wrote, 'If the whole plot is walled in, the totally private compound enables complete freedom of design and activity to be undertaken within it'.[50]

Keith and Margaret Ingham now had five children, and had outgrown Greystones. Wanting to stay in the area but with building plots hard to come by, they were fortunate to buy a half-acre plot nearby. However, *House and Garden* reported that it 'was not their dream site', being 'in the middle of an area of large, unlovely houses', nonetheless 'it had several mature trees to commend it'.[51] Henck Snoek's photographs ably show how Ingham made dramatic use of the trees and illustrate his belief in placing buildings carefully in their landscape. As he had told BDP colleagues at a staff conference in 1968,

> I should like to see the formation of more specialist groups like the Housing Unit … I would also like to see considerable attention focused on landscape design and I am not being funny when I say we ought to be putting the creepers on our working drawings. The beauty of Britain is not so much buildings, but the natural features. Just as much as we want to produce integrated buildings, our buildings should be integrated with the landscape.[52]

Despite the landscaping potential the site had considerable constraints, including a building line set well back and a ground landlord's stipulation that no part of the structure should be within eight feet of the site boundaries.[53] Ironically this created the very conditions – what Grenfell Baines had called the 'gap-toothed grin' – that Ingham sought to avoid and one of the less desirable aspects of what Mellor saw as the '… persistent suburb.'[54] It potentially placed the house in a landscape rather than integrating it. Writing of the problem in 1970 Ingham argued that 'too often houses are surrounded by useless and overlooked garden areas'.[55] His first response to this creation of 'useless space' was to occupy it by other means. Employing the same strong super-graphic identity he was simultaneously adopting at Preston Bus Station, he placed an enormous internally lit house number, moulded in yellow plastic, on the front lawn – turning signage into Pop Art.[56] Manufactured by Glasdon, the company created by his friend

Don Sidebottom, it represented dissatisfaction turned into defiance. Elsewhere Ingham incorporated one of the litter-bins designed for the bus station into the open-plan kitchen, its diagonally placed Helvetica typeface showing his interest in graphics.

To achieve the necessary accommodation, Ingham had to build a second storey if sufficient outdoor private space was to be realised. The result was a house effectively in the centre of a series of courts as opposed to a more readily understood courtyard house. On the first floor he arranged a row of bedrooms like ships cabins, complete with sliding doors, two feet back from the edge of their ground floor 'podium'. One of his passions was sailing and his work often contained symbolic or constructional nautical references.[57] The careful positioning of the bedrooms allowed a continuous angled strip rooflight that ran around the edge of the house. Enamoured by the play of light he had seen in houses on a trip to Greece, he designed this section to allow reflected light to bounce off the white external walls down through the rooflight and onto the white internal walls of the ground floor. Further light effects were produced by the play of light off the pool to the far end of the house over which the living room projected. Artificial lighting was also incorporated to create dramatic effects in the evening just as he had experimented with at Greystones.

Despite the apparent internationalism of the design language, which sees Ingham continue to play with a De Stijl elementalism, the house remains firmly sited in its locality. The beach pebbles used modestly to clad the chimney stack of Greystones here metaphorically slide down the building to become a more pervasive landscape element. The house, now demolished, sat surrounded by a sea of beach pebbles on which floated six-feet-wide stone flags forming a broad jetty of paving connecting public and private space. Ingham's symbolic regionalism, somewhat sentimental at Greystones, is here used in an altogether more mature and considered way.

June Park's survey of 1960s houses identified several distinct trends, including 'the courtyard house or bungalow where the outside space forms an additional room, both

(Previous page)
Figure 8. Set amidst
mature pines in Regent
Avenue, and with the
accommodation
screened from the road,
Ingham used the same
'super graphics' for
No. 10 as used on
Preston Bus Station,
The local paper
reported on it 'giving its
surroundings a much
needed jolt'

warmer and more private than the average garden'.[58] Though part of the trend, this approach may also have been informed by an awareness of tropical architecture first encountered when Ingham was a student at the Bartlett School, a possibility reinforced by the luxuriant semi-tropical planting to the internal courts.[59] More plausibly it has been suggested that Ingham wanted the screen so he didn't have to look at the local 'area of large, unlovely houses.' The luxuriant planting became well established within a year, with a three-inch deep covering of beach pebbles proving 'very successful in restraining the growth of weeds and maintaining the ground in a moist condition even in the driest summer weather'.[60] Plans and written instructions show that he intended to cover over half of the wall surface with luxuriant vegetation, enfolding the house just as Greystones had been.

If the house had been an end in itself, confirming the rise of the architect's house as a 1960s' genre and the architect as celebrity in an age of a growing media presence for architecture, then its coverage in the professional press would have been entirely justified. However it also works as an experiment in housing provision that is not readily apparent without reference to Ingham's wider radical ideas. He was clearly referencing Regent Avenue when he wrote that 'with the pressure of higher densities related to the basic desire for privacy not enough use is made of land'.[61] Contemporary with the house was a report he wrote for BDP entitled '"In Wall" Housing', and subtitled, 'Making a start – an approach to low-cost housing'.[62] Ingham's witty draft front cover illustration to the report shows a caravan or mobile home (embodying an almost throw-away 1960s aesthetic) set in a well-designed compound complete with car, pond, and garden gnome. To the perimeter wall is a large house number in the same clear type used in both Preston and Regent Avenue, and a section of beach-pebble paving. The humour in the illustration, and the use of sub-Archigram cartoon storyboards to explain the concept, reinforced the design of No. 10 as 'a radical approach to the supply of housing to first-time purchasers'.[63]

Very much a discussion document, the report talked of 'growing a home' from a simple base unit like a caravan, if that was all that could be afforded, to the ultimate realisation of a large permanent family home such as the Inghams now enjoyed. Various types of layout, construction, and base units were considered in the report from a caravan, via units designed with standard ex-catalogue building products, to more industrialised production. 'It is tempting to propose', Ingham wrote, 'a further variation on the compact, optimised, high technology package associated with shipbuilding or space programmes rather than the building industry'.[64] Considering all the options the report favoured the use of the TRADA Housing Unit System, a three-dimensional timber module capable of easy expansion.[65] Seen in the context of this report, Regent Avenue is the finest realisation of Ingham's radical ideas about the continuous development of a site for family living, 'rather than gain space through the usual method of moving house'.[66]

Hulton Park, Bankfield Manor and the architecture of everyday

If Ingham's love of the Modern Movement in his work of the late 1960s went against the architectural tide, his last two major house designs, Hulton Park and Bankfield Manor, fully embraced both the developing emphasis on the vernacular and the 'culture of quotation' that preceded post-modernism and demonstrate a growing unease with doctrinaire modernism.

In 1958 Hulton Hall, near Bolton, was demolished, bringing to an end nearly a thousand years of its estate's occupation by the same family, latterly Sir Geoffrey Hulton. In 1972 Ingham was commissioned to design a new house at Hulton Park, near Little Hulton, for Sir Geoffrey and his wife.[67] Set in a landscape with mature planting and on the edge of a new housing development, Ingham's design was a single-storey brick construction beneath an assertive monopitch roof. The building delights in its brick

Figure 9. BDP staff photographer Roger Park's photograph of No. 10 shows one of the private courtyards created by Ingham, the two floors separated by a narrow clerestory of continuous glazing to refract and reflect light from the surrounding water

Figure 10. The ground plan for No. 10 clearly shows Ingham's determination to make the house part of the landscape whilst at the same time creating privacy

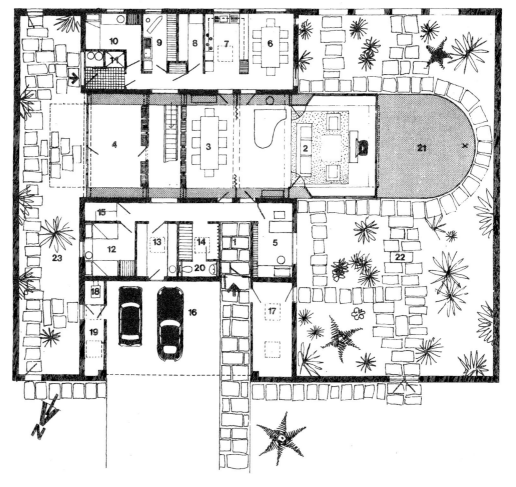

Figure II. A humorous, and unused, concept sketch by Ingham for the front cover of BDP's report on low-cost housing. His sketch again incorporates 'super graphics' and beach-pebbles as at No.10 together with a garden gnome fishing in the pond

detailing, with narrow slit windows to the clearstory on each façade. It provided both family accommodation and a connected office wing (with integral garage) for the business of the estate. Its forms, allied with the use of brick, share in the neo-vernacular of Darbourne and Darke's Lillington Gardens (1961-72), RMJM's Hillingdon Civic Centre (1973-78) and look forward to fellow BDP architect Francis Robert's Ealing Broadway Centre (1979-85). They are also reminiscent of the Expressionist architecture then being re-evaluated by figures such as Dennis Sharp, with whom Ingham worked on *Architecture North West*. [68]

Still fewer stylistic vestiges of the Modern Movement – save white walls – remain in Ingham's last substantial house, Bankfield Manor, completed in 1985.[69] Designed for Don Sidebottom, it was conceived as a modern manor house on the edge of a lake near Poulton-le-Fylde. The client had originally wanted a classical building, but Ingham persuaded him against this and produced a neo-vernacular house with more roof than wall. Close to Glasdon's Blackpool factory, it had to double as a base to entertain business guests and contained a striking circular staircase of transparent acrylic as an advertisement of the company's products. Its disproportionately large roof seems to hark back thirty years to the New Empiricism but is best understood as Ingham's homage to the work of Arts and Crafts architects, especially Lutyens and Voysey, who he came to regard highly in later life. It also reflected his deeply held love of 'everyday architecture', – a subject he had earlier championed through commissioning a series of wallcharts from David Gentlemen for European Architectural Heritage Year in 1975.

Ever eager to promote the regions over the metropolis, and the vernacular over the polite, he conceived the posters as a compliment 'to the RIBA wallsheet series on well known architects of major buildings such as Wren, Inigo Jones and Vanbrugh. This uniquely British vernacular architecture, much more than the Cathedrals and Stately homes, forms the real character of this country. It forms the fabric of the towns and countryside we love.'[70] An increasing awareness of the threat to these environments led him to establish, together with fellow members of the RIBA Planning Advisory Group, Francis Tibbalds and Percy Johnson-Marshall, the influential Urban Design Group. It was founded, as he recalled on the occasion of the fiftieth issue of *Urban Design Quarterly* in 1994, to express 'our anger at the unsatisfying nature of the environment

Figure 12. Completed in 1972 the house at Little Hulton was not only a home for Lord Hulton, but part of a new housing development (Photograph courtesy of BDP/Norman Butler)

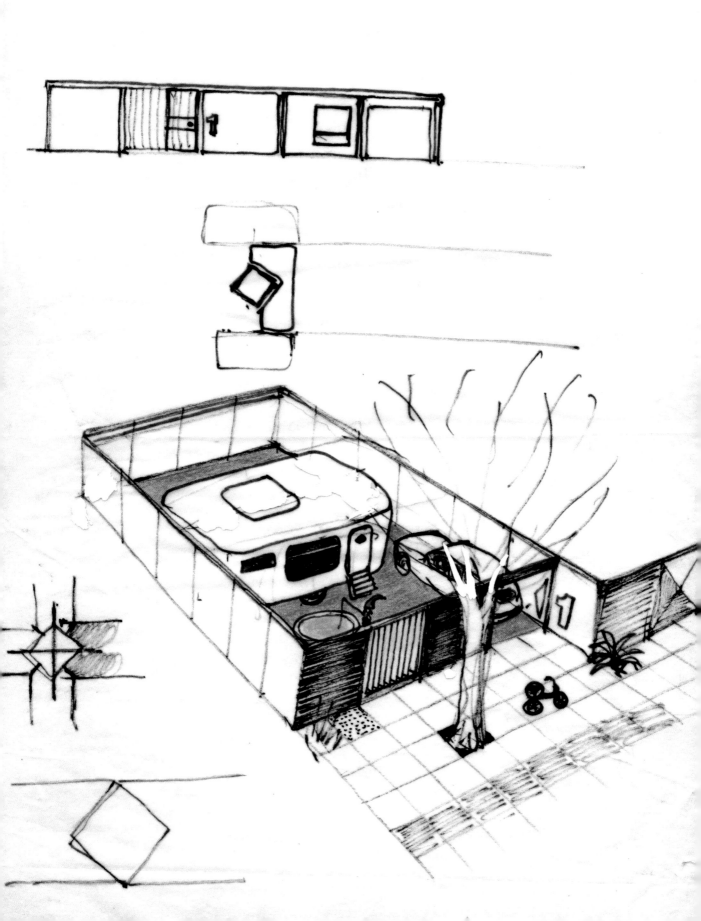

being created cumulatively by architects, planners and road engineers'. [71]

Bankfield Manor sits contentedly in a landscape designed by Derek Lovejoy and Partners. After its completion Ingham took a series of photographs from an increasing distance until it appeared as nothing but a large orange roof in a green landscape. Working together they took a typically flat 'Fylde' field and created a lake with gently undulating banks which composes itself for views from a sunken sitting area in the drawing room. The nautical theme is emphasised in both Ingham's presentation drawings, which placed a yacht on the lake, and the large port-hole window to the side elevation. Ingham had by this date left BDP, convinced that his outspokenness and individualism had destroyed his chances of becoming a full partner despite its appreciation of his being made a Vice-President of the RIBA in 1977, a position never before held by a salaried architect from private practice.

It has been suggested that Ingham put professional and personal recognition before practice to his detriment. Despite the variety of expression employed in his houses he could well have sympathised with Peter and Alison Smithson in 1965 when they wrote their survey of the 'Heroic Period of Modern Architecture'.[72] Despite coming to an end in 1929 they famously proclaimed that 'This heroic period is the rock upon which we stand'. Like them one suspects that Keith Ingham was on the same rock when he wrote that 'I still have a (now secret) love of the pure white (when white) hard peopleless forms of the Modern Movement, perhaps in future to become an erotic indulgence of consenting intellectuals in private.'[73]

1. This article is largely based on material held in the Keith Ingham Archive in Manchester Metropolitan University Library Special Collections. The Archive is currently uncatalogued and grateful thanks are due to Jeremy C. Parrett, Special Collections Archivist, and colleagues for access. The article discusses what the author considers to be Ingham's most interesting housing projects but is not comprehensive and does not include his conservation work or his significant contribution to the development of urban design.

2. Keith Ingham, 'Comment', *Architecture North West*, no.23, June/July 1967, p.6.

3. Owen Hatherley, *A New Kind of Bleak: journeys through urban Britain*, London, Verso, 2012, p. 76. On the history of Building Design Partnership see Hugh Pearman et al, *BDP: 61/11 Continuous Collective*, London, BDP, 2011. Other earlier examples of multi-disciplinary practices emulating the Gropian philosophy included Farmer and Dark (by 1953) and the Design Research Unit (founded in 1943), without embracing the profit sharing approach of BDP.

4. Hatherley, ibid., p.76. On GG see Elain Harwood, 'Sir George Grenfell Baines', *Oxford Dictionary of National Biography* [http://www.oxforddnb.com/view/rintable/89956 accessed on 23/08/2013]. See also British Library, National Sound Archives, National Life Story Collection, interviews with Louise Brodie, 5-12 January 2000.

5. A comprehensive history of BDP has yet to be written despite its important contribution to post-war British architecture. These early years, when it operated under a variety of names including the Grenfell Baines Group (1941), Grenfell Baines and Hargreaves (1950), the Grenfell Baines Partnership, and finally the Design Group (April 1961) before Building Design Partnership was created in December 1961, seem particularly unclear and overlooked.

6. Hatherley, op.cit., pp.75-6.

7. See, for example, Keith Ingham, introduction, *St.Annes-on-Sea and its Future*, St.Annes, 1974.

8. Biographical information on Ingham can be found in Alan Powers, 'Keith Ingham', *The Independent*, 3 May 1995; Lesley Jackson, 'Keith Ingham', *The Independent*, 26 May 1995; Dennis Sharp, 'Keith Ingham, North-west individualist, dies', *Architects' Journal*, vol.201, no.18, 4 May 1995, p.14; Obituary: Keith Ingham, *rudi.net* (Resource for Urban Design Information) at http://www.rudi.net/books/12118 [accessed 22/05/2012] – includes reminiscences by John Billingham, Neil Parkin, and Arnold Linkden.

9. Powers, ibid. Ingham's student scrapbooks contain a newspaper cutting of Holford's Paternoster scheme of 1956.

10. The Mondrian reference was inferred after the completion of the house and is said to have pleased the architect. I am grateful to Gaye Smith, Keith's partner and the former Librarian of the Faculty of Art and Design at Manchester Metropolitan University, for this information.

11. Alan Powers, 'Tom Mellor', *The Independent*, 24 December 1994.

12. Churchwood was reviewed in the *Architectural Review*, vol.117, no.700, April 1955, pp.257-8, alongside houses by Patrick Gwynne and Eric Lyons. It was subsequently included in Sherban Cantacuzino, *Modern Houses of the World*, London, Studio Vista, 1969. On Markelius see Eva Rudberg, *Sven Markelius, Arkitekt*, Stockholm, Arkitektur Forlag, 1989, and on the important role of landscape during these years Marc Treib (ed.), *The Architecture of Landscape, 1940-1960*, Philadelphia, University of Pennsylvania, 2002.

13. On Whitehead, see Alan Peat, *David Whitehead Limited: Artist Designed Textiles, 1952-1969*, London, Oldham, 1993; and Mary Schoeser, *Fabrics and Wallpapers*, London, Harper Collins, 1986. Ingham's scrapbooks from the 1950s contain many adverts from *Architectural Review* and *House and Garden* for David Whitehead – in one instance alongside cuttings of the recently completed Hunstanton School (1950-3) by Peter and Alison Smithson – noted commentators on Gropius, Le Corbusier and ads (*Ark*, no.18, November 1956).

Acknowledgements:
A great many people
and institutions have
helped with this article.
They are Bernadette
Bone, Richard Brook,
Mats Edstrom,
Peter Jenkins, Alison
MacKenzie, Christina
Malathouni, Jeremy
C. Parrett, Gaye Smith,
Otto Saumarez Smith,
the RIBA and English
Heritage libraries,
Charles Wilson and,
unwittingly, the late
Keith Ingham – whom
the author met regularly
in 1990-5

14. Tom Mellor, 'The End of the Beginning: notes on the future of architectural design in Britain', *Town Planning Review*, vol.24, no.1, April 1953, p.48. On 'The New Empiricism', see Reyner Banham, 'Revenge of the Picturesque: English architectural polemics, 1945-1965,' in John Summerson (ed.), *Concerning Architecture: essays on architectural writing presented to Nikolaus Pevsner*, London, Allen Lane, 1968; and useful recent discussions in Robert Gregory, 'Heroism versus Empiricism', *Architectural Review*, vol.227, no.1235, January 2000, pp. 68-73, and Peter Carolin, 'Sense, Sensibility and Tower Blocks: the Swedish influence on post-war housing in Britain,' in Elain Harwood and Alan Powers (eds.), Twentieth Century Architecture, no.9, *Housing the Twentieth Century Nation*, 2008, pp.99-112.

15. Mellor, ibid., p.50.

16. Ingham's archive contains his own photographs of window details of Churchwood, openings made into the wall of the Lytham Hall estate, and the war memorial. His father, Arnold, was a keen amateur cinematographer with works deposited in the North West Film Archive. I am grateful to Catherine Kitching of Fylde Borough Council for information on the war memorial.

17. Keith Ingham, 'In praise of simplicity', *Building*, (Doors and windows supplement), vol.252, no.7502, 26 June 1987, pp.10-11. See also 'Letting in a Breath of Fresh Air', *Housing Design Awards 1987* (a *Building* publication), 30 October 1987, pp.7-9.

18. The competition was announced simultaneously in *Ideal Home*, vol.78, no.5, November 1958, p.3; *RIBA Journal*, vol.66, no.1, November 1958, p.10; and *Architects' Journal*, vol.128, no.3321, 23 October 1958, p.593. It is discussed in David Jeremiah, *Architecture and Design for the Family in Britain, 1900-70*, Manchester University Press, 2000, pp.178-82. On the Ideal Home exhibitions see, Deborah Ryan, *The Ideal Home through the Twentieth Century*, London, Hazar, 1997.

19. *RIBA Journal*, vol.66, no.1, November 1958, p.10.

20. *Architects' Journal*, vol.130, no.3360, 10 September 1959, p.147.

21. *RIBA Journal*, vol.66, no.12, October 1959, p.411.

22. Arne Jacobsen's work, which Ingham greatly admired, was the subject of the first one-man exhibition held at the RIBA, in February 1959.

23. Steen Rasmussen's influential *London: the Unique City*, originally published in English in 1937, was re-issued in 1948. On Highworth see Kenneth Powell, *Powell and Moya*, London, RIBA Publications, 2009, pp.6-7.

24. George Grenfell Baines, *Ideal Home*, vol.80, no.4, October 1959, p.75.

25. *RIBA Journal*, vol.66, no.12, October 1959, p.411.

26. 'Good taste – on the surface!', *Ideal Home, Small Homes Supplement*, vol.81, no.4, April 1960, pp.36-7; Margaret Casson, 'What is the interior designer's role?', ibid., pp. 77-9. Lady Casson, from her position as a tutor in design at the Royal College of Art, acted as consultant to a number of organisations such as London Transport and the C.O.I.D. The leading Manchester department store, Affleck & Brown, created a demonstration house within the store to display the new styles of interior design and furnishings that *Ideal Home* was promoting.

27. Copy amended by hand held in Keith Ingham Archive, MMU Library Special Collections.

28. *Ideal Home, Small Homes Supplement*, op.cit.

29. 'A 'link' for neighbours', *Ideal Home*, vol.80, no.4, October 1959, p.74.

30. ibid.

31. Michael Young and Peter Willmott, *Family and Kinship in East London*, London, Routledge and Kegan Paul, 1954.

32. 'Home progress: We exchange views with the Minister of Housing', *Ideal Home*, vol.81, no.4, April 1960, pp.23-25.

33. See Susanne Schmid, 'Between L. S. Lowry and Coronation Street; Salford cultural identities', in Christoph Ehland (ed.), *Thinking Northern: Textures of Identity in the north of England*, Amsterdam, Rodopi, 2007, pp.347-62.

34. Mellor, op.cit., p.50.

35. G. Grenfell Baines, 'Tomorrow's Estates', *Ideal Home*, vol.81, no.1, January 1960, p.51.

36. 'Small House competition', *Architects' Journal*, vol.130, no.3360, 10 September 1959, p.152.

37. 'The Small House Scheme', *Ideal Home*, vol.80, no.2, August/September 1959, p.6.

38. *Ideal Home*, vol.79, no. 5, May 1959, p.87.

39. See Joan Ockman, 'Architecture and the Consumer Paradigm in the mid-twentieth century', in Helena Mattsson and Sven-Olov Wallenstein, *Swedish Modernism; architecture, consumption and the welfare* state, London, Black Dog, 2010, pp.170-87.

40. 'Panorama Showhouse', *Evening Chronicle*, (supplement), 28 March 1961; 'Housing, Stockport', *The Builder*, vol.208, no.6344, 18 December 1964, pp.1305-6.. Panorama houses were also built by Arnold Ingham & Son at Gretdale Avenue, St. Annes, according to undated material in the Keith Ingham Archive. Other MHLG winners included housing by Eric Lyons at Blackheath, and Tayler and Green at Loddon. In 1961 Grenfell Baines & Hargreaves had designed a house called 'Les Ruisseaux', at St. Brelade, Jersey, for an 'A. Kemp Esq'.

41. *Architecture North West*, no.23, June/July 1967, p.6.

42. *The Book of Small House Plans*, London, *Ideal Home* and RIBA, 1959, p.2.

43. *Architecture North West*, op.cit., p.6. Ingham referred to 'rat trad' as the 'Volkswagen of housing'.

44. 'House at Wigan', *Architecture North West*, no.23, June/July 1967, p.14. It is believed that the house survives, but it was given a low-pitched roof in the early 1990s.

45. *Evening Gazette*, 3 February 1969, p.7.

46. 'Keith Ingham's house', *Architects' Journal*, vol.152, no.34, 26 August 1970, pp. 473-6 (part of an extended article on architects' own houses that included those of John Winter, Maurice Taylor, Colin Smith, Philip Pank, J.S. Bonnington and Peter Aldington); Juliana Rusakow, 'Architect's own family house built within a series of courts', *House and Garden*, vol.24, no.5 (240), June 1969, pp.70-5. *Building Trades Journal*, vol.165, no.4949, 7 July 1972, p.1.

47. June Park, *Houses for Today*, London, Batsford, 1971, pp.63-7.

48. *House and Garden*, op.cit., p.70.

49. ibid.

50. *Architects' Journal*, 26 August 1970, op.cit., pp.473-4.

51. *House and Garden*, op.cit., p.72. The Inghams seem to have fallen foul of the observation in the *Ideal Home Book of Small House Plans*, p.7, that 'The situation is fast approaching where people will seek a district with available land rather than a piece of land in the district of their choice.'

52. BDP, 'Symposium Report; Product and Philosophy' (conference held at Elevethan Hall, 1968), p.54.

53. *Architects' Journal*, 26 August 1970, op.cit., p. 474.

54. Tom Mellor, 'The persistent suburb,' *Town Planning Review*, vol.25, no.4, April 1955, pp. 251-4.

55. I am grateful to Charles Wilson, one of Keith's former colleagues, who with Mary Smallbone and John Gravell was an assistant architect on Preston Bus Station, for this recollection.

56. On this general trend see David Robbins (ed.), *The Independent Group: postwar Britain and the aesthetics of plenty*, Cambridge, MIT Press, 1990.

57. Keith delighted in sailing his Seabird Half Rater, a sailing boat that originated in the West Lancashire Yacht Club in 1898 and was constructed in Lytham. A keen member of both the Seabird Association and the Blackpool and Fleetwood Yacht Club, he regularly sailed from the family's holiday home near Abersoch – an interesting conversion of a traditional Welsh cottage. The boat often featured in his photography and graphic design.

58. Park, op.cit., p.8.

59. University College London held a conference on tropical architecture in March 1953, which developed into the Diploma Course in Tropical Architecture at the Architectural Association the following year directed by Maxwell Fry. Between 1947 and 1964 Fry and Drew researched and published on the subject, espousing a form of modernist regionalism responsive to climate and culture. There are also affinities between housing at Tema Manhean, Ghana, West Africa, by Fry, Drew, Drake and Lasdun which considered the idea of extendable housing and Ingham's 'In Wall' housing. I am grateful to Viviana d'Auria, University of Leuven, for this information, presented at 'The Influence of Fry and Drew' conference, University of Liverpool, 10-11 October 2013.

60. *Architects' Journal*, 26 August 1970, op.cit., p.475.

61. ibid., p.473.

62. BDP, '"In Wall" housing' (report, n.d.)

63. ibid., p.2.

64. ibid., section 4.4. Despite his commitment to craftsmanship Ingham was not opposed to the use of technological solutions – with their attendant risk of de-skilling – where appropriate. Both his work at Blackpool Zoo, for example, including the first permanent air-supported structure in the country in 1971, and his work as an industrial designer for Glasdon's and the reinforced plastics division of English Electric, falls outside the limits of this article.

65. Grenfell Baines had been placed fourth in a competition for the Timber Development Association House in 1945.

66. BDP: '"In Wall" housing', op.cit., p.1.

67. The original location and condition of this unpublished design is currently unknown. Sir Geoffrey Hulton died in 1993.

68. Dennis Sharp, *Modern Architecture and Expressionism*, London, Longman, 1966. The Ingham Archive contains part of *Architectural Design*, vol.37, no.12, December 1967, a year-by-year history of the Modern Movement. He kept the part for 1924-1935 with Hugo Häring's Gut Garkau Farm of 1924 which has some similarities to the house at Hulton Park. Ingham knew Geoffrey Darke through committee work for the RIBA when he was a Vice-President, including the Housing Design Award. Other members of the Editorial Board of *Architecture North West* included J. Roy Parker and John Billingham.

69. This account draws heavily on the tour notes from Twentieth Century Society, 'North West Weekend' (University of Lancaster, 2-4 July 1999), and information from Gaye Smith and Don Sidebottom. Bankfield Manor and its landscape survive and have only been modestly altered since change of ownership.

70. Information held in Keith Ingham Archive.

71. Keith Ingham, "UDQ50', *Urban Design Quarterly*, no.50, April 1994, p.5. Shortly before his death in 1995 Ingham was putting a lot of effort into the production of a book on Urban Design. Eventually produced as the *Good Place Guide; Urban Design in Britain and Ireland* (2002) by John Billingham and Richard Cole, they acknowledge (pp.12-13) that 'Keith Ingham was a key figure in the early days of working on a "Good Place Guide"'.

72. The article was originally published in *Architectural Design*, vol.35, no.12, December 1965, and later revised and published as a book, Alison and Peter Smithson, *The Heroic Period of Modern Architecture*, London, Thames and Hudson, 1981.

73. Alan Powers, 'Keith Ingham', *The Independent*, 3 May 1995.

Matthew Whitfield

7 A Merseyside Maker: The houses of Jo Parker

Joseph Parker (1926-2000) was a characterful person who created characterful buildings. He was given free reign by his older partner, John Nelson, and the two seldom collaborated on designs, so that Parker's singular designs under the firm's name of Nelson and Parker can be taken as being his alone. They began with a sequence of modest, well-crafted houses and developed into a far more florid output, but consistent qualities are found through all his work. These were an attention to detail, a keen sense of materiality, a rootedness in place and people to create schemes closely related to their sites and clients, and an architectural confidence that did not rely on external influence or fashion. Parker was concerned with numerous strands of modernism in the realisation of his architectural projects, but primarily he focused on the contribution of craft, especially where that craft was idiosyncratic, responsive and personal, and expressed something of the ineffable – of fun, and love – in the final result.

The matter of Parker's variable name is worthy of some attention before that of his buildings. J. Roy was a professional signature he devised as he was establishing his architectural credentials in his early thirties, considering it to be modern and stylish, but later he let it fall out of use. Jo was how he always signed his name for friends, family and close professional connections, eschewing the usual 'e' as non-essential, preferring the clean lines of the two-letter name and rejecting any criticism that it was the female version as irrelevant.[1] Therein lies a flavour of the man and his character.

Parker was educated at the University of Liverpool's School of Architecture, graduating in 1953 after completing his National Service. His architectural heroes were typical of his generation and included Mies van der Rohe and Frank Lloyd Wright, whose influence was pervasive in his work though seldom in a literal way. Among contemporaries, Parker particularly admired Denys Lasdun, but he found Le Corbusier a problematic figure because of what he viewed as his doctrinaire approach to town planning and design. Overall, he was far more interested in the specificity of his schemes and the development of a personal style than identifying with any particular icons. He and his cohort of Liverpool graduates in the immediate post-war period found themselves without a grand master to look up to: Parker remembered his teacher, Gerald Beech, as lacking the experience and force of personality to guide his students in any particular direction. Although they were the same age James Stirling had graduated from Liverpool ahead of Parker in 1950, and became an architectural centre of gravity all of his own; they were not friends as students and although Parker admired his work he was not an identifiable influence. Instead, under the auspices of the Liverpool Architectural Society, meeting monthly at the Bluecoat Arts Centre, Jo was part of a group of young architects and practices like Peter Carmichael and Hall, O'Donahue and Wilson who were rooted in their immediate region and who looked to one another for support, sharing ideas and a sense of collegiality.[2]

The bulk of Parker's practice was in small private houses, though there was a significant amount of work for restaurants and theatres, and at the Liverpool Playhouse he designed a restaurant within a theatre. These two forms of display and showmanship reflected the passions of the man who, by means of an ever-present exuberance in his detailing and a spirited belief in the handmade, was an exceptionally theatrical architect. This approach grew out of his private interests: Jo was a huge fan of opera and theatre and was interested in the architecture of the stage, joining the Theatres Trust and developing a passion for the conservation of historic performance spaces. One of his heroes was Frank Matcham, the grand master of late Victorian and Edwardian theatre whose designs for Blackpool's Grand Theatre and Tower Ballroom Jo would have been familiar with whilst growing up in the town. The Everyman Theatre that he designed in Liverpool in 1975-7 was the culmination of these passions. Converted from the nineteenth-century Hope Hall, a former chapel, concert hall and cinema, Parker retained some historic features but created a striking identity on Hope Street and a fashionable thrust stage internally that helped to define the contemporary work that the company

Figure 2. The main room of the semi-open plan living space at No.1 Ingestre Road with exposed timber construction and 'floating' brick fireplace to the right (Phil Sayer)

produced. The bricks from the old theatre were reused in the rebuilding of 2011-14, along with a restyled version of Parker's red neon lowercase lettering.[3]

The house that Parker built for himself and his family encapsulates these essentials and illustrates the architectural journey that he made over the decades of his greatest professional activity. The site on Ingestre Road is an extraordinary one, lodged between the boundary wall of a nineteenth-century villa and the teetering edge of a disused sandstone quarry in Oxton, a Wirral village that had developed into a high-status suburb of Birkenhead and Liverpool since the 1850s. Just as all around the mature trees and aged sandstone textures mask the extent of suburban development, fading it into a naturalistic backdrop, so the first phase of Jo's house sought to disappear behind the high boundary wall.

This single-storey, flat-roofed structure was completed in 1957 to a simple plan. The largely glazed hallway is a link sited between two evenly-sized wings: to the east is a semi-open plan living room and kitchen; to the west are two large bedrooms, one single bedroom and a modest bathroom. But for an angled boundary path to the east (leading down to the former quarry, now transformed into a municipal park) against which the house abuts, the plan would be perfectly rectangular. There is geometric rectitude and sparseness employed along every elevation and the plan is as easy to read externally as it is internally, lacking extraneous wings or unusual massing. Partly, this appearance is drawn from the requirement to fit the house efficiently into a tight, narrow site; partly it is due to an evident reluctance to be fully visible either from the road or by the users of the park below; and most of all it is inspired by a guiding maxim of creating a pure and legible space in accord with an undiluted modernist impulse.

The simplicity of the scheme reflects the modesty of the brief. This was a project with a budget of only around £3,500 for three permanent adult residents (Jo, his wife Kathleen and his mother-in-law Margaret Horrocks) and two full sized bedrooms. A lot of the work was done by Parker himself and without recourse to expensive materials or heavy construction. The building materials were straightforward, cheap, and relatively

Figure 3. Portrait of Jo Parker in 1975, when he was President of the Liverpool Architectural Society

easy to assemble: a single thickness of unbroken brickwork for short stretches bookending more considerable sections of glass panels in timber frames and panels of vertical weather boarding. Owing to the prefabricated components of boarding and windows all this was assembled within sixteen weeks; it was a pared down structure that was a cost-effective response to a simple brief but with elegance evident in the result.[4] The limited palette of materials and surfaces achieved not only a sparse, raw finish that can be identified with the New Brutalism first codified by Reyner Banham two years earlier in 1955, but also contained the possibility of something more wilful.[5] For instance, where brick was used as the external walling it was left exposed internally, but one or two touches hinted at a purely decorative impulse that Parker would not suppress just to achieve consistency.

The very first approach to the house speaks of this impulsiveness, as the wall that separates the kitchen from the hallway is extended outwards towards the boundary wall to create a barrier along the north elevation, framing the space between the gate and the front door. The effect is to create a smaller, more welcoming area on the main approach to the house, a function underlined by the decorative pattern of projecting and recessed headers and stretchers in the extended wall. On the southern elevation facing the quarry, the hardwood beams supporting the flat roof structure were projected outwards beyond the building line in an exaggerated manner, although reduced in length by later owners due to decay in the timber and now less discernible. Parker loved this device and it appears in numerous later domestic projects. Inside, the brick fireplace was conceived as an apparently floating wall which housed hidden shelving as well as disguising the flue and, in the manner of the 'welcome wall' adjacent to the front door, was given a vertical sequence of projecting bricks to emphasise its constructional method. Parker exploited every opportunity to display structural components, most notably in the living area where the timber structure of the roof was exposed. Brick walls were left bare, while the timber boarded panels, packed with aluminium and plywood insulation, were plastered and painted white internally. This approach may have been brutalist in a taxonomical sense, but for Parker it was never just about rawness. The joinery was of a very high quality and combined the qualities of pure functionality – virtually all of the storage was built-in, reducing the need for furniture – and the expression of materiality, by the stains, varnishes and expert finishes used on a variety of hardwoods. Parker was rooted in his locality and liked to use craftsmen with experience in the local shipbuilding industry, so that while Ingestre Road avoids literal nautical themes, the skill of luxury shipbuilding shines through in many places, from the simplest internal door to more elaborate cupboard joinery.[6]

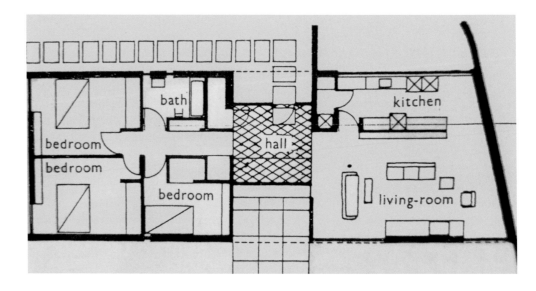

125 A Merseyside Maker: The houses of Jo Parker

Figure 8. The interior of the Ingestre Road linking block demonstrates the Parker's interest In creating unusual volumes with idiosyncratic joinery and brickwork (Phil Sayer)

Figure 9. The bathroom at No.I Ingestre Road (Phil Sayer)

If the original 1957 house contained the core of Parker's architectural ethos – that of an essentially disciplined modernism with a close attention to craft detail and some interesting idiosyncrasies – then the 1976 extension, designed after two decades of intense work on other projects, marked the culmination of his architectural evolution and was a monument to his charming caprices. Viewed from the garden, the first impression of the south elevations is that there are two separate buildings joined by a glazed link, evidently belonging to different eras and possibly by different architects. Parker saw the two phases, two decades apart, as separate attempts to achieve similar goals with wildly different methods.

An extension was required by the mid-1970s for numerous reasons. The Parkers' daughter Jane was born in 1963 and as a teenager required more space and privacy, while increasing anti-social behaviour in the area made necessary a secure garage, which extends to the edge of the site across an existing driveway and part of the garden. Again, Parker took on a good deal of the work himself, with a local carpenter assisting on the extensive internal joinery.[7] There is the same attention to craft detailing, especially in timber, from handrails to internal doors, and imaginative tiling choices in the bathroom, reflecting the style of the late 1970s in their chunkier style and bold colourways.

The two-storey addition, housing a garage, workshop and miscellaneous storage at ground level with an additional bedroom, study and bathroom on the first floor, creates a contrast in height between the two wings, but this is less significant than the unusual geometry of the later phase. To the south, the glazed link slopes up towards a pyramidal roofed pavilion built of a brick that closely matches that used in 1957 but which has a much freer geometry in almost every way. Where brick walls meet at oblique angles, the bricks, rather than being mitre-cut, project in alternate courses like interlinked fingers, a device used inside and out to be both decorative and expressive of its materials. Elsewhere, individuality is created from the external expressions of internal functions, with a large window divided by timber mullions for the master bedroom and, adjacent,

an odd oriel window, a sort-of square frustum or truncated pyramid set on a large sill of slate. Viewed from the northern elevation on Ingestre Road, the core block with its pitched pyramidal roof is easily readable, but what defines the view are two towers to the front and western flank with mono-pitched roofs (again, clad distinctively in slate). The towers provide concealed top lighting for the walk-in shower in the bathroom and an alcove in the bedroom designed for a significant piece of furniture. More important than the contribution that the towers make to the rooms is the way their over-scaled forms act as landmarks for the building as a whole. Where the younger Parker sought to use contextual good manners and to hide his work behind historic walls, he now had the confidence to create height and massing even when it was not functionally necessary.

The main shift came from the internal plan itself which, whilst following an overall functional logic, makes a virtue of its wilfulness. The journey from the old house to the new encapsulates the delight that Parker took in subverting expectations. The glazed link between the two phases could have been straight but instead is angled and lined with mirrored panels, reflecting the greenery of the garden immediately outside and creating a self-consciously confusing and delightful space. More interlocking brickwork corners form the base of the stairwell, which twists through more angles underneath a steeply sloping varnished timber roof; a highly engineered double timber beam appears to diagonally tie together the complex structure of angled walls and window panels but is in fact a handrail. The main bedroom is dominated by large floor to ceiling windows and the top-lit alcove, whilst the unusual shape of the other rooms makes odd demands on this one: each wall is restless in some way, either because of unexpected angles or a particular surface treatment, from vibrant orange flock wallpaper, still in situ, to reeded timber cladding and vertical strips of glass bricks, in addition to the window and top lighting. The bedroom designed for the architect's daughter narrows into an extraordinary oriel window which offers a view, as though from the prow of a spaceship, over the park below the garden. It is in the bathroom where the eccentricity reaches a

climax: a complex polygonal plan is accompanied by a deeply sloping timber ceiling, a top-lit walk-in shower below the lantern tower, and the culmination of the room is a wash basin located at the end of a mirrored, tapered space with an *Alice in Wonderland* quality of strangeness and disorientation.

It is between these two poles of Parker's work, between the calm discipline of unobtrusive modernism and the riot of spatial playfulness, that his work from the late 1950s to the late 1970s may be appreciated and understood. It is evident from the earlier work that the apparent dichotomy between these two positions is not as marked as may first appear. The first published example of a Parker design, before he had built anything, was in a 1953 compendium of new house designs, *New Elizabethan Homes*, in which he proposed a flat-roofed single-storey dwelling, one of only two examples in the book and daring for the British architectural scene of 1953. A simple rectangular plan was divided by a spine wall – extended out to beyond the front elevation, as at Ingestre Road – and accommodation was laid out tidily either side of it, with an open-plan living space and bedroom/storage areas respectively. This house was described by Parker as a 'reach-me-down design, to be as efficient and pleasing to as many people as possible on a number of differing sites'; in other words almost a prototype for semi-mass housing for those with a little money and land.[8]

An almost identical version of this plan was realised on Bidston Hill on the Wirral four years later, at approximately the same time as he built the first phase of his own house but not before considerable controversy. The local planning authority, Birkenhead Corporation, initially rejected the design in 1955 as it was thought too radical for its semi-rural location.[9] Eventually built following a successful appeal via the Ministry of Housing and Local Government against representations from the council and local objectors, the house was an even more flexible and reproducible version of that which Parker had worked up in 1953. The client was a young art teacher, a Mr J. Mahon who, like Parker, was in his early thirties and desirous of affordable modernism. The construction was mainly of prefabricated components, including long runs of the insulated timber boarding such as those he employed at Ingestre Road, with only three short brick walls in the building, and a flat steel roof deck with a span across the whole structure.[10] The building is still standing but has had virtually all of its original character destroyed; new owners have added a porch with a pitched roof, and due to re-cladding and redecoration the simplicity of Parker's late-1950s ethos has been undermined.

Figure 12. Charleville, on Bidston Hill, was Parker's first two storey house, a fact that was disguised by the fall of the land on the site. An extension to the right (not by Parker) is stylistically sympathetic but disrupts the rectangular plan of the original house (author)

Charleville (now The Cedars), completed in 1959 for C. V. Brown, is another small two-bedroom villa in the Bidston area. It is a modest but creative essay in brick and timber (textures now familiar to Parker) this time over two floors, and won a local RIBA bronze medal in 1959.[11] The lower floor is set into the steeply sloping site and provides the structural integrity of concrete foundations and brick walls, whereas the upper (or ground) floor is entirely of timber, with a shallow pitched roof, and is cantilevered over the lower floor at the edges giving the impression – especially from the driveway – that this is a standalone bungalow in timber. The impression is given of a simple wooden cabin carrying strong North American overtones, a theme that recurs in Parker's work if only because of his enthusiastic use of timber, but the pitched roof here loosens the strictures of his modernism and creates a more traditional sense of vernacular building within woodland. What draws the house away from the rustic is the prominent feature of the brick stairwell on the front elevation, a bull-nosed projection with blank walls except for some clerestory lights and which connects both floors in visual and practical terms.

Another 1959 house, Caracas, was commissioned by the Venezuelan consul to Liverpool and his family. It featured in the construction press as a laudable case study of economical and efficient construction and design methods, and the Liverpool Architectural Society used the house as an exemplar in their 1959 symposium on 'Modern Homes'. It was Parker's largest commission to date, as the client called for numerous bedrooms to house five children and two maids, a requirement that he approached methodically. Describing his design ethos, Parker explained that:

> All elements are reduced to their basic essentials and this type of logic operates throughout the design in relation to all elements. On the large scale, the problem as a whole is broken down into constituents. In [the case of Caracas] for example, the entrance, the kitchen and dining block, the living room and the bedroom block. Each of these I treat in a manner best suited to the problems. I find the visual and structural separation of such elements both sound economics and good aesthetics.[12]

At Caracas these principles translated into a plan and set of elevations redolent of Ingestre Road. A long single-storey range contained all of the living and service spaces in a semi-open plan fashion, whilst a two-storey bedroom range, clad in hardwood and given a monopitch roof sloping down towards the single-storey block, was separated

from it by a glazed entrance porch or linking block. This scheme was cited by Parker as a significant early example of his rational design philosophy, but the quirks were already evident, including a rubble-walled chimney stack exposed half way along the single-storey living room block with an external stone shelf provided for an object or garden display, whilst the stairwell within the bedroom block was lit by a long window that was projected outwards from its base at around 45 degrees.

Parker harnessed these idiosyncrasies to create his first true tour-de-force in 1961-2 at Maeldune, Blundellsands, just north of Liverpool along the Lancashire coast, with the benefit of further ideological gestation, an engaged client and an exemplary site. This was Parker's first completed house of the 1960s and saw a freer approach to plan, volume and form than he had previously attempted. At its heart, Maeldune (named after a Celtic prince who sought adventures along the west coast of Britain) contained a typically logical Parker response to the arrangement of accommodation, similar to that he had outlined in the building of Caracas. A living/service floor at 'ground' level was positioned underneath a first floor bedroom/studio storey, but numerous design features elevated the scheme from basic functionality into something altogether more sculptural.[13]

The site was the most important factor in the design, carved out of sand dunes on the seaward side of the Blundellsands estate, an upmarket Victorian suburban development laid out on sinuous roads around a large park adjoining a station on the Liverpool, Crosby and Southport Railway. The coastline had always been unstable, and some nineteenth-century houses had been destroyed by erosion, but improved post-war flood defences meant that belatedly the seafront could be re-developed with some degree of confidence. The client, John Hamilton, liked to indulge his passions of gardening and observing the regular stream of international shipping that plied across Liverpool Bay; the site, and Parker's scheme, was to offer him opportunities to enjoy both.

The semi-basement was constructed of granite setts arranged into four curvilinear forms with shallow barrel vaults in concrete. The excavated dunes were landscaped to create a mini, cultivated dunescape – an intriguing design to stretch the interested gardener.[14] This solid base acted as a bulwark against the shifting sands with the main accommodation, rich in hardwood timber and glass panels in the usual Parker manner, positioned on top. A dramatic stair tower rises though the rear of the plan, serving the entire house and culminating in an observation room clad in copper externally that peeps over the top of the main building like a submarine conning tower and provides an

Figure 14. In plan, the organic inspiration for Maeldune is made more explicit

(Overleaf)
Figure 15. Maeldune, pictured before the major alterations to the fenestration in 1993

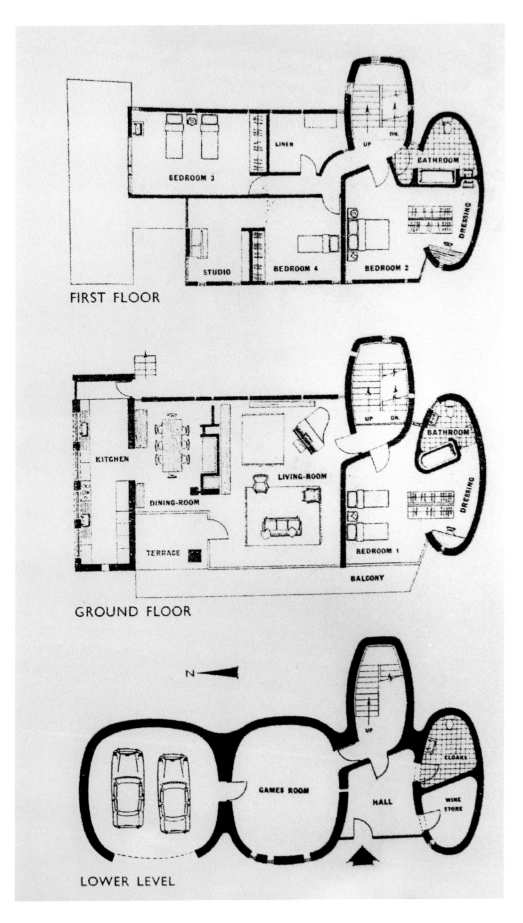

FIRST FLOOR

BEDROOM 3

LINEN

UP

DN.

BATHROOM

DRESSING

STUDIO

BEDROOM 4

BEDROOM 2

GROUND FLOOR

KITCHEN

DINING-ROOM

LIVING-ROOM

UP

DN.

BATHROOM

DRESSING

TERRACE

BEDROOM 1

BALCONY

N

LOWER LEVEL

GAMES ROOM

UP

CLOAKS

HALL

WINE STORE

excellent view to the sea, as Hamilton had demanded. This combination of rounded
forms – in the stair/observation tower, a further brick bulge to the south that housed a
range of ancillary services, the granite basement and the organic landscaping – and the
rectilinear core of the house with its crisp timber mullions, extensive glazing and flat roof,
was an attempt to create a sense of modernity emerging from the landscape, but also
presented a range of sculptural opportunities by juxtaposing different geometries into
a satisfying synthesis. The tower to the rear is the most distinctive feature, making the
house a minor landmark along the coast and giving Parker a chance to exercise his
penchant for strong vertical features. Numerous internal and external changes to the
house, including the insertion of a large patio door, substantial internal alterations and
new picture windows on the top floor of the seaward elevation were carried out by new
owners in 1993 despite a spirited campaign to prevent them, and this has continued
with a more recent campaign of unsympathetic works including new horizontal timber
cladding.[15] Parker's most distinctive individual building has been irretrievably
undermined.

One of Parker's more intriguing schemes was a small development in 1965 of five
detached houses and three bungalows for middle class purchasers, entirely speculative
in nature, in the smart suburbanised coastal village of Parkgate on the Wirral. This foray
into mass housing was, in design terms, a success. He reined in any outré visual quirks to
attract buyers drawn to a more disciplined modernism, who perhaps in the south east of
England might have bought a Span property. Yet although there is nothing outlandish
about these houses, clustered around Hamilton Close in a conventional suburban setting
(named after Emma Hamilton, Horatio Nelson's mistress and nearby Ness's most
famous daughter) they demonstrate much of the design flair that characterises Parker's
one-off commissions.[16] The primary construction method is of post-and-beam timber
framing with limited load-bearing brick walls on the ground floors, and the familiar
timber cladding of the upper floors lends an appropriate texture to the sylvan setting.[17]
The first floor of each house is cantilevered over the ground level to provide larger
bedrooms, while the L-shaped living rooms form a continuous circulation route around
a central service core and are almost fully glazed.

Schemes by Parker from the late 1960s and into the 1970s show a balanced

Figure 17. House in
Fulwood Park, Liverpool
(author)

combination of the practical modernism of his earliest houses with a more emphatic
execution. A relatively small house in Fulwood Park, Liverpool, was commissioned by
a doctor and his family. The park was a residential scheme of the 1840s adjacent to the
Mersey that had gradually increased its original density by allowing additional building
within its one-acre plots. Less striking than some of his other designs of the mid-1960s,
this was an exercise in partial contextualisation to the extent that it blended into the
setting of heavily wooded surroundings; there was, naturally, no attempt to respond to
the large Italianate villas that are the predominant housing type in the park. The single-
storey structure was a simple affair of two pavilion blocks containing Parker's usual
separation of functions, connected at right angles and with a timber pergola extending
out at the front to incorporate a car port.[18] A key requirement was for the house to act as
a foil for the owner's sculpture collection, positioned inside and out at various key display
points and sightlines, and the accommodation itself was an unassuming component of
the client's desires.

There were numerous opportunities for more striking interventions. The Brown
family, who had commissioned Jo to build their first home – Charleville in Bidston, by
1967 required a new property that was larger and on one level.[19] A repeat commission
was naturally a high accolade, but Parker avoided reproducing the first earlier building
that had so evidently pleased the client. The Browns' new house, named Colonus, was
constructed around a mile from the Hamilton Close scheme on Albert Drive, Parkgate,
amongst other individually built homes. The single-storey scheme was conceived as a
series of pavilion rooms linked together around a three-sided courtyard with generous
timber-framed glazing, but the overall impression is of a distinctive pale grey brick mass,
creating a light tone in contrast to the overt solidity of the constructional method.
Double brick piers at the corners created an emphatic weight of structure that was new
for Parker, but some of the old organic devices remained, not least the extensive use of
timber internally and a further use of thick roof beams extended out from the structure
at eaves level to provide a touch of the vernacular amongst the urbane brick. It is the
urbanity that ultimately shines through, however, not least in the bold choice of large
circular windows on numerous elevations, a striking feature for an architect not typically
given to such simple geometry. More dramatic still was No.1 Townfield Lane, built in

Figure 18. Colonus,
Neston, Wirral.
Whilst emphasising
solidity and with strong
geometry, this later
work maintained the
signature rustic device
of exaggeratedly
projecting external
beams (author)

Figure 19. No.1
Townfield Lane, 1973
(Elain Harwood)

1973, perhaps for an Egyptian client, where the overscaled tie-beams and infill of glass blocks between brick piers is reminiscent of Parker's addition to his own house.

One of Parker's favourite commissions grew out of his lasting and warm relationship with Gordon Deering who owned Mariners, a small chain of seafaring-themed restaurants for which he was retained as interior architect with a free reign in design matters.[20] Mallard Hey, as the Deerings named their new home, had an intriguing site, for it replaced dilapidated courtyard buildings on a farm adjacent to Scarisbrick Hall, designed (principally) by A. W. N. Pugin and E. W. Pugin. The Gothic Revival *tour de force* of the Pugins' hall was a clear influence for Parker, who further refined his use of brick to create a surprising and expressive building.[21] Entirely modern in conception, there was nevertheless a Gothic sensibility to the playful yet thoughtful use of material, texture and form: U-shaped structural piers (as at Colonus) created the core structure of the building with glazing of variable widths inserted between them to create a set of syncopated elevations with verticality emphasised again and again. In places, the piers were thrust rhythmically upwards in places and topped with monopitched rooflets in slate (seen later at the Ingestre Road extension), creating an interesting skyline that echoed the Pugins' spires and crockets. The bricks were expensively matched to their older neighbours, while the planning and scale was such that the house became an intrinsic part of the historic farmyard complex rather than a jarring addition.[22]

Parker's houses have experienced a high rate of attrition and unsympathetic alteration. This situation has not been helped by the low profile that the architect maintained during his professional life and the relatively sparse coverage that his buildings received in the architectural press so that even on Merseyside the houses are not fully appreciated as a body of work. Happily the architect's own home at Ingestre Road is currently owned by enthusiasts who have reversed unsympathetic alterations with great care and are excellent custodians of and proselytisers for Parker's work. The house, along with other schemes including Hamilton Close, retains a good deal of integrity and stands as testimony to a meaningful and distinctive local architectural scene of the 1960s and 1970s.

Acknowledgements: Thanks to Peter de Figueiredo, Julian Treuherz and Jane Parker for their invaluable help with sources, recollections and – most of all – the time and enthusiasm they gave to assist in the writing of this article. Grateful thanks are also due to Geoff Beard, Martin Holden, Tom Byrne and Sue Lunt

1. Pers comm., Jane Parker, 7 January 2014.

2. ibid.

3. The new building by Haworth Tompkins won the Stirling Prize for 2014.

4. *House and Garden*, vol.13, no.11, November 1958, pp.86-7.

5. Reyner Banham, 'The New Brutalism', *Architectural Review*, vol.118, no.708, December 1955, pp.354-61.

6. Jane Parker, 7 January 2014.

7. ibid.

8. 'The Parker House', in Margaret Sherman, ed., *New Elizabethan Homes*, London, *News Chronicle* Book Department, 1953, p.48.

9. *Architect and Building News*, vol.207, no.12, 10 February 1955, p.173.

10. *Architectural Design*, vol.27, no.10, October 1957, p.376.

11. *The Builder*, vol. 200, no.6157, 19 May 1961, pp.936-7.

12. *Interbuild*, vol.7, no.3, March 1959, pp.20-3.

13. Daily Mail *Book of Bungalow Plans*, London, Associated Newspapers, 1965-6, pp.54-6.

14. Report by Elspeth Hamilton, 1993, compiled for the Twentieth Century Society, in English Heritage London Historians' Files OUT 206.

15. *Building Design*, no. 1146, October 1993, p.2.

16. *Architecture North West*, no.18, August 1966, p.12.

17. *Wood*, vol.30, no.2. February 1965, pp.32-3.

18. Daily Mail *Book of Bungalow Plans*, London, Associated Newspapers, 1965-6, pp.20-2.

19. Daily Mail *Book of Bungalow Plans*, London, Associated Newspapers, 1968-9, pp.51-2.

20. Jane Parker, op.cit., 7 January 2014.

21. June Park, *Houses for Today*, London, Batsford, 1971, pp.72-3.

22. *Building*, vol.220, no.6679, 21 May 1971, pp. 67-73.

Neil Swanson

8 Cedarwood: *Women's Journal* House of the Year 1960

Figure 1. Cedarwood, the garden elevation (Phil Sayer, 2014)

Figure 2. Cedarwood: view of street frontage taken just prior to opening in 1960; note Austin A99 on the drive. From *Women's Journal*, March 1960 (John Mills Photography)

On 24 February 1960 in the leafy Liverpool suburb of Woolton queues of eager fans waited in line to encounter the future. They waited, not at St Peter's church hall for the recently renamed Quarrymen (now known as the Beatals [sic] after Stuart Sutcliffe joined John Lennon and Paul McCartney), but for the opening of the *Women's Journal* House of the Year.

This was an exciting event for many Liverpudlians. They had watched with increasing curiosity as the unusual boxy building on Woolton Hill neared completion. As they stood patiently waiting for entry, they read breathless publicity garnered from national and local newspapers and journals, outlining the heady aspirations of the architects and the project sponsors. As they inched past the gate emblazoned with the name 'Cedarwood' and across the drive to the secluded, shady front door, they anticipated the discovery inside of airy, colourful rooms filled with the latest furniture and gadgets. According to local legend, over 66,000 people visited during the spring of 1960.

For some (including a young Stephen Bayley, the future design critic who grew up just a cycle ride away), the house and its interior were inspirational.

> I can only have been eight years old when the house was finished, but I remember it vividly. My response to it was un-learnt, but nonetheless profound. I made my poor father take me there as often as possible. It was like primitive religious observation: I didn't have the words to describe it at the time, but Cedarwood represented all the stylish and exotic values I yearned for. I loved Liverpool, but it was suffocated by its past and uncomfortable in the present. Cedarwood, by contrast, was optimism.[1]

In 1960 Liverpool was emerging from the long, drab years of post-war austerity. The export drive had gathered pace and the city's ships and sailors and stewards were bringing home the new products of American affluence from across the Atlantic, and New York jazz, delta blues and Elvis were being absorbed into the emerging Liverpool music scene.

The two architects of Cedarwood, Dewi-Prys Thomas and Gerald Beech, both

Figure 3. Dewi-Prys
Thomas (left) and
Gerald Beech (right),
architects of Cedarwood
seen examining a
model of the house.
From *Women's
Journal*, March 1960
(John Mills Photography)

taught at the Liverpool School of Architecture from the late 1940s.[2] Thomas (1916-85)
was born in Liverpool into a family with a strong Welsh heritage. A talented draughtsman
who initially wanted to be an artist, he graduated with first class honours in 1939. During
the war he worked in Cardiff for T. Alwyn Lloyd before returning to Liverpool in 1947 as
a senior lecturer, a position he retained until 1960, the year of Cedarwood, when he was
appointed head of the Welsh School of Architecture in Cardiff, remaining there until
his retirement in 1981. During his time in Liverpool, Thomas designed innovative houses
in Liverpool and the Wirral, including the listed Entwood in Birkenhead from 1959.
At Birkenland, an earlier house of 1957 on Bidston Hill in the Wirral, Thomas responded
to the spectacular views westwards towards Wales, devising an elegant solution to
building on a complex sloping site with a design that refers at several points to Alvar
Aalto's Villa Mairea in Finland of 1938-9. Two rectangular volumes of light timber
construction are positioned around an overlapping entrance space, while the expressively
angled lowest step of the main staircase is a direct quotation. Later in Cardiff Thomas
found the pressures of academic life limited his architectural output.[3] Following his
retirement from teaching, he completed the designs for Y Pencadlys, the remarkable
headquarters of Gwynedd County Council in Caernarfon. His legacy and influence
on the architectural life of Wales is celebrated in the Dewi-Prys Thomas prize awarded
triennially for good design in the Principality.[4]

Gerald Rushworth Beech (1921-2013) also studied at Liverpool, where he shared
a studio with the architect turned historian Quentin Hughes, gaining a diploma in
architecture with distinction in 1947 and a diploma in civic design in 1948 before
qualifying in 1952. From 1948 he was a studio instructor and lecturer, and from 1968 to
his retirement in 1988 was a senior lecturer.[5] Throughout his academic career he ran his
practice, Gerald Beech and Partners, through which he worked with talented and
capable young architects. Many of his commissions were associated with the University,
including railings and gates in Abercromby Square, completing the University's Bedford
House Staff Club and designing the beautiful Wyncote Sports Pavilion in Allerton,
winner of a Civic Trust Award in 1964. His private houses had a simple, clean quality
that belied some complex plans, exemplified by that of 1962 for a building contractor,

T. E. Dennis, at Heswall on the Wirral, a single-storey brick box bisected by a largely glazed steel-framed living room.[6]

Thomas and Beech collaborated on only one house, on the '*Women's Journal House of the Year*' project known as Cedarwood, which they completed in 1960 and which is the subject of this essay. They also designed a Friends' Meeting House in Heswall, built in 1961-2.[7]

The two collaborators were among many of their generation influenced by the pragmatic and expressive modern architecture of northern Europe that emerged after the war, with its concern for materials, textures and a response to landscape. Cedarwood was built in a former gardeners' yard, on a site dominated by the tall brick and sandstone wall of the kitchen garden and fronting on to Beaconsfield Road in the former grounds of a large mansion, Stoneleigh, which was one of many sold off in the late 1950s. Here in a desirable part of south Liverpool, two-storey detached houses and bungalows were built as speculative homes, set in lawns behind low brick walls in typical suburban fashion. Several plots with mature trees and distinctive features were reserved for individual houses, some of which were designed as one-off commissions by Liverpool-based architects, including Victor Basil, the American James Hunter, and Gerald Beech himself.

Writing about Cedarwood, the architects outlined their intentions to create a house with 'ideas capable of further development in the coming decade'.[8] Two key themes underpinned their thinking. The first was to make a 'prototype which, if adopted for a whole estate, would allow the unity of 18th-century terraces while retaining the detachment so many people still prefer'.[9] The second was to make a 'background for civilised living' … a 'modern house designed for the modern family; the family that requires privacy in urban areas but also the most free relationship between living space and outdoors; that requires "cave" as well as "tent"; that requires wellbeing and warmth internally despite lavish window area and sun in all rooms sometime during the day; that requires the broadest feeling of spaciousness for entertaining, on occasion, but a more intimate atmosphere for normal day to day life: that requires maximum returns in comfort and standards of living with minimum drudgery and maintenance'. In short it was a house in which 'each member of the family can develop his [sic] different personality and interests in the fullest possible way'.[10] Knowledge of the connections made by Dewi-Prys Thomas in his history lessons between Welsh vernacular and the origins of architectural form in ancient Greece suggest that these analogies of 'cave' and 'tent' reflect his thinking. The L-shape made by the house and garage could even be seen as a farmyard transposed to suburbia.

Thomas and Beech developed a simple and direct architectural response to the site: the building would extend the full width of the plot (50 feet / 15m) on the ground floor, avoiding the 'dank corridor that usually squeezes between detached houses on narrow plots'.[11] The ground floor would be narrow (18 feet / 5.5m front to back) with a solid, masonry wall with small openings facing north across a car court to the road beyond, and a more open, glazed south face looking over a patio and reflective pool to the garden. The ground floor walls, which would extend out into the garden to create boundaries, enclose exterior space and form the structure for a garage, and also support four laminated timber beams which overhang at front and back. On these rest the upper storey, in effect a large wooden box (27 feet / 8.2m square), containing the bedrooms and bathrooms. The independence of the 'box' was emphasised by long horizontal clerestories inserted over the brick walls between the upper and lower storeys, a device that became widely used in 1960s houses where structural timber was involved.

In developing this form Thomas and Beech let the site inform the building; this was no 'statement building' with the grand front familiar in nearby suburban houses of the time; instead, this house presents a closed, discreet public front to the street, and the front door is set in a corner, reached diagonally across an open, hard-paved car court,

**Figure 4. Cedarwood:
south elevation,
architects' drawing 1960**

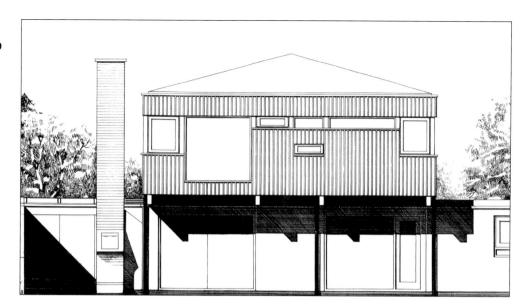

**Figure 5. Cedarwood:
north elevation,
architects' drawing 1960**

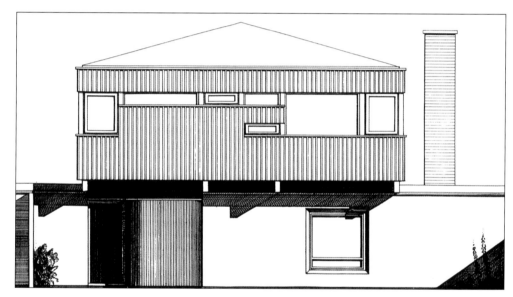

**Figure 6. Cedarwood:
Ground floor plan**

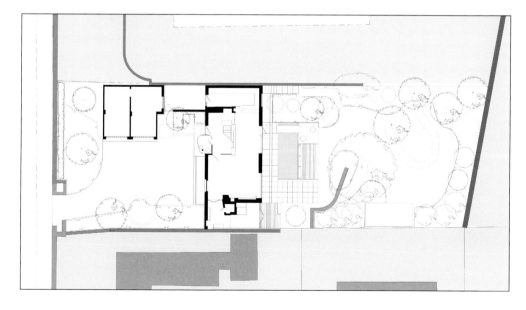

framed by heavy, solid single-storey Tyrolean rendered walls. The light timber box of the upper floor seems to hover on these, detached by the shadow of the overhang and the light through the glazing strip beneath. The crisp timber detailing and carefully proportioned window openings of the upper storey contrast with the roughness of the ground-floor walls.[12]

At Cedarwood, references to Villa Mairea can be found again in the use of vertical timber siding as cladding to the upper floor, contrasting with a white rendered masonry ground floor, and in the curving timber slatted wall next to the front door that wraps round the cloakroom beneath the overhanging upper storey. The robust modelling and chamfered window recesses of the ground floor walls recall the influential Ronchamp chapel designed by Le Corbusier and completed just five years previously. At first glance there are also similarities with Trevor Dannatt's well-publicised Laslett House in Clarkson Road, Cambridge of 1958, with its carefully ordered Western Red Cedar upper floor projecting over a brick ground floor, making a freestanding compact villa-like volume. At Cedarwood the upper floor overhangs much further, to the back and front, suggesting a more romantic approach, while the lower storey extends to either side.[13] The few windows facing the street at Cedarwood is contrasted with the openness of the garden front, with full height sliding windows to the open plan living room and dining room. In this fluid, open interface between inside and out, perhaps can be detected the American influence of the Case Study houses, with their large sliding glazed openings, just beginning to become possible in England with the development of float glass by Pilkington's between 1953 and 1957 in nearby St Helens.

The architects also took care over the internal layout and finishes. To counteract the narrowness of the ground floor layout, they designed the living area as a spacious open-plan L-shaped room that could be subdivided by glazed doors and screens that folded back into the wall. When the screens were open, long views extended from the kitchen at one end of the house to the conservatory at the other. The architects described how, from her key position in kitchen 'the housewife … is able to keep an eye on the children wherever they are playing downstairs'.[14] In contrast to the adaptable and flexible ground floor, the upper floor, with its four bedrooms and bathroom, provided 'very private territories'.[15] The architects made use of strip windows in different but harmonious proportions to create a unified façade, with enclosed and intimate atmospheres in each room.

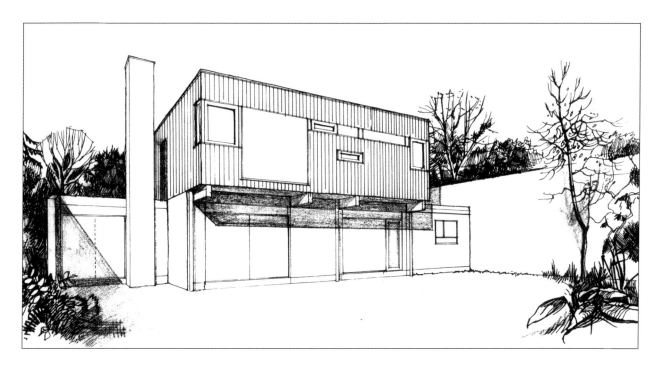

Thomas and Beech made extensive use of timber throughout the building. Except for the Sapele woodblock flooring and doors from West Africa, all timber came from Canada, whose trade commission was at the time promoting exports. Hemlock from the Pacific coast was used for structural timbers, with grainy Douglas fir for the laminated beams which carry the upper storey and the tapered steps of the staircase, while fragrant western red cedar was used for architraves and skirtings and for the dramatic panelling of the central 'spine' wall. Douglas fir was used in a free-form cloakroom enclosure by the front door, and upstairs as a plywood for structure and floors and on the landing walls as panelling in which the soft grain is 'scoured away so that the hard grain leaps into relief producing a decorative "watermark" effect'; similar textured effects were used on pelmets in the bedrooms.[16] Together, the warm tones and textures of the timber were designed to give a 'warmly pleasing appearance and natural friendliness … durable, light, strong and with excellent thermal insulation'.[17] Today, over fifty years after completion, the timber is still in place and has developed a beautiful patina.

The architects developed complex and sophisticated designs for several key features of the building. The fireplace was designed as a carefully proportioned composition of planes with the fire as the focus and niches for the telephone, telephone directory and coalscuttle, backlit through blue glass, and anchored by a black tiled plinth. The staircase was designed to hang from steel rods (made by the local blacksmith) fixed to the beams above the hallway, so that it appears to spring weightless from the cedar-clad 'spine wall' which itself is pierced by coloured glass openings. Sliding reeded-glass panes and glazed-fronted cupboards were designed as a translucent screen between the kitchen and dining room.

The construction of the house, by a well-established local building contractor, J. W. Jones and Sons, led by Howell Jones and his foreman Eddie Ellis, made use of several features which were innovative at the time. The bedroom walls were finished in dry-linings using plasterboard and paper, which did not require lengthy drying out periods, would not crack as a result, and could be decorated immediately. The freestanding chimney was made of slate waste bricks, a new product from Dinorwic Quarry in North Wales. Floors and roofs were insulated with fibre glass and use was made of double-glazing. The electric underfloor heating (installed in an age when nuclear power was expected to reduce energy costs to a minimum) extended under the

Figure 9. Sitting
Room showing feature
fireplace and view
through doors to the
conservatory (right)
(Neil Swanson, 2010)

Figure 10. Staircase
showing suspended
steps and bust niche
in wall (Phil Sayer, 2014)

entire ground floor, including the conservatory, and even outside under the car court
at the front.

The costs of the house project were borne by *Women's Journal*, the London based
magazine that awarded Cedarwood the accolade of its 'House of the Year 1960'.
Beginning in 1958, an executive home was chosen from a different part of the country
each year, save in 1960 and 1965 from an estate being developed commercially. In doing
so, the magazine was simultaneously linking itself and its readers with innovative
contemporary design outside London, and at the same time offering a setting in which
potential sponsors, manufacturers and retailers could pay to display and promote their
latest products. They were very successful in attracting the best of British product design
of the time. The list includes Baxi, who supplied the fire, and Bilston, whose Atlanta bath
(also selected for the Design Centre) was fitted in the bathroom. Marley provided floor
tiles; Formica's colourful and durable worktops and surfaces still grace the kitchen and
bathroom; and Lionite supplied the innovative folding screen between the living and
dining rooms. Rotaflex provided the light shades, in spun cellulose acetate formed into
ovoid and spherical shapes.

The furnishings and decorations were supplied by Liverpool's premier department
store George Henry Lees, whose interior designer Ian Mackenzie worked closely with the
architects to create a series of sumptuously coloured room settings filled with the latest
furniture and household appliances available from the store. Highlights include Sorrento
and Tiber seating by Everest in the living room, and the Austin A.99 Westminster in black
and tartan red on the drive. Architecture students from the Liverpool school provided
drawings which adorned the walls. Only one piece was specially commissioned: an
abstract tapestry called *Old Man of the Sea* designed by Stephen D. Lee and hand worked
in needlepoint by Arthur H. Lee and Sons of Birkenhead, which was positioned at the
top of the stairs but which sadly has been lost.

The garden was designed as an integrated counterpart of the house. The connection between interior and exterior through sliding glass doors was almost seamless, reinforced visually by the band of upper level windows and framed by the deep overhang of the upper level 'box'. A large pool, crossed by a delicate timber bridge to a pebbly 'beach', was designed as a focus close to the house. The pool reflects the low winter sun into the house, creating beautiful shimmering reflections on the ceiling. Further away from the house the garden develops an informal character, shaped by two interlocking grassy mounds which form an 'infinite vista' when viewed from the living room. Two birch trees (now mature) form sculptural and shady canopies over the garden in summer, while letting winter sun flood the house. An east-facing roof terrace was built over the kitchen (accessible via steel and timber steps from the garden) and a heated, glazed conservatory provides a space at the west of the site, connected to the living room.

The *Women's Journal* House of the Year opened to much fanfare on 24 February 1960. The March edition of the magazine featured a full colour description of the building, including interviews with the architects and others linked to the project, plus a fashion shoot combining glamorous models in gritty Liverpool Dockland locations with smartly dressed couples at a cocktail reception in Cedarwood. A programme of events was advertised for the four-week period that the house would be open to the public, including lectures by the architects and landscape architect Arnold Weddle, then teaching at Liverpool University and who would later become the first professor of landscape architecture in the United Kingdom at Sheffield University. The magazine even included the recipe for a special celebratory meal 'Poulet au Lee', which was served at Lee's department store restaurant throughout the March opening times.

Figure 13. Stairs and hallway (Phil Sayer, 2014)

The project received some notice in the architectural press, including a short description in the *Architectural Review*, expressing approval and suggesting that the concept 'would give, in a complete development of this type, a reasonable combination of terrace-house continuity and detached individuality'.[18]

The Guardian for Wednesday, 24 February 1960 had extensive coverage of the house, announcing that 'a new age of elegance opens tomorrow'.[19] Correspondents in the 'Mainly for Women' section discussed contemporary issues raised by the house: Anne Brooking tackled open plan living in an article in which the pros ('it's more fun, there's more room for jiving') and cons ('the noise! The lack of privacy! The cooking smells!') were set alongside the 'for and against television debate', and concluded with a last word from the children: 'no one ever shouts at us to close the door now!... A new era perhaps?'[20] Discussing contemporary furniture, Mary Stott debated the influence of Utility furniture and the Swedish furniture selected by the more discerning for its ease of use and adaptability; she noted the recent trend, pioneered by the Conran group, to create heavier, bulkier furniture, perhaps as a 'reaction against the very light "stick-like" Italian-influenced furniture'.[21]

Timber as a building material was given a mild boost by Eugenie Fordham, who drew comparisons between the 'bold and exciting overhung first floor' at Cedarwood and the medieval jettied buildings in the Shambles in York. Mary Reynolds, writing about kitchen design, cited research carried out by the Council for Scientific Management in the Home to support her utilitarian advice, while *The Guardian*'s 'Household Correspondent' enthused about the 'labour saving gadgets' (while also pointing out the derivation of the word gadget from Gadge – an instrument of torture), including the Swanmaid dishwasher ('for one glorious wash-up in the evening') and the English Electric Liberator (for its 'gorgeous automatic grapple with washing day'). Best of all,

Figure 14. Dining room
(Phil Sayer, 2014)

though, is the description of the duvet, then new: 'a heavenly gadget ... a blissful cloud of the lightest down ... it supplants bed-making and is merely put on top of the sheet; no blankets summer or winter'.[22]

The Guardian's Women's Page editor appreciated the flexibility of the layout, 'not exactly open plan, but with screens and glass doors to subdivide space', and the possibility of 'living with the garden'. She wondered whether the living room could accommodate a whole family, but pointed out the warmth of the timber finishes, the double glazing and the underfloor heating, and the freedom this gave to occupy the bedrooms as 'private living quarters'. She pointed to the complication of separating dining from kitchen, but enjoyed the worktops of cheerful citron Formica, with blue used in the bathroom. She cast a sceptical glance at the 'attractive staircase with the vertical metal rods instead of banisters – would it not inevitably become a climbing frame for the young?'[23] She wasn't wrong on that score.

It was left to 28-year old Geoffrey Moorhouse, later to become a well known writer and journalist, to strike a more curmudgeonly note in his architectural review for *The Guardian*, pointing out that the house was for 'a fairly uncommon modern family, to be found somewhere in the middle of the supertax range'. He had a point: the cost was estimated at £10,000, which included furniture and fittings worth about £6,000, leaving construction costs of approximately £4,000 at a time when a typical three-bed semi cost less than £1,200. However, Moorhouse acknowledged that the architects had succeeded in producing 'a basic form which might well be developed further in domestic building in the next decade'. He admired the flexibility provided by the sliding screens and the possibility of re-aligning the partition walls upstairs. He complemented the 'interest at the back of the house ... the rhythm in the façade and the ambitious attempt at landscaping on a modest scale'. Most of all, he was excited at the architects' handling of

Figure 15. Living room
(Phil Sayer, 2014)

Figure 16. Bedroom
overlooking garden
(Phil Sayer, 2014)

Figure 17. Bathroom
with Formica surfaces
and wall panels
(Phil Sayer, 2014)

the frontage, and their ambition to produce a building type 'which might evoke the concord that one associates with the terraces of the eighteenth century, while still retaining the detached character demanded by the Englishman in the mid-twentieth century'. Moorhouse agreed with the *Architectural Review* that Cedarwood represented a house which 'might well bear repetition on a large scale ... [in a form in which] the units would appear to flow into one another and thus achieve a sort of unity'. Despite this he concluded his review by asking 'whether the House of the Year 1960 can be adapted sufficiently to fulfil a need and not, as now, merely to provide a luxury'.[24]

Moving in almost forty years later, we found the house to be in good condition, a testament to the quality of its design and construction. The only major work has been to replace one of the laminated timber beams which had sagged due to structural deficiencies resulting from the poorly understood glue technology of the time. Cedarwood has proved to be a very comfortable and stimulating home for our family. It did not lead to the 'extensive flowing estates' envisaged by some, but its influence can be seen in individual houses built subsequently in south Liverpool and in places like Parkgate on the Wirral, where a small group of timber framed houses designed by Nelson and Parker develop ideas seen in Cedarwood. The house was described by Pevsner as 'immaculately detailed', and is featured in Quentin Hughes's book *Liverpool*, where he described the house as 'A little gem of a house, lovingly detailed'.[25] In 2007 Cedarwood was listed at grade II★ on the advice of English Heritage.

We still have strangers ringing our doorbell, remembering the thrill of the house when it first opened. Some even claim it was the inspiration behind the Beatles' song *Norwegian Wood*. Perhaps John Lennon, who lived just five minutes away with his Aunt Mimi on Menlove Avenue, was as inspired by the panelled timber house on Woolton Hill as by the rest of his home city.

153 Cedarwood: *Women's Journal* House of the Year 1960

Figure 18. Kitchen with surfaces in citron Formica (Phil Sayer, 2014)

1. Stephen Bayley, correspondence with the author; 17 July 2011.

2. Jack Dunne and Peter Richmond, *The World in One School, The history and influence of the Liverpool School of Architecture 1894-2004*, Liverpool University Press, 2008, p.66.

3. Biography of Dewi-Prys Thomas at www.dew-prysthomas.org./biog-en.html, accessed 5 January 2014.

4. ibid.

5. Papers of the Gerald Beech Partnership Archive 1959-74, Liverpool University Library Archive.

6. Penelope Whiting, *New Single-Storey Houses*, London, Architectural Press, 1966, pp.21-5.

7. Clare Hartwell, Matthew Hyde, Edward Hubbard and Nikolaus Pevsner, The Buildings of England, *Cheshire*, London, Yale, 2011, p.397.

8. Architects' report, quoted in '*Women's Journal* House of the Year', *Women's Journal*, March 1960, p.20.

9. ibid., p.20.

10. Architects' report, quoted in 'The House of the Year', *The Guardian*, no.35348, 24 February 1960, p.11.

11. ibid., p.20.

12. Nikolaus Pevsner, The Buildings of England, *South Lancashire*; Harmondsworth, Penguin, 1969, p.158.

13. Trevor Dannatt, *Buildings and Interiors 1951 / 72*; London, Lund Humphries, 1972, pp.25-7.

14. Architects' report, quoted in 'Women's Journal House of the Year', op.cit.

15. ibid., p.20.

16. ibid., p.21.

17. ibid., p.21.

18. 'Mass Sophistication', *Architectural Review*, vol.127, no.757, March 1960, pp.153-4.

19. 'The House of the Year', *The Guardian*, no.35348, 24 February 1960, pp.11-16.

20. ibid., p.12.

21. ibid., p.12.

22. ibid., p.13.

23. ibid., p.14.

24. ibid., p.11.

25. Pevsner, op.cit., p.158; Quentin Hughes, *Liverpool*, London, Studio Vista, 1969, p.68. See also Derek Abbott and Kimball Pollitt, *Hill Housing*, London, Granada, 1980.

Figure 19. Advert for Dulux paint, featuring Cedarwood in background, from *Women's Journal*, March 1960

You're right – they used

DULUX and **DU-LITE**

Fiona Fisher

9 Kenneth Wood: Modern Surrey Houses of the 1950s and 1960s

There is a long-standing prejudice against suburbs, often perceived as 'subtopian' deserts of architectural mediocrity. The architectural and design practice that Kenneth Wood established at East Molesey in Surrey in 1955 is one example that proves the contrary, operating primarily in a local context to produce good modern buildings of modest scale after the removal of wartime building restrictions. Although little-known today, Wood's work was published and exhibited in Britain, and internationally in the 1950s and 1960s, when it was critically well-received. Projects included street improvement schemes at East Molesey and Chertsey, church halls and church extensions around Kingston upon Thames and in north London, a village centre at Oxshott, and a youth club and a school at Kingston, but it was for the design of individual modern houses, mostly in Surrey, that Wood's firm became best known. The architectural contribution of successful suburban firms such as Wood's has been largely overlooked, as discussion of the post-war suburb as a site of subtopian development has hindered a broader appreciation of progressive architectural forces within that arena.

In the late nineteenth century, Surrey became closely associated with the emergence of an idealised domesticity, epitomised in the 'Surrey Style' architecture of Edwin Lutyens and the Surrey houses of C.F.A. Voysey.[1] According to *New Estates Magazine*, Surrey was the county 'to which, above all the others, the Englishman can return from overseas, and find the many sided peace of home'.[2] Speculative housing developers found a ready market between the wars for houses in the 'Surrey Style' and, although a number of notable one-off modern houses were completed before 1939, Surrey's towns and suburbs were expanded and rebuilt predominantly in local and historical styles.[3] As Ian Nairn noted in his introduction to the Surrey volume of *The Buildings of England* (1962), this architectural conservatism continued after the Second World War. 'Modern architects still find it more difficult to put up modern buildings in Surrey than almost anywhere else, whilst misinterpretations and malformations of traditional Surrey vernacular multiply without hindrance.'[4] Nevertheless, the natural attractions of the county, its proximity to London, and the availability of land on which to build made it 'a haven for the discreetly sited private house' and Wood was one of a number of architects, among them Michael Manser, Powell and Moya, Leslie Gooday and Stefan Buzás, who designed modern houses for Surrey clients in the 1950s and 1960s.[5]

Kenneth Brian Wood was born at Silvertown in east London in 1921 and spent his early childhood in London and Kent. Following a secondary education at Dartford Grammar School, he enrolled in the autumn of 1937 at the Regent Street Polytechnic for evening studies in engineering services. Wood's training was interrupted by the war, during which he served in the Royal Air Force and on secondment as a ferry pilot with the Air Transport Auxiliary. In 1946, after his release from military service, he resumed his training and returned to his job as a junior draughtsman/surveyor with Matthew Hall and Company. He was soon sent on loan to Reginald Blomfield's architectural practice, which was short of staff.[6] Wood's experience working there alongside student architects, some of whom were also studying at Regent Street, furthered his developing interest in architectural design and thoughts of changing professional direction. On completing his engineering services examinations he re-applied to the Polytechnic to study architecture and was accepted for admission in autumn 1948 as one of a number of mature students on the course. During his training he worked for firms in London and the South East, including Dudley Marsh at Herne Bay, Farmer and Dark and the Regent Oil Company in London.

Wood's first position on qualifying was with Eric Lyons at his practice in East Molesey in Surrey.[7] Lyons was at that time working on the Parkleys housing development, a scheme of 175 flats and a parade of shops arranged in low-rise blocks on an eight acre site at Ham. Along with Oaklands (1948), a small scheme of 24 flats at

Figure 2. Vincent
House, Kingston
upon Thames.
Garden elevation.
RIBA Library
Photographs
Collection, London
(RIBA 40731)

Whitton, Parkleys established the principles for subsequent housing schemes with
Span, a development company established in the expectation of finding a market for
affordable modern houses in attractive landscaped environments that were managed by
the residents, creating a sense of community and place.[8] Ian Nairn described Parkleys
as 'a delightful and delightfully landscaped estate whose tile-hanging makes a genuinely
C20 comment on the native Surrey style'.[9] As Wood's own projects demonstrate, he was
sympathetic to Lyons's contextual approach to design, as well as his emphasis on
economy of form and construction. During his time with Lyons, he worked on Parkleys
and the Soviet Trade Delegation project at Highgate (36 flats, an assembly hall and a
nursery), as well as the design development of Lyons's sketches for a house for Span
partner Geoffrey Townsend at Walpole Gardens in Twickenham. In 1955, at the age of
33, Wood established his own architectural and design practice at East Molesey, close to
that of Lyons who continued to employ him on a part-time basis until 1956.[10]

   During this hopeful period of expanding opportunities, it was Wood's non-
domestic projects that launched his practice.[11] His wider reputation was established
with a run of five houses for private clients in Surrey – Whitewood at Strawberry Hill
(1958), Wildwood at Oxshott (1958), Vincent House at Kingston (1959), Nathan House
at Oxshott (1960), and Fenwycks at Camberley (1960). These early projects were
followed by Hampton House at Hampton (1961), Atrium at Hampton (1962),
Tanglewood at Hampton Hill (1962), Oriel House at Haslemere (1963), Dykes at
Virginia Water (1963), Torrent House at Hampton Court (1964), Little Boredom at
Cobham (1968), and Picker House at Kingston (1968).[12]

Wood's houses of the 1950s and 1960s reveal something of the pattern of land use in Surrey at that time. His first house, Whitewood, was planned for a small suburban plot in an area of mainly mid- to late-Victorian housing at Strawberry Hill, near Twickenham. The single-storey courtyard house was designed to minimise visual impact on nearby residents and to ensure privacy and a favourable outlook for Wood's clients. A similar approach was employed for two later houses, Atrium and Tanglewood, the latter designed for a tricky quarter-acre plot with development restrictions. These single-storey, compact and inward-looking suburban courtyard houses employed borrowed views to create a sense of interior spaciousness and can be contrasted with several larger houses that Wood designed for semi-rural settings with attractive open views of the Surrey landscape. Oriel House at Haslemere was built on the site of a former orchard and several other houses were built on sub-divided garden plots. Among them were Nathan House, built on part of the garden of the Knott Park Estate at Oxshott which was sold for development in 1953, and Picker House at Kingston, which was built on part of the landscaped grounds of a mid-Victorian mansion that was parcelled for development in 1954. In contrast, Wildwood at Oxshott was built on Crown land and is notable as an example of a house designed for a new development area. So, too, is Torrent House, a Civic Trust Award winner in 1965 that was completed on a former industrial site.

The publication of several of Wood's early projects helped him to develop a reputation for modern domestic design that was furthered when Vincent House was selected for display at the *Architecture Today* exhibition in 1961, positioning his practice at the forefront of national architectural developments at that time. Sponsored by the Arts Council of Great Britain and the Royal Institute of British Architects, the exhibition took place at the Arts Council Galleries in St James Square from 28 June to 29 July 1961, and was timed to coincide with the Congress of the International Union of Architects then being held in London.[13] The organising committee aimed to showcase the best British architectural design of the period and Wood responded to an open call for submissions. Other leading firms were invited to participate.[14]

The residential category in which Vincent House was exhibited included local authority work and speculative schemes and featured low-rise, high density suburban and village housing alongside Corbusian-inspired urban mass housing. Among the designs exhibited alongside Vincent House in the residential category were James Stirling and James Gowan's flats at Langham House Close, Ham Common; the LCC's Alton Estate (West) at Roehampton; Eric Lyons's Span housing at Corner Green in Blackheath; and the Park Hill development in Sheffield by Jack Lynn and Ivor Smith. A number of private houses were shown, although none was depicted in the exhibition catalogue, which placed a visual emphasis on the use of modern materials and mass production techniques. The private houses – a weekend house of timber construction at Fawley Bottom, near Henley on Thames, by Lionel Brett; a brick and timber single-storey courtyard house at Hampstead by Trevor Dannatt; a two-storey brick and steel-framed house at Hampstead by H.C. Higgins and R.P.H. Ney; a timber-framed house with linked pavilions by W.G. Howell and John Killick at Keston; a two-storey brick house at Highgate by Leonard Manasseh; High Sunderland, the single-storey timber-framed house near Galashiels that Peter Womersley created for textile designer Bernat Klein; and a house at Kano in Nigeria by the Architects' Co-Partnership – reflect more fully the plural practices and forms that continued to evolve within British modernism in the 1950s as it broadened away from Scandinavian and purely functionalist influences. In the same year, Wood's Hampton House, a highly commercial venture to showcase the work of a newly-formed housing development company, was named as *Ideal Home* magazine's House of the Year.[15] The company was established by Charlotte Parker, an interior designer and ceramicist, who was joined in the venture by Norman Barker, an entrepreneurial individual with no knowledge of design or construction. Although adept at marketing, the couple's lack of experience and financial resources soon led to the failure of the business.

As well as participating in national competitions and exhibitions, Wood was involved in organising and exhibiting in several group shows by members of the Kingston upon Thames District Chapter of the South Eastern Society of Architects. These included Architecture Week (1961) and 'Design 66' (1966), both held at Bentalls, the local department store, and 'Architecture at Habitat' (1969), held at the Kingston branch of Habitat which had opened two years earlier. Local exhibitions were an important vehicle for modern architecture as well as the work of individual architects and firms, and give an indication of the range of the profession in Surrey, as well as the spectrum of modernist practice in the county at that time, which ranged from Wood's humanist brick and timber designs to the steel and glass aesthetic of Michael Manser. Among practices that participated were: Eric Lyons and Partners, J. E. K. Harrison and Associates, Alan and Sylvia Blanc, Michael Manser Associates, Robert Baillie, Norman and Dawbarn, J. H. Lomas, Scherrer and Hicks, W. S. Hattrell and Partners, Jack Godfrey Gilbert, Fred Greenwood, Noel Moffett and Associates, Scott, Brownrigg and Turner, Broadway and Malyan, and Derek Lovejoy and Associates, who exhibited two architectural projects, a house at Woldingham and offices at Croydon.

Wood valued the historical component of his studies at the Regent Street Polytechnic, and it was as a committed modernist with a strong respect for architectural tradition that he approached the design of public and private projects throughout his career. Early houses such as Wildwood, which incorporated a central galleried living area of post and beam construction, reflect his knowledge of British vernacular architecture, hall houses in particular. They also suggest his awareness of new tendencies within British modernism of the late 1950s, evident in a growing acceptance and use of mixed materials – brick and timber – in conjunction with pitched, rather than flat roofs in domestic design. Clear, too, is his attention to the progress of modern architecture in North America, to the work of Marcel Breuer, whose internationally disseminated House in the Garden (Museum of Modern Art, 1949) was a point of reference, and to regional developments, notably the modern timber and glass architecture that evolved in the San Francisco Bay Area.

Wood's interest in timber construction was furthered in 1957 by his participation in an architectural competition to promote the use of Canadian timber in British domestic design. The competition, sponsored by the British Columbia Lumber Manufacturers' Association (BCLMA), emulated Canada's Trend House programme of 1952 to 1954, in which leading Canadian architects had designed a series of regional show homes to promote the domestic use of native forest products.[16] The BCLMA competition, part of a wider set of marketing initiatives by the Canadian lumber industries in 1950s Britain, presented a materially based vision of domestic modernity to consumers. From the three hundred architects who put forward proposals for timber houses, ten were selected to form an architectural panel. The panel was devised to have geographical reach across the United Kingdom and Wood was chosen alongside Leslie and Peter Barefoot (Suffolk), Edward Butcher (Dorset), Munce and Kennedy (Belfast), C. Wycliffe Noble and Partners (Surrey), James Houston and Son (Ayrshire), Bartlett and Gray (Nottingham), Philip R. Middleton and Partner (Middlesbrough), Robert Paine and Partners (Canterbury), and Nelson and Parker (Liverpool). Models of their competition houses, which drew to varying degrees on Canadian domestic prototypes, were exhibited at the Building Centre in London from 26 March to 3 April 1958. The house plans were made available to consumers on a £25 royalty basis through the Timber Trade Development Association and were publicised in *Housing Trends*, a brochure that featured the ten designs alongside Wells and Hickman's Canada Trend House, which had been shown at the 1957 Ideal Home Exhibition.[17] Wood's competition house, Design 109, provided 1,380 sq ft of living space and featured a

Figure 3. Design 109
for the British Columbia
Lumber Manufacturers'
Competition.
Courtesy of Kenneth
Wood

split-level living area with a dual aspect fireplace that served upper and lower zones. The house was timber framed with brick gable ends and was partially clad in Western Red Cedar weatherboarding. The design was subsequently completed for a client on Debden Road in Saffron Walden, Essex.

As one of the British architectural panellists, Wood was offered the opportunity to see the work of the lumber industries at first hand. He travelled in Canada, as well as visiting Chicago and New York, in May 1958 and recorded his impressions in photographs and writings that formed the basis for articles on Canadian architecture and timber construction that he published and broadcast on his return.[18] In Vancouver, a flourishing centre of art and design with an evolving regional architectural culture of post-and-beam modernism, Wood visited buildings by Semmens and Simpson, William Wilding and John C. Porter as well as several speculative housing schemes.[19] Although the rapid suburbanisation of Vancouver's North Shore and 'wholesale stripping' of development areas disturbed him, he found much to admire in the local architecture, noting that although the workmanship was somewhat rougher than that found in the United Kingdom, designs were often imaginative, an 'easy familiarity' with timber products resulting in buildings that were comfortable and 'honestly modern in approach'.[20] He particularly admired the spatial efficiency of dwellings designed for steeply sloping sites, which used the local topography of Vancouver to advantage to create houses that were more varied in plan than was typical in Britain at that time.[21] Already attracted to timber as an economic alternative to lightweight metal and glass structures, Wood's visit convinced him of the exciting possibilities that it offered for the spatial development of the interior and the creation of thermally efficient open-plan living environments of individual design. On his return he became an advocate for the expanded structural use of timber, counting himself among a 'growing number of younger and more progressive architects' who were turning their attention to timber for its 'definite advantages over other systems'.[22] Although never exclusive, this interest in

Figure 4. Fenwycks,
Camberley. Garden
elevation.
RIBA Library
Photographs Collection,
London (RIBA 25168)

timber construction is reflected in a range of projects for private and commercial clients, an important example being the cluster of buildings that Wood designed as a new district headquarters for the Forestry Commission at Santon Downham in Suffolk (1969).

Many contemporary writers situated Wood's timber-framed houses within a national history of domestic architectural development. Michael Manser, for example, commented on the relationship between Fenwycks at Camberley and medieval half-timber buildings. 'Despite the hundreds of years between them – and the radically modern detailing of Fenwycks – an ancestral similarity breaks through, particularly downstairs, where the brick base and timber-framing inside are most apparent.'[23] Similarly, an article published in *Illustrated Carpenter and Builder* described Fenwycks as 'the modern development of the Tudor half-timber house'.[24] Wood promoted historical continuities in his own writing, as a means of addressing resistance to timber construction among lenders, insurers, and the wider building trade. 'As a nation we are excessively conservative in our architecture, but surely we cannot think that housebuilding in timber is in any way revolutionary if we remember that the use of timber as the main structural material in a house originated and was perfected in this country three and four hundred years ago.'[25] In contrast to the historical accent of British writings, French magazine *Votre Maison* described Fenwycks as a surprising avant-garde home, emphasising its progressive use of traditional materials.[26]

This combination of tradition and modernity appealed to Wood's clients who, when viewed collectively, appear forward thinking although not radically so in their domestic aspirations and tastes. Most were professionals working in the creative fields of art, design, or music, among them a professional flautist, three employees (aircraft designers and engineers) of the Hawker Aircraft Company in Kingston, a graphic and packaging designer, a fine artist, an interior designer and ceramicist, a music arranger, and the conductor of the BBC Welsh Symphony Orchestra. Some came to Wood

Figure 5. Oriel House, Haslemere. Detail of the oriel windows. RIBA Library Photographs Collection, London (RIBA 81416)

Figure 6. Oriel House, Haslemere. Living room. Colin Westwood/RIBA Library Photographs Collection, London (RIBA 81417)

through personal recommendation, others through enquiries made at the RIBA and one through a chance meeting in a council office queue.[27] Their budgets varied enormously. Wood's first private commission, Whitewood at Strawberry Hill (1958, 1,300 sq ft), for his friends Peter and Vicky Jones, was completed for under £3,200. In contrast, the house at Kingston that Wood designed for businessman and art collector Stanley Picker (1968, 4,975 sq ft) cost close to £81,000.[28] What these clients shared was a belief in a type of easy, un-ostentatious modern way of living that corresponded with Wood's commitment to the design of unselfconscious buildings that would derive their character over time, through the process of inhabitation.

Wood's designs take their cue from the built and natural environments in which they are located. Many combined structural brick and timber in the way of vernacular Surrey houses and several incorporated weatherboarding, another characteristic feature of the local architecture of some parts of the county. His contextual approach to materials is perhaps best exemplified by the two houses that he completed for the conductor John Carewe: Oriel House at Haslemere, for which he sourced a local brick; and one of the few houses that he designed outside Surrey, the Old Mill at Felin Dawel in Glamorgan, a semi-derelict building that was partially reconstructed using reclaimed materials. Wood's respect for the natural and historic landscapes in which he worked is also evident in his approach to the siting of his buildings. Where possible, he preferred to retain existing planting, an approach that he shared with Eric Lyons. This can be seen from Whitewood, which was planned around mature fruit trees on its suburban plot, to later projects, such as Nathan House, for which a path through the old rose garden on which it was built was preserved.[29] The undulating Surrey landscape

presented the opportunity for Wood to introduce variety to the plans of several of houses, as he had observed in Canada. The gentle incline of the Vincent House plot in Kingston was used to create a dais for music and dining within the ground floor living area, while at Camberley the underlying topography was expressed in the split-level interior that Wood created for Fenwycks. Dykes at Wentworth and Picker House at Kingston (see Figure 1) were both conceived for steeply sloping plots, the design for the latter using the fall of the plot to create a dramatic galleried entrance with a lower, double-height living area. For Wood, the incorporation of split-level living spaces was never a matter of fashion, but always an outcome of the contours of the site and the views out; the Surrey landscape offered a variety of opportunities for experimentation.

A similar strategy to that adopted in relation to natural environments can be seen in Wood's planning of Torrent House, a project in which he worked with an existing structure, a redundant single storey electricity substation that had been used to power local trolley buses. At a time when the movement for re-use centred on country houses and disused agricultural buildings, Torrent House was unusual in adapting an industrial building. The brick and concrete substation, on a riverside plot at Hampton Court, had a flat roof that was split into upper and lower levels. Wood designed a lightweight cantilevered floor to sit on top of the existing structure, using the variation in roof levels to define upper (dining) and lower (living) zones, which gave both the benefit of unobstructed river views. The exterior made visual reference to the boathouses that could be found along the riverside nearby. The house was given a Civic Trust Award in 1965, in which it was commended 'for imaginative (indeed witty) transformation of a typical subtopian eyesore'.[30]

Wood's skill in designing private houses lay in his ability to interpret and balance

Figure 8. Wildwood,
Oxshott. View from
the kitchen to the
dining area.
RIBA Library
Photographs Collection
(RIBA 3743)

the specific and generic needs and desires of clients whose lifestyles were, in several
cases, characterised by overlapping domestic and professional interests. Several of
these clients had working requirements for their homes. Whitewood was designed with
a central artists' studio and adjoining wings that accommodated a garage/workshop
to one side and family accommodation to the other. Peter Jones, who was beginning to
establish himself as a fine artist, used the workshop for commercial picture framing and
the studio to paint, often working alongside his wife Vicky, who designed fabric pictures
which she sold through London department stores. Torrent House at Hampton was
also conceived as a live-work space and incorporated a ground floor studio for client
Peter Devenish, a graphic designer. Several of Wood's clients required spaces for
musical rehearsal or performance. Music arranger Stephan Quehen, client for
Tanglewood at Hampton Hill, wanted somewhere to work at night without disturbing
his family or neighbours and Wood arranged the living accommodation to provide
buffer zones around his study. Acoustics were also a design consideration for Vincent
House, for professional flautist Douglas Whittaker, who needed space to rehearse
and also wished to stage musical performances in his home. Personal interests
played an important part in the development of several designs. Whittaker was a
serious photographer and Wood's plans for Vincent House incorporated a small
darkroom. Elisa and Nigel Money were keen ornithologists and the central
galleried living area at Wildwood was created to give views of the surrounding
woodland from both floors of the house. Peter Jones and his family enjoyed staging
puppet theatre performances and Wood's design incorporated a domestic
interpretation of a proscenium to create an occasional stage.

Several clients wished to display or exhibit works of art in their homes and this

Figure 9. Wildwood, Oxshott. View from the living area to the dining area. RIBA Library Photographs Collection (RIBA 3742)

Figure 10. Fenwycks, Camberley. The split-level living area. RIBA Library Photographs Collection (RIBA 25170)

influenced the designs of Vincent House and Picker House in particular. For Vincent House, Wood created a first floor gallery with clerestory lighting suitable for hosting small formal exhibitions of art. Stanley Picker's substantial collection of contemporary and modern painting and sculpture was at the heart of the brief for his house at Kingston and its later gallery addition.[31] Practical concerns also gave rise to specific preferences among clients; Elisa Money's memories of an oppressively hot kitchen at a former home was one of the factors that informed the arrangement of the ground floor rooms of Wildwood.[32]

Although the Surrey landscape and diverse personal requirements of his clients gave rise to individual spatial responses, Wood's belief that a house should provide an undemanding backdrop to everyday life is expressed in a consistent aesthetic approach to the design of the interior. This can be seen in his preference for natural materials, neutral tones, and low-maintenance fixtures and fittings, as well as his concern for flexibility of use; a modernist pre-occupation that generated a range of post-war architectural responses. His houses of the 1950s and 1960s incorporate a variety of movable, removable, and adaptable interior elements that allowed the alteration of the interior according to social requirements. A folding timber wall at Wildwood allowed part of the living area to function as a playroom and adjoining cloakroom, or as an occasional bedroom with en suite bathroom. Curtains running on tracks concealed between timber elements were another integral aspect of Wood's architectural conception for the house that allowed temporary spatial re-configurations of the interior; those running the length of the gallery, for example, provided visual privacy to the sleeping accommodation when required. Built-in storage at Fenwycks was designed to be removed to allow the conversion of the master bedroom into two smaller rooms, while at Vincent House removable partitions fulfilled the same function. Wood was not only concerned with the day-to-day flexibility of the living environments that he created, but also with their ability to sustain family life over time; his designs were shaped in response to the emphasis on rootedness and stability that was a distinctive feature of British culture in the 1950s and was informed by his own historical understanding of the house as a site of organic change.

The concept of the developing home took hold in North America more quickly than in Europe, where traditions of heavy construction made the alteration of existing buildings more difficult and costly. During the Depression, it evolved as a means of offering pay-as-you-build options to consumers. Britain's post-war material shortages and building restrictions created a similar context in which phased development became attractive and Wood was one of a number of architects who began to experiment with adaptable domestic forms.[33] The rapid growth of the suburban locations in which he completed his early Surrey projects alerted him to the speed with which relatively new buildings could become obsolete as populations grew and user requirements changed. His concern with adaptability, which was closely related to his interest in timber construction, is reflected in a number of public buildings that he designed for future expansion, the earliest of which was a parish hall for St Mary at Chessington (1955).

Fenwycks was completed in 1961 in two stages, as intended in Wood's initial designs. The clients, Mr and Mrs Paton, had a young family and wanted to create a house that could be extended and sub-divided to create separate self-contained accommodation as their children reached adulthood, or for sub-letting should they then find themselves alone. Wood's design allowed for easy alteration of the interior within the original perimeter of the building, as well as its simple modular extension. At the time of its completion in 1960, the house had a floor area of 2,000 sq ft. and cost £6,600 to build.[34] In its initial form it contained a lobby and entrance hall, a garage and store, and a living area with adjoining patio on the lower level; a kitchen and a dining area at mezzanine level; and four bedrooms and a bathroom a half floor above. The timber construction of the intermediate level dining-room and kitchen allowed the extension of both spaces. Services for the extension were planned and incorporated in the initial build; coiled electrical wiring, for example, was concealed between the walls of the stage one building, ready to be unwound and used as required.[35] The lower floor was arranged to allow conversion of the garage to a self-contained bedroom, dressing room and bathroom. Services for the future bathroom were also incorporated in the original build, along with provision for the relocation of the garage. Twelve years after its completion Fenwycks was extended in line with Wood's initial plans. The living/dining area was extended to include a sun room, the kitchen was enlarged to include a breakfast area and additional storage space, and the east wing of the house was altered to provide self-contained accommodation for an older family member. The house, which is significant as a British example of a fully realised developing home, featured in promotional materials published by the Council of Forest Industries of British Columbia to demonstrate the adaptability of timber buildings.[36]

In his introduction to the Surrey volume of *The Buildings of England*, Ian Nairn commented on a selection of modern post-war buildings, 'All these buildings are in either a straightforward projection of traditional forms or a crisp industrial vernacular of glass and steel. That they are all "quiet" buildings does not mean that they are dull, incidentally: the worth of all the examples mentioned here is unlikely to burn out as some of the pyrotechnics of the 1940s have burnt out.'[37] The houses that Wood's firm designed in the 1950s and 1960s can be counted among those 'quiet' buildings. Based on knowledge of traditional local building forms and designed in response to the Surrey landscape, they reflect his personal aspiration for a humane and socially responsible architecture that respected, but did not copy tradition, as well as his assimilation of regional tendencies within modernist architectural practice, notably those of the Canadian west coast. Surrey, with its ready supply of land and clients and its rich history of progressive domestic design, provided an ideal context for Wood's investigations into the possibilities that timber construction offered for spatial inventiveness and for the creation of modern houses to meet the immediate and long term needs of their users.

I am grateful to
acknowledge that the
research for this article
was completed with the
support of an Arts and
Humanities Research
Council Early Career
Fellowship [Grant
Number: AH/I002928/I]
held in 2011/12

Kenneth Wood died in
January 2015 as this
publication was nearing
completion. I would like
to acknowledge the
generous spirit in which
he assisted my research

1. References in this article are to pre-1965 Surrey, which included what are now the London boroughs of Kingston, Merton, Richmond, Sutton and Croydon. On the 'Surrey Style' see Roderick Gradidge, *The Surrey Style*, Kingston upon Thames, Surrey Historic Buildings Trust, 1991.

2. Arthur W. Haslett, 'Beautiful Surrey', *The New Estates Magazine*, vol.1, no.3, 1934, p.2.

3. For inter-war examples see Jeremy Gould, 'Gazetteer of Modern Houses in the United Kingdom and the Republic of Northern Ireland', Twentieth Century Architecture, no.2, *The Modern House Revisited*, 1996, pp.111-28.

4. Ian Nairn, in the introduction to Ian Nairn and Nikolaus Pevsner, The Buildings of England, *Surrey*, 2nd edition revised by Bridget Cherry, Harmondsworth, Penguin, 1971, p.74.

5. ibid., p.78.

6. Wood recalled only that the firm to which he was loaned as a draughtsman was Blomfield's. It seems likely that it was the firm of Reginald Blomfield, which was continued by Austin Blomfield after his father's death in 1942. Kenneth Wood, in discussion with the author, October 2008.

7. Wood was elected an Associate of the Royal Institute of British Architects in February 1954 and worked for Eric Lyons from c.1953 to 1956.

8. On Span and suburban living see Alan Powers, 'Models for Suburban Living', in Barbara Simms, ed., *Eric Lyons and Span*, London, RIBA Publishing, 2006, pp.23-33.

9. Nairn and Pevsner, op.cit., p.75.

10. Wood and Lyons were also professionally involved in the 1960s. Wood worked alongside Lyons at Chertsey when he was appointed co-ordinating architect for a street improvement scheme that ran parallel to the town centre development, for which Eric Lyons was the consultant architect. Lyons also invited Wood to join Walter Greaves, Richard and Su Rogers, Stout and Litchfield, Carol Møller and Peter Aldington on the panel of architects for the Redhill Wood area of Span's New Ash Green development in Kent.

11. Projects from the 1950s include church halls at St Mary's, Chessington (1955) and at St George's, Tolworth (1957), the redesign and extension of Emmanuel Church, Tolworth (1958), and the design of two parish halls for St. Mary-at-Finchley, North London (1960).

12. Other domestic projects were completed in Wales, Sussex and Essex.

13. *Architecture Today* exhibition correspondence and minutes, ACGB/121/28, V&A Archive of Art and Design, London.

14. ibid.

15. 'House of the Year', *Ideal Home*, vol.83, no.6, June 1961, pp.49-60.

16. Eleven Trend Houses were built across Canada in the winter/spring of 1953-4 and opened to the public in the spring/summer of 1954. See Allan Collier, 'The Trend House Program', *Journal for the Society for the Study of Architecture in Canada*, vol.20, no.2, June 1995, pp.51-4.

17. The BCLMA competition featured in: *Architect and Building News*, vol.213, no.13, 26 March 1958, pp.406-11; *Architects' Journal*, vol.127, no.3291, 27 March 1958, pp.460-5; *International Prefabrication and New Building Technique*, April 1958, p.240; *The Lady*, vol.147, no.3816, 10 April 1958, pp.498-9. The exhibition was the subject of a British Pathé news item, see http://www.britishpathe.com/video/canadian-style-homes, accessed 17 October 2012.

18. These included: 'Timber Construction in Canada', *Architects' Journal*, vol.128, no.3318, 2 October 1958, pp.485-92; 'Wooden Walls', *The Listener*, vol.60, no.1539, 25 September 1958, pp.458-60; 'The Structural Use of Timber', *Architecture and Building*, vol.34, no.2, February 1959, pp.67-74; 'Canada's Architectural Development: A View From Another World', *Canadian Architect*, vol.4, no.2, February 1959, pp.42-5.

19. *Western Homes and Living* magazine, launched in 1950, was important in disseminating the style. See Sherry McKay, 'The Object of Living: *Western Homes and Living*', in Alan C. Elder et al, eds., *Modern Life: Art and Design in British Columbia 1945-1960*, Vancouver, Vancouver Art Gallery/Arsenal Pulp Press, 2004. See also Rhodri Windsor Liscombe, *The New Spirit: Modern Architecture in Vancouver, 1938-1963*, Montreal, Canadian Centre for Architecture/Douglas and McIntyre, 1997.

20. Kenneth Wood, 'The Role of Timber in Canadian Building', p.2 (notes for an article for *The Builder*); 'Romance and Commonsense. The Story behind Canadian Timber Homes', p.2 (notes for an article for *New Homes* magazine) and general notes from Wood's 1958 visit to North America, p.2, Kenneth Wood, private papers.

21. *The Listener*, op.cit., p.459, and 'General Notes' from Wood's 1958 visit to North America, Kenneth Wood, private papers.

22. 'Building Homes of Timber', *Financial Times*, no.22545, 13 November 1961, p.40. The article appeared under the by line 'a correspondent' in a section devoted to building and contracting.

23. Michael Manser, 'Halfway House', *Home*, September 1961, p.71.

24. 'A Timber House has Warmth and Elasticity', *Illustrated Carpenter and Builder*, vol.150, no.4358, 10 March 1961, pp.730-1.

25. 'Building Homes of Timber', op.cit., p.40.

26. 'Une Etonnante Maison d'Avant-Garde', *Votre Maison*, Christmas 1962/January 1963, pp.56-9.

27. Elisa Money and Kenneth Wood's chance meeting led to Wood's commission for Wildwood. Author's interview with Elisa Money, 27 October 2011.

28. Average national house prices rose from £2,230 in 1956 to just under £5,000 in 1969. See Chris Hamnett, *Winners and Losers: Home Ownership in Modern Britain*, London, Routledge, 1998, p.23.

29. Interview with Janet Mundy, 17 October 2011.

30. Civic Trust Award 1965, London, The Civic Trust, 1965, p.80.

31. The project is covered in detail in Jonathan Black, David Falkner, Fiona Fisher, Fran Lloyd, Rebecca Preston, Penny Sparke, *The Picker House and Collection: A Late 1960s Home for Art and Design*, London, Philip Wilson, 2012.

32. Author's interview with Elisa Money, 27 October 2011.

33. An early British example is the house that Tayler and Green completed at Kingston in Surrey in 1950. See 'House at Kingston-on-Thames' in F. R. S. Yorke and Penelope Whiting, *The New Small House*, London, Architectural Press, 1954 (3rd edition), pp.20-3.

34. *Illustrated Carpenter and Builder*, op.cit., p.730.

35. 'A House in Harmony', *CMC Look*, Spring 1961, p.10.

36. See, for example, B. C. Wood, The Council of Forest Industries of British Columbia, c.1971, p.8.

37. Nairn and Pevsner, op.cit., p.75.

Jon Wright

10   Houses and Housing in South Devon by Mervyn Seal

**Figure I. Kaywana Hall
(Seal's own home) from
above (Mervyn Seal)**

Torbay's fresh air and mild climate has been attracting visitors since the Napoleonic Wars, and the railways brought many more from the 1850s onwards. Branded the 'English Riviera' by the Great Western Railway, the towns of Torquay, Paignton and Brixham are clustered around a large, sheltered natural harbour, and retain distinct identities despite sharing a common local authority since 1968. In the post-war period, the area attracted people with wealth and leisure time, the legacy of whose lifestyles are reflected in the flamboyant modern designs of Mervyn Seal. He was the recipient of numerous housing design awards and a significant regional architect whose career ended in an unhappy withdrawal from private practice but whose work – which was almost unknown beyond the region – has recently captured attention and deserves to be better known. Seal's concentrated cluster of houses in the Torbay area tracks the wider architectural thinking of the decades in which he was active, studiously and inventively reflecting the significant stylistic movements of the post-war decades from European modernism to neo-vernacular and post-modernism.

Despite a wide range of projects, it is Seal's domestic buildings that will remain his most impressive legacy. His early career was dominated by a succession of private houses and speculative developments, mostly in partnership with an entrepreneur builder, Michael Kent, who facilitated Seal's moving to South Devon in the late 1950s and who allowed him to set up in independent professional practice. These projects, along with the award-winning Oakland Park in Dawlish, dominate this first critical look at his work.

Of Seal's early designs, it is the four 'butterfly roof' houses that are likely to remain his lasting legacy. Stylish fusions of traditional techniques and materials and modern architectural thinking, the houses are significant essays in the 1930s-40s modernism of Le Corbusier and Frank Lloyd Wright that filtered through British architectural schools in the 1950s and informed a generation of young architects. They can also be seen as regional modern interpretations of the foremost typology of nineteenth-century Torbay architecture, the private villa with a view, while also tracking the idiosyncratic evolution of an architect whose response to site and design flair give all four houses an impressive individuality.

The butterfly roof, which allows for so much internal modulation, was one of the earliest departures within modernism from the insistence on flat roofs. Le Corbusier designed the first of these at a house in South America for Ortúzar Matias Errazuriz in 1930, with a single all-purpose living room in the centre. The principal bedroom was planned on a gallery at one end reached by a ramp and the guest room at the other end was approached by an external bridge. The roofs are therefore high at each end and dip down in the middle, one being longer than the other. The house was to have been built in local stone with a wood and pantile roof. It was never realised, but became famous through Le Corbusier's own books, and was published by F. R. S. Yorke in *The Modern House* (1934).[1] Marcel Breuer adopted the same type of roof in 1945 for a project for a low-cost veterans' house; for the spacious Geller House in Long Island, which was published in the *Architectural Review* and *House and Garden*; and for a demonstration house erected in the garden of the Museum of Modern Art in New York in 1949 that attracted many visitors. The butterfly roof solved problems of flat roofs, and eliminated gutters and drains at the roof edge; Breuer argued that a single internal drain eliminated winter freezing, while the expansive roof allowed a house to be built piecemeal beneath it, perhaps including a temporary car port until additional bedrooms could be inserted.[2]

It is likely that Seal got the idea, consciously or otherwise, from F. R. S. Yorke's *The Modern House*, a book he had owned since he first dreamed of becoming an architect at age fourteen and which he still refers to as his 'bible'.[3] Over these four houses Seal explored the possibilities of what was domestically achievable beneath this roof shape, coming up with an impressive variety of arrangements for his self-designed interior fittings and furniture. In the architectural history of the United Kingdom, they remain aesthetically unique.[4] They were also houses built for relaxed,

fun living and in that they contain something of their creator's personality.

Mervyn Thomas Seal was born on 28 April 1930. In 1946 he took the examination for admission to the Civil Service and joined the Bath and Avon District Surveyor's Department as a junior assistant the same year. After a year at the Ministry of Works in London, he was stationed in Singapore for his national service with the Royal Engineers. On his return in September 1949, Seal was accepted at the Royal West of England Academy in Bristol on the basis that the sketches and paintings he had sent from Singapore were 'satisfactory'. The School had been in existence since 1921 following pressure from the students of design classes being run by the Bristol Society of Architects. By 1949, the academy felt bold enough to begin its prospectus thus –

> It is the aim of the school to further the interests of architectural education in the West of England, not so much by training clever draughtsmen as by providing that fundamental instruction and discipline in the Art, Science, Theory and History of Architecture, which in addition to experience in architect's office, shall prepare the student for the independent practice of his profession.[5]

Whilst studying, Seal won several prizes for design but concedes that his bookish work was not strong. His architectural career began on leaving the academy in 1954, when he joined the regional firm of Gerrard Taylor and Partners.[6] After just a year with the firm, Seal joined the City of Bath Planning and Architect's Department as a junior assistant helping design a number of maisonettes, flats and houses and designing the Le Corbusier-inspired Haycombe Crematorium (1957) for the city.

As is often the case with young architects, Seal's first commission came from his parents. Obtaining an improvement grant to convert an old coach house in Lyncombe Vale, Bath, he convinced his sceptical parents to demolish and rebuild the top storey and to use the surviving ground floor as a garage and entrance. While it could hardly be termed conservation, it was nevertheless a rarity for the time, and anticipated the rash of barn conversions nationwide over the next few decades. It was an early expression, too, of Seal's elevated living arrangements inspired by Le Corbusier, with the main living spaces above the service areas.

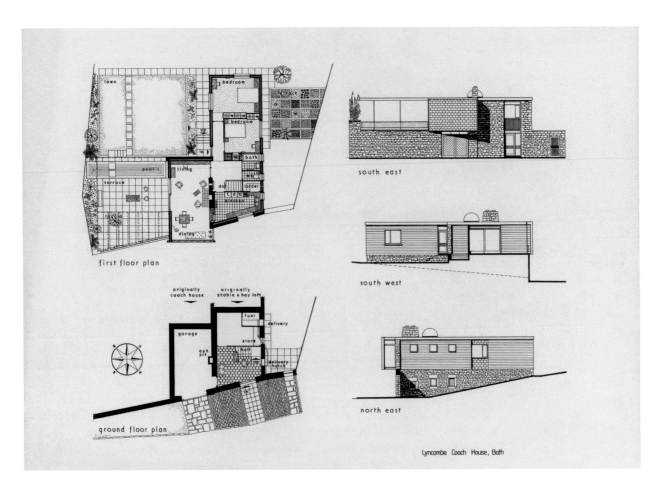

first floor plan

bedroom
bedroom
bath
lawn
pool
terrace
living
dining
dn
larder
kitchen
in
up

ground floor plan

originally coach house
originally stable & hay loft
garage
fuel
delivery
store
hall
ash pit
up
delivery hatch

south east

south west

north east

Lyncombe Coach House, Bath

Figure 3. Lyncombe
Coach House, Bath,
plans and section, 1957
(Mervyn Seal)

Figure 4. Lyncombe
Coach House, Bath, 1957
(Mervyn Seal)

In 1958, Seal designed Bridge House for his family in Shropshire, a modest, elegant modern home that allowed him to expand the vocabulary of Lyncombe Coach House and express his architectural vision to the full. A prototypical house for those that would follow in South Devon, Bridge House is a small, narrow dwelling, constructed from a mixture of basic and traditional materials that expresses its modernity through simplicity of form and a clever response to its site. With a rear entrance at ground level, the house gradually extends out from a carport constructed of reject burnt bricks that supports a lightweight timber frame above, which was clad in slate with large areas of glazing. Seal made use of the building's height and concentrated an expanse of glass at the living room end to take advantage of the views over the surrounding parkland. Here Seal established several principles at the forefront of his architectural thinking, namely the significance of site in the design, the use of traditional building techniques and the necessity for moderate costs. In addition, the house gave him the freedom to incorporate built-in fixtures and fittings.

In 1959 Seal was the recipient of an RIBA Small House Design Award for plans for a modest semi-detached courtyard house featuring a central patio that Seal described as 'almost a necessity'.[7] The bungalow was a rational and practical design which featured built-in furniture and a kitchen also designed by Seal.

Le Corbusier and Wright were the obvious and long-lasting fascinations of the period. Wright, in particular, was a powerful force in British domestic architecture throughout the post-war period – the most potent message being, perhaps, that it is not only possible, but actually quite easy to design modern dwellings with limited means. British architects everywhere were challenged to provide quality homes despite post-war restrictions, and for many Wright's fresh approach to timber and masonry provided the answer. Seal remembers that as a student he was able to retain a dual loyalty: 'I was never an exponent of either one, but there was always vocal discussion about either one at college and I was just a good listener'.[8] For some architects of Seal's generation, Wright was displaced by the attraction of a more rational approach to domestic design offered by Mies van der Rohe and others, but for Seal the twin voices of Le Corbusier and Wright were always in his head when approaching a house design. 'It was Wright for materials and Corbusier for the ideas.'[9]

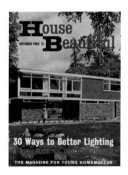

Figure 5. The cover of
House Beautiful, October
1958, featuring Bridge
House, Condover
(Mervyn Seal)

Seal's growing preoccupation with an elongated open-plan interior, first expressed fully at Bridge House, was entirely suitable for Parkham Wood (1960), a highly visible addition to the cliffs above Brixham.[10] Thinking primarily of the interior character of the house, Seal sought to emulate Le Corbusier's 'large capricious spaces' and like many of his contemporaries was impressed by his Unité d'Habitation at Marseilles. 'I saw the Unité on a grey, wet day and was disappointed, but I had seen, studied and appreciated the plan of the flat interiors.'[11]

At Parkham Wood, the only stipulation was for 'a three-bedroomed house', and Seal was given the freedom to expand the vocabulary of Bridge House both inside and out to create a dramatic and thoroughly modern family home. Raised on five high brick piers set at right angles to the cliff edge and cantilevered out on narrow concrete beams, Parkham Wood is a house perched on the edge of a cliff – a cliffhanger. Having partially excavated the foundations, Seal chose to leave certain pinnacles of rock exposed beneath the house to allow contours of the cliff face to be integral in the final design.

The clients owned the adjacent Parkham Wood Hotel, so Seal's other preoccupation for the house was privacy. The rear wall was kept devoid of any windows, reserving all the glazing for the eastern elevation, which commands dramatic views over Brixham Harbour and the sea beyond. To accentuate the dramatic outline of the building, an asymmetrical M shape, Seal outlined the profile with deep projecting eaves that continued down the side-walls, framing the almost completely glazed façade whilst acting as a brise soleil. A concrete balcony was cantilevered off the brick piers with the steep driveway nearly two floors below. To provide access to the front, Seal punched

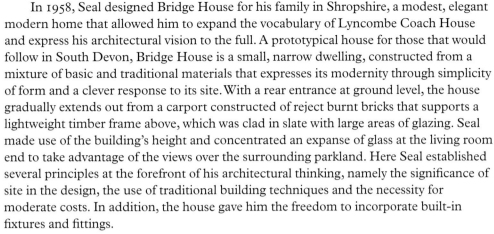

Figure 6 and 6a.
Bridge House,
Condover, Shropshire,
with plan from *House
Beautiful* (1962), 1958
(Mervyn Seal)

FIRST FLOOR

GROUND FLOOR

SIDE ELEVATION

Figure 7 and 7a.
Parkham Wood,
Brixham and plan (1960).
The house was a highly
visible addition to the
cliffs above Brixham
(Historic England,
James O. Davies for
picture; Mervyn Seal
for plan)

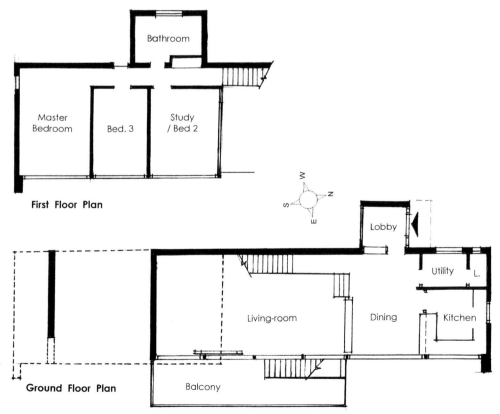

Bathroom

Master
Bedroom

Bed. 3

Study
/ Bed 2

First Floor Plan

Lobby

Utility   L.

Living-room

Dining

Kitchen

Ground Floor Plan

Balcony

**Figure 8. Marina Park,
Brixham showing the
sculpture by Brian
Stringer (Mervyn Seal)**

through the balcony to accommodate an external stairway. Designed by him,
but constructed by the blacksmith of the 150-year old Uphams Shipyard in Brixham,
the staircase, which featured an innovative 'fishbone' design of thin, angled steel support
for each tread, which was of Utile mahogany – it was the first such design, which Seal
would repeat internally at Kaywana Hall and at select blocks at Marina Park.

Determined that the drama and interest of the exterior should be repeated internally
Seal designed a number of interesting internal vistas by modulating the internal spaces
around the central living space. By including blue and red Devon limestone from
Buckfast, he was able to demonstrate the use of local materials, a feature repeated in all
his subsequent butterfly houses.

Seal and his collaborator Michael Kent had meanwhile embarked on what would
prove to be a major development of Berry Head, a series of related schemes that were
phased, mostly for reasons of cash flow. As a student in the 1950s Seal had produced a
thesis on housing design, where he promoted the idea of segregation between traffic
and pedestrians through landscaping. Approached by Kent for a design-and-build
development on land above Brixham Harbour, Seal embarked on the development of
Heath Court (1959), followed by a single dwelling, Marina House (1961), and further
housing projects at Heath Rise (1961) and Marina Court (1961). The headland was
transformed over a three-year period. At Marina Park (1962), the last of the
developments, Seal saw the opportunity to finally put his earlier ideas about landscaping
into practice. So that Kent could see what he had in mind, Seal took him to visit Eric
Lyons's developments for Span at Ham Common and Blackheath in London. Kent was
impressed with the designs and they proceeded to work on a comprehensive, speculative
scheme for the site. The site itself was an unremarkable patch of heath on the Berry Head

headland, but Seal's appreciation for the natural landscape led him to make the best of it and, one might argue, to try to improve upon it. Marina Park was the recipient of a Housing Design Award with the assessors stating that 'the architect, faced with an open site, has created an environment with an exceptionally interesting use of space in and around the buildings by the planning of a series of courts for pedestrians and with partial traffic segregation with car parking facilities adjacent to each court. The architect has used to the full the natural levels of the ground.'[12]

There are two key pieces of art on the site. The main entrance from Heath Road, under the colonnade, features a ceramic panel designed by local artist Roger Kerslake. Constructed from bottle glass impressed in clay, it sets a tone for the estate and creates an interesting and attractive central feature. For the second artwork, Seal and Kent approached the local art college in Newton Abbot, which ran a competition for a sculpture that was to sit in the courtyard. Brian Stringer completed the winning design, which mused on the seascape beyond, in 1962. One final project, Broughton Close begun in 1963, a crescent of detached houses in Plymouth which won a Housing Design Award in 1967, marked the end of the highly productive collaboration between Seal and Kent.

Purchasing a steeply sloping, heavily wooded site with unknown geology would perhaps have bothered some looking to build a family home but Seal was emboldened by the success of Parkham Wood, both as an expression of his architectural principles and of the possibilities of the conjunction of lightweight, elevated structures on precarious sites. He designed and self-built the second of the butterflies, Kaywana Hall, as his own home. Kaywana means 'old water' in Guyanese; Mervyn and his wife Maria had read the Kaywana Trilogy by the author Edgar Mittelholzer, considered to be the first professional novelist to emerge from the English-speaking Caribbean. The novels were set on West Indian plantations and Seal chose the name for its exoticism. He purchased the plot on the aptly named Higher Contour Road in Kingswear for £700 in 1961, and began planning a four-bedroomed house. In contrast to Parkham Wood, where the long

Figure 9 and 9a (overleaf). Kaywana Hall, with plan, 1961 (Mervyn Seal)

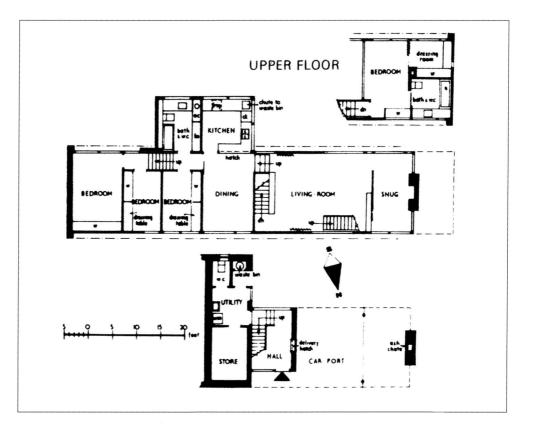

elevation faces the view, Seal deliberately sited the house at right angles to the steep slope, primarily to benefit the orientation and to create the drama of the gable end floating high in the treetops. To support this elevation, which contained the master suite, the structure was more adventurous than Parkham Wood, with Seal supporting the floor plate solely on the single, slender, reinforced stone chimneystack from which the room precariously extends as a cantilever eight feet out from the support. It was a lighter structure than Parkham, being timber-framed on either side and this allowed for glass on both main facades. Here he produced abstract compositions of glass and panels of greenish grey Cornish slate, and the dynamism of the rear elevation was highlighted with two strips of red Vitroslab that gave the building a sporty elegance. Internally, Seal used exposed Parana pine for the ceiling, and the walls were made of Agba strip. Of all the four butterfly houses, Kaywana Hall was perhaps the most exuberant and daring, but has subsequently been the most altered.[13]

The difficult sites were all part of the challenge for Seal. Having made his name as 'the man who builds houses that look like butterflies in Torbay', he was asked by his friends, Mr and Mrs Sanders, to design a third after they had seen Kaywana Hall.[14] Faced with a completely level site, Seal sought to compensate for the absence of drama in the immediate landscape by extending the possibilities of the internal layout. Elbury Hall (1962) was designed with virtually all the rooms on one level. Unencumbered by the need to design a lightweight structure, Seal constructed the house with traditional cavity walling, allowing for the use of pre-cast concrete beams for the impressive internal ramp and the elevated master bedroom. There is also a structural element to the ramp, as it cantilevers out from the stone base of the house to support the walls. The ramp is the key feature of the house and Seal made it four feet wide to omit the need for a balustrade and counteract the narrowing effect often produced by stairs. Mrs Sanders underlined the

Figure 10. Plan of Elbury Hall

Figure 11. Internal ramp at Elbury Hall, near Brixham (Mervyn Seal)

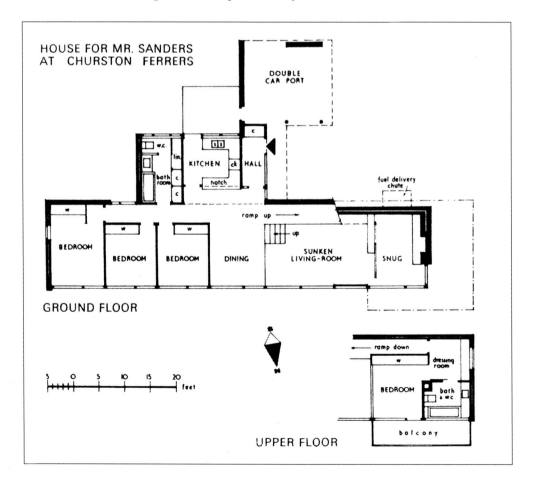

HOUSE FOR MR. SANDERS AT CHURSTON FERRERS

DOUBLE CAR PORT

w.c.

lin.

KITCHEN   ck   HALL

both room

c

c

hatch

fuel delivery chute

w

w   w

ramp up →

BEDROOM

BEDROOM   BEDROOM   DINING   SUNKEN LIVING-ROOM   SNUG

up

GROUND FLOOR

5   0   5   10   15   20   feet

ramp down

dressing room

w

BEDROOM   both & w.c.

balcony

UPPER FLOOR

Figure 12. Coridon House, Babbacombe, Torquay 1963 (Mervyn Seal)

practicalities of the arrangement and expressed them in a contemporary interview. 'Walking up and down the ramp is, of course, quieter than using stairs, and vacuum cleaning is very much simpler too.'[15] For Seal, the ramp was essential for bringing out the sculptured quality of the living space and it is echoed by the sloping parana pine ceiling, which runs unbroken over the entire living and dining area. Corbusian influence is also clear in the rear fenestration, designed with privacy in mind to allow coloured light in during the daylight hours and out at night through a series of small unevenly spaced apertures. The façade is an uninterrupted eighty-foot screen of double-glazing that looks out over a sloping lawn to the sea.

The fourth and final butterfly house was Coridon House, whose name was derived from *Lysandra coridon*, the official term for the Chalkhill Blue butterfly. Achieving what was arguably his most successful interior layout, Seal planned the most important rooms to be on the upper entrance level due to the heavily sloping site, cantilevering the generous floorplate to provide the requisite area and make room for an internal garage. Conversely, the lower floor is moderate in size, accommodating only a second bedroom, utility room and store, thereby minimising the area of foundations and disturbance to the site. In contrast to the previous houses, the chimney, constructed of Seal's beloved Buckfast stone, is centrally positioned – Seal's response to the clients' demands for a division between the kitchen diner and the living room. Above the long slate hearth was a recessed unit for a television, books and a drinks cabinet finished in rosewood, while large sliding doors on either side of the chimney gave access to a wide balcony from both sides of the house. Coridon was the last of the butterflies, although Seal turned down a number of other clients who wanted one. He continued to design other notable private

homes like Kilmorie (1965), a whitewashed modernist villa, again on a cliff edge,
but as the decade waned and the practice expanded, he concentrated his efforts on
larger scale projects.[16]

   Oakland Park (1969-73) originated out of a national competition for developers
sponsored by Devon County Council, who were the owners of the site. In their brief,
the council in conjunction with Dawlish Urban District Council emphasised that the
scheme should belong to Devon and form a model estate that would illustrate a way of
developing new housing using the intricate scale and character of the many small towns
and villages requiring new development. Marketed as a 'return to village life', Oaklands
and its sister development at North Hill in Brixham (1975) mark a significant departure
from his previous work.[17] Drawing inspiration from the local vernacular village
architecture and streetscapes, Seal successfully integrated modern urban planning and
historicist styling. The medieval wooden door grates were an idea that came to Seal
whilst on a skiing holiday in Bavaria, so that they were vernacular but hardly local.
Seal argues, too, that with the intervention of a professional architect the buildings
went far beyond simply 'copying' pre-existing forms. Indeed, Oakland Park's
townscape illustrates Seal's thinking about the relationship between building and
landscape, forming an impressive, enclosed environment of its own. Incorporating
a number of communal areas, connecting pathways and lanes, Oakland Park creates
its own landscape, unlike the award-winning Stoke Hill Estate in Exeter (1966-67),
also by Seal, which slotted into the existing topography. Planning officers nationwide
invited developers to view Oakland Park as a potential template for future schemes
and Seal's approach became one of the most widely adopted for small-scale

**Figure 14. The Studio,
Brixham Road,
Paignton, 1976
(Mervyn Seal)**

housing development nationally, though few schemes have the intimate, natural feel
of the original.

Seal continued to design large apartment blocks in Torbay, the best being the
brutalist Braddons Cliff (1972), Deans Prior (1974), and Lyncombe Crescent (1974).
All display Seal's ability to design intelligent, large-scale buildings that manage to treat
their surroundings well. Their success secured the practice notable commissions
elsewhere in the county. The peak of Seal's practice can be measured precisely by
the construction of a highly unusual office on Brixham Road, Paignton, in 1976.
The Studio was a bold series of curved brick frontages arranged asymmetrically around
a central drum that contained a spiral staircase; the interior is arguably the strangest of
any purpose-built architects' offices ever constructed in Britain. Plasterwork formed
organic tentacles in the ceiling for the light fittings, while the custom-made furniture and
workstations were conceived as part of the structure, as if organically grown. On the front
was emblazoned the firm's logo, a 20-foot diameter brass copy of Leonardo da Vinci's
Vitruvian man – the height of braggadocio. The same logo featured on Seal's planning
drawings, which were returned from Torbay Council meetings with a skirt drawn over
the offending parts of the image.

Seal's architectural career ended in the recession of the early 1990s when his
financial investments in property led to bankruptcy, followed by a decade-long legal fight
to successfully recover some of what he had lost. Following the Twentieth Century
Society's interest in Parkham Wood and its listing by English Heritage in 2009, he has
been piecing together and archiving his working life, reconnecting with the buildings,
estates and spaces that he and his firm designed and built, and revealing one of the most
astonishing and previously little known clusters of regional modernism in Britain.

Figure 15. An interior of the Studio in 1981 (Mervyn Seal)

1. F. R. S. Yorke, *The Modern House*, London, Architectural Press, 1934, p.37. In his *Oeuvre Complète*, vol.2, Le Corbuser illustrated a house in Japan by Antonin Raymond that copied many features of his design, a building also featured in Raymond McGrath, *Twentieth Century Houses*, London, Faber & Faber, 1935.

2. *Architectural Review*, vol.202, no.610, October 1947, pp.115-16; Isabelle Hyman, *Marcel Breuer, Architect*, New York, Harry N. Abrams, 2001, pp.124-8, 344.

3. Mervyn Seal to the author, July 2012.

4. Seal did inspire one more butterfly house in the area, self-built by an associate of his practice Ian Hobson, who worked with Seal for fifteen years; it was completed c.1972 and remains in Brixham.

5. Prospectus for the Royal West of England Academy, 1949.

6. Gerrard Taylor and partners were a notable south-west practice. Mollie Taylor was responsible for Kilowatt House in 1935-8, Bath's pre-eminent Modern Movement house.

7. Mervyn Seal to the author, July 2012.

8. ibid.

9. ibid.

10. The Twentieth Century Society requested English Heritage to list Parkham Wood as a 'rare, surviving example of Mervyn Seal's idiosyncratic, dramatic private houses'. It was listed in 2009 at Grade II.

11. Mervyn Seal to the author, July 2012.

12. From a report in Mervyn Seal's collection.

13. The building was not in a particularly good state when new owners employed another Devon architect, Stan Bolt, to remodel it. The new Kaywana Hall was completed in 2008. Bolt's design retained the roofline, the chimneybreast and the fishbone staircase but little else. The house now operates as a luxury B&B.

14. Mervyn Seal to the author, July 2012.

15. Quoted by John F. Lewis, in 'The Exotic Butterflies of Devon', *Ideal Home*, vol.84, no.12, December 1963, pp.56-63, which featured Parkham Wood, Kaywana Hall and Elbury Hall and included a sketch of the forthcoming Coridon House.

16. The records for this house are lost and its clients unknown. It has been altered so heavily that it is now virtually unrecognisable.

17. Marketing material for Oakland Park from Mervyn Seal + Associates, 1972.

Elain Harwood

II Stout and Litchfield

Stout and Litchfield was a London practice, strongly associated with the Pimlico
area in which the partners made their homes and later with Docklands. But their most
memorable houses owe much of their character to the broken-down plan and cranky
roofs of their very first house, built in the Cotswolds and a response to sensitive local
conditions. This article draws extensively on an interview made with Roy Stout and the
late Patrick Litchfield in October 2001, and quotations not otherwise referenced are
from that day.[1]

Roy Stout (1928-) and Patrick Litchfield (1931-2002) met while studying at the
Royal West of England Academy (RWA) in Bristol between 1948 and 1953. The RWA
was an independent school of architecture rather like the Architectural Association until
it was absorbed by the university in 1958, and similarly had premises in a large mid-
eighteenth century house, No. 25 Great George Street. It was a small school, with about
twenty students a year who formed a close-knit group and learned much from each
other; Litchfield believed you never developed a really close understanding with another
architect unless you had been students together. Many were ex-servicemen, especially in
the two years above Stout and Litchfield, while their contemporaries included Donald
Insall, Raymond Stride and Gerald Treglown (who formed a commercial practice in
Bristol); housing specialist Peter Randall and university lecturer Graham Wilton were
slightly younger. Stout and Litchfield produced their thesis with a group of friends that
included Frederick Mark, Roger Mortimer and Noel Keating. These five vowed that they
would all move to London and set up in partnership together, but Mark went to work for
John Madin in Birmingham and Mortimer for J. T. Design in Bristol; Keating moved to
London with Stout, but subsequently returned home to Ireland. Meanwhile, after a brief
spell working on shop conversions and housing in his native Bournemouth, Litchfield
had to do his National Service – two years older, Stout had already done his – but luckily
he was stationed at an RAF base outside London and could meet at weekends.

Keating and Stout joined the London County Council (LCC). Stout worked under
Colin Lucas, formerly of Connell, Ward and Lucas, who had entered Robert Matthew's
new Housing Division as a group leader in 1950 rather than return to private practice.
He worked mainly on the Roehampton Lane Estate (now Alton West) from 1953 until
1962, when it was almost completed. Stout's last and most important projects there were
the library, which featured very tall, conoid rooflights, and the Adult Education Centre
(now demolished) in a team led by John Partridge that also included Tom Kay. Stout was
also responsible for the design stages of the LCC's estate at Cedars Road, Lambeth
(1961-8), also with Lucas as group leader. Here he broke down the housing units into
linked blocks lining the road that reflected the form of the three-storey paired villas they
replaced, though it was a mixed development of flats and maisonettes. Within each unit
he set the flats in small groups around a stair, with a courtyard and walled garage
enclosure. This was the first evidence of a breaking down of form and the use of a white
brick, both features that were to become important in his later work with Litchfield.
The size of each block is comparable with that of the two villas that were retained,
a Trades Union headquarters and an old people's home.

By the time that the Roehampton Library was completed John Partridge had left the
LCC, having been denied a sabbatical to work up a scheme for the competition to design
Churchill College, Cambridge, with Bill Howell when they won through to the second
phase. Stout knew two groups of people working on schemes for this most important of
post-war competitions, for Litchfield had joined Richard Sheppard and Partners and
worked with William Mullins on the design that eventually won; Sheppard had himself
trained at the RWA and employed a lot of Bristol students. The Churchill College
competition offered Britain's leading modern practices and many young architects the
chance to design a major monument after a decade's diet of low-budget schools and
public housing. Sheppard was more established in the world of university building than
most, for the practice had recently designed Weeks Hall, its first phase of student

accommodation for Imperial College in Princes Gardens, Westminster, and was known to the scientists and engineers who predominated at Churchill. Churchill offered something more, however: the chance to create a modern monument that would stand alongside Cambridge's most venerable colleges for many centuries to come.[2]

The scheme built at Churchill College was far more simple and rational than that which won the competition. Litchfield and Mullins designed the first buildings to be constructed, flats for married graduate students set away from the main accommodation. These apartments with private gardens were arranged on a pinwheel plan in which the college's vocabulary of brick, exposed concrete floor plates and copper roofs was first explored. If the resulting plan resembled, with regrettable irony, that of a swastika, it was notable as another early example of breaking down a large scheme into its component parts, gaining intimacy and avoiding overlooking. Litchfield also worked on the first phases of the main college, including the quadrangles closest to Storey's Way and the central block that houses the college's library, reading room and lecture theatre. Peter Phippen and Peter Randall worked on the second and slightly less lavish phase of student quadrangles, so the RWA tradition continued.

In their evenings and weekends, meanwhile, Stout and Litchfield entered many competitions themselves, all in a Corbusian style. These included designs for Toronto City Hall in 1958 and offices for Somerset County Council at Taunton in 1960. 'Although none of the designs were successful we gained valuable experience of working together', Litchfield later considered.[3] Finally, in 1962, a commission for a house at Shipton-under-Wychwood, Oxfordshire, enabled them to set up their own practice, supported until 1966 by two days a week teaching at the Architectural Association.

The commission came through an old friend of Litchfield's, the barrister Milton Grundy. He wanted a weekend house in the Cotswolds, and nearly acquired a medieval property before in 1959 he secured a half-acre site formed out of the garden of the Old Prebendal House on the edge of Shipton near the river. He asked for a house with three bedrooms, each with its own bathroom, view and access to the garden, set apart from an open-plan living and dining area. The brief was thus to provide a mix of sociability and privacy for Grundy and his guests.

A condition of building on the site – from Grundy as well as local planners – was that despite its concealed location the house should have stone walls and Cotswold slate roofs; this meant that the house had to have to have at least a monopitch roof. Somewhere, too, having experimented with neo-Corbusian designs for cross-wall structures with large areas of infill glazing, Stout and Litchfield began to turn towards more faceted plans and a softer massing. For Litchfield, Shipton marked 'a simple reaction against the rigidity of structure, breaking down scale, accepting that you could put a roof on – and that you didn't have to stick to right angles'. It was the 'dream job' for such an exploration, but Stout and Litchfield accepted that they had had to thoroughly understand functionalism in order to react against its formal order, and they admitted that an element of constructivism continued to inform their work. 'Having to put a pitched roof on helps to express the unit', they explained.

Stout and Litchfield's work has some similarities with that of Stout's slightly older colleagues from the LCC who formed the basis of what later became Howell, Killick, Partridge and Amis (HKPA). An influential scheme in the development of a modern vernacular for Stout and Litchfield was a house of 1952-3 at Wisborough Green, Sussex, built by Bill and Gill Howell for a friend of Bill's mother, Mrs M. Trestrail. It was a small, rectangular bungalow of brick, concrete blocks and timber, with a store linked by a covered way, which in its honest expression of its materials and chunky detailing anticipated the terrace of houses by the Howells with Stanley Amis for themselves and friends in Hampstead. The Howells explained that for economy they 'decided to make a virtue of necessity, and make the house an essay in these materials in their own right. It seems to us that the bulk of post-war house-building, though using this range of materials, has failed to make much of them – certainly in the interiors.'[4] There were full-height windows to the principal living space, internal partitions of timber and glass, and timber ceilings. For Stout it inspired details such as the windows cut down from the clerestory and the small projecting buttresses between them. The Hampstead houses, their homespun brutalism tempered by their tiny scale, were to be influential on another architect who served time at the LCC, Peter Aldington, whose career ran roughly parallel to those of Stout and Litchfield and whose houses similarly captured the spirit of their romantic settings.

Despite considering their design and materials very carefully for the house at Shipton, Stout and Litchfield's initial scheme was turned down as 'aesthetically unsuitable' because of its unusual plan.[5] On appeal, a public enquiry was held at Chipping Norton, described by Litchfield as 'a thunderstorm'. Nikolaus Pevsner spoke on their behalf, declaring that their model was 'absolutely charming' despite admitting that he 'liked flat roofs', while Richard Sheppard, Hugh Casson and Eric Lyons all wrote letters of support. It was agreed that the house could be built, but only after a long delay.

Stout and Litchfield separated the various elements of their building into a series of linked units rather than create a formal villa. Each was set at an angle and each element was itself wedge-shaped, the difference between the diverging angles of the walls made up in an extra curve to part of the roof. They had noticed this feature in groups of local farm buildings, where the roofs varied because of the introduction of acute and obtuse angles. The individual elements of the Shipton house were broken down into six separately defined units with low links, the largest being the kitchen and dining area across the north side of the group. Their layout emphasises the pointed end walls of rough local stone, 1'4" thick (hefty for the time), particularly those of the three bedroom units of identical size and plan arranged like the leaves of a fan to the east. Shipton was one of the first buildings to be photographed by Richard Einzig, after he also left the LCC to pursue an independent career, and the house's striking images proved extremely popular with architectural magazines. Grundy also had connections to the film world, which is how the exterior came to be used in *A Clockwork Orange*. Part of the interest was its shock value at a time when most modern houses had flat roofs and big windows – the angles of the Shipton house make the areas of stone walling most prominent in photographs, particularly before some additional windows were cut into them.[6]

To the west is a sitting room, and a covered loggia leads to stores, a pavilion and a loggia that enclose a courtyard. The roofing is of Cotswold stone slates. Most of the furniture was built-in, much of it like the dining table and bench seating, worktops and the living room sofa supported on blocks of concrete faced in quarry tiles, which also line the floors.

Grundy also wanted a garden. Stout and Litchfield wanted the low-lying house to be surrounded by a lake or pond and suggested John Brookes, perhaps the most noted plantsman and designer of gardens for private houses at this time, who worked at some of their later houses. But Grundy then visited Kyoto with the artist Viacheslav Atroshenko, and they were inspired to create a Japanese garden; much of the design was by Atroshenko, who painted a mural along the western wall in 1971, but Grundy also employed a Japanese designer, a Mr Kasamoto, and the garden is a careful balance of Japanese ideas and plants below an existing canopy of mature firs, cedars, oaks and a large horse chestnut. The house appears to grow out of a pool, and is reached across steppingstones over gravel to the entrance, with to the rear a raked gravel garden inspired by the Ryoan-Ji temple at Kyoto; beyond the bedroom wings are mosses and a stream.

One scheme that never materialised for Stout and Litchfield was for St Cross College, Oxford, where W. E. (Kits) van Heyningen, father of the architect Joanna van Heyningen, was the first principal. It was their largest project, commissioned in 1966 and designed through most of 1967, and included a dining hall, seminar rooms, library and common rooms, together with a computer centre that reflected van Heyningen's special interest in this area, arranged in a series of quadrangles within a perimeter wall of residential accommodation.[7] It was to have been a facetted composition with elongated conoid rooflights like those of Roehampton Library; otherwise the design somewhat resembled HKPA's later work in brick at Darwin and Sidney Sussex colleges in Cambridge; it was only finally abandoned in the late 1970s when Stout and Litchfield learned that van Heyningen was retiring.

Meanwhile Stout and Litchfield established a reputation for town house conversions, beginning in Aldeney Street, Pimlico. This was the bread and butter of the practice, a succession of renovations in the Pimlico area undertaken as the leases fell in; Stout estimated that they must have realised some twenty of these schemes, and in 1972 *Building Design* described them as 'the Kings of the conversion business'.[8] Stout and Litchfield's own house on the corner of Winchester and Clarendon streets is the best known of these jobs today. The scheme was devised in about 1969 and they moved in in 1970, Litchfield occupying the basement, where the surrounding area – with its arcaded walls supporting the roadway above – became a tiny garden, while Stout with his wife and four children took the first, second and third floors.[9] The office was for many years in part of Litchfield's flat on the ground floor and was thus deliberately small, with a staff of no more than six. Assistants in the 1970s included Lloyd Stratton, a Cornish student who stayed with them for most of the decade before joining the Architects' Co-Partnership, and David Burn.

There were also more private houses. First was one at Bishop's Stortford for Stout's uncle, in the garden of his former house, which also had a slightly broken plan. It was followed by Pyramids at South Harting in West Sussex, built in 1965 for a parliamentary secretary and keen gardener, Gillian Jacomb-Hood. Her brief was for a weekend house that maximised natural light and views of the South Downs, and which again sought separate guest accommodation, this time with its own kitchenette as well as a bathroom. The house had also to accommodate her antique furniture, of which the most problematic was a tall grandfather clock. The plan is again a series of linked pavilions, but this time they are square, with wedges limited to the lower spaces that link the principal rooms to a central living room treated like an internal courtyard set at an angle to the rest, which are skewed towards the view. Each pavilion, including that for the double garage (now converted to another living room), has an open pyramidal roof, clad in cedar shingles externally and boarded in Columbian pine internally, supported on a series of concrete ring beams that form lintels to the large windows set within walls of white bricks from nearby Midhurst. The tallest pyramid serving the living room appears like a mother hen nursing the huddled group of roofs when seen from afar. Again Stout and Litchfield also designed the built-in furniture, mainly cupboards and wardrobes.[10] The total cost was £10,000.

Figure 4. The Shipton house in its Japanese setting (see also cover) (Historic England, James O. Davies)

Figure 5. The kitchen/dining room at Shipton-under-Wychwood (Historic England, James O. Davies)

Stout and Litchfield also brought their segmental style to London and its suburbs. First, in 1966, was a house in Worcester Park for the Nolan family who had previously lived at Connell, Ward and Lucas's The Firs, built in 1935 at Reigate in Surrey as four bedsits. The Nolans had occupied this unusual property as a single house, a curious arrangement that had led the parents and their guests to sleep in rooms above those of the children, with the dining room and kitchen on the children's level. This so suited them, at a time when the separation of adult and children's spaces was becoming fashionable, that it was repeated in the new house, which comprises four two-storey monopitch wedges set in pairs and linked by a glazed stairwell. Construction is of white sand-lime bricks, which became a popular material with the practice; though cheaper than Midhurst stocks, Stout thought they 'looked well' if pointed with white mortar; the roofs were this time of slate, though again with pine boarding inside.[11] The house was built on a shoestring, costing under £9000.

Stout and Litchfield's next London house, in Kingstown Street near Primrose Hill, was a modern interpretation of a mews house, built behind a villa in Regent's Park Road for Lukas and Caroline Heller. Mrs Heller was the daughter of Edward Carter, librarian of the RIBA and later of UNESCO, so had grown up surrounded by modern architecture in Paris. The scheme, designed in 1967 and realised the next year, was for two garages with a self-contained flat for Mr Heller's arthritic mother on top and accommodation for a nurse or housekeeper behind. The Hellers asked that it should be designed so it could also make a viable modern-day mews house for letting. A separate loggia and sauna screened it from their own house. The specification was higher than for Worcester Park, using the London stock and slate roofs common in mews buildings. However, all the corners are rounded, rather like HKPA's houses for visiting mathematicians at the University of Warwick, built in 1968-70. Stout and Litchfield's last job, in 1990-1, was to add an extension on Kingstown Street for a new owner, Robert Seward.[12] They also used similarly chamfered units in white Midhurst brick in a scheme of old people's flats designed in 1967 for the Greater London Council in Atkins Road, Clapham Park. Completed in 1972 with David Burn as the principal assistant, each unit was carefully defined. The regular pattern of three-storey flats, all orientated north-south to meet the council's specifications, was interrupted by a single-storey clubroom containing small halls that can be linked together, a little piece of Shipton dropped into urban London. Despite the six monopitch roofs that give a village-like feel to the clubroom, the overall regular plan is more formal and the cranked corners and curves, making full-height ribs like a minimal order on the elevations, again resemble HKPA's educational work of this period.[13]

Kingstown Street was followed in 1970-1 by a house in Bishopswood Road, Highgate, for the architectural historian Paul Oliver, then just becoming interested in vernacular architecture. Stout and Litchfield described it as 'two Shipton pavilions set back to back with the central brick wall taken out', so that it resembles a rectangle that has been cut in half on a skew with one part then slid along this fault line. At roof level, two rising ridges form a cross, one facing one way and one the other, and this division across the centre of the house also occurs in plan and section. There is a narrow frontage, and the principal rooms are on the upper floors. Oliver and his wife Valerie had no children, which determined their brief for an interflowing space between the kitchen, dining, living and office areas, each a half level above the last with the living room and office topped by open, boarded roofs. The white Midhurst bricks and high roof ridges stand out defiantly in their largely Victorian setting, giving the building an impact despite its small scale and later alterations that have seen the addition of a second garage and new glazing.[14]

Anthony Pretor Pinney appeared in the office unannounced in around 1967 carrying photographs cut from an article on Italian hill towns, an interest that had led him to be recommended to the practice. His family had bought the manorial estate of

Figure 6. Pyramids,
South Harting, 1965
(author)

Somerton Randall or Randle in Somerset in the 1780s, and erected a neo-classical house, but when they extended their estates in the early nineteenth century they had adopted an older manorial name for their property, Somerton Erleigh. Pretor Pinney sold Somerton Randle in 1962 but kept the name of Somerton Erleigh for its replacement. He wanted a 'modest house that would fit in with the rural scene', but thought that a courtyard plan would suggest continuity with the remains of a Roman villa on his estate.[15] The scheme had a long gestation; although it was designed in the late 1960s it was then put on the back burner and realised only in 1972-3.

The new Somerton Erleigh is a synthesis of ideas developed at Shipton-under-Wychwood and the Olivers' house, in that it consists of 'back to back pavilions' that create triangular clerestories at their junctions and make the most of good views to the north and east. A magnificent beech tree determined its precise location on the open hillside, with long grass sweeping right up to the house at the request of the planners that it should sit lightly in its setting. The main structure is of concrete block, but the outer walls are clad in reclaimed local blue lias stone, whose thin shards enhance the building's broken profile; the shapes of the small, high gables and narrow flues reflect the client's interest in hill towns. Kitchen, living, bedroom and children's areas each occupy one side of the courtyard, the major spaces opening into it from sliding doors off a continuous circulation area defined by a timber arcade that resembles a cloister. The main living room was large enough for Pretor Pinney's surviving family portraits and old furniture. Outside, a separate entrance serves a small estate office.

Stout and Litchfield also prepared several unbuilt designs for Peter Gresswell, an exceptionally sympathetic developer and author of *Houses in the Country* for Batsford in 1964 and *Environment: An Alphabetical Handbook* published by John Murray in 1971; he was responsible for persuading the Electricity Board to put underground all the wires in his own village of Stanton St John for European Architectural Heritage Year. Their schemes included four houses at Charlwood and a proposal in 1971 at Milborne Port, on the Dorset-Somerset border near Sherborne, for a compact group of 18-20 houses at the centre of the village with monopitch or asymmetrical roofs. These schemes were contemporary with Somerton Erleigh, so that work in the southwest dominated the office for a time.

One more white brick house was built in the London suburbs, Lake House on
Coombe Hill near Kingston-upon-Thames. The clients, Guy and Monica Libby, knew
Gillian Jacomb-Hood, for Monica Libby was a parliamentary secretary like her and Guy
was her stockbroker. They visited Pyramids, and although Guy Libby had little interest in
architecture himself he appreciated the house's qualities. Lake House was designed in
1973-4, in a lengthy process during which the accommodation was enlarged and outdoor
terraces reduced; it was not completed until 1976. The setting is unusually picturesque,
for although it is a tight plot cut from an early twentieth-century house, Kingfishers,
it adjoins an artificial lake that is all that survives of Coombe Court, the model for John
Galsworthy's 'Robin Hill', the fictional house in *The Man of Property*, the first of the
Forsyte novels (Galsworthy's father was a property developer in the area). The Midhurst
brick stands out in a suburban London context, but the dominating feature is the series
of slate roofs designed as a series of square hips. Their deep eaves are a development
from their earlier houses, an English detail in a house that otherwise again nods to
Mediterranean imagery and where the abstracted shapes of Somerton Erleigh are still
recognisable. There were lots of trees, some of which survive, and the house had to be
wriggled between them, but the architects forsook their usual odd angles to produce a
series of rectangles of different shapes and heights huddled against that of the double-
height living room. A stair within this space serves two bedrooms on the tiny upper floor
inserted between the other roofs; otherwise the accommodation is on a single floor,
though with steps within the house. Martin Richardson wrote of this being 'an exuberant
house, almost baroque in its sculptured pleasures'.[16]

Figure 10. Lake House,
Coombe Hill, 1973-6
(author)

Stout and Litchfield also extended a house at Staplefields, West Sussex called Whitehouse Cottage, making additions in red brick and white-painted weatherboarding that included a large living room and gallery at one end and a study, bedroom, bathroom and a conservatory added at different times to the other. In the early 1980s there was also a new little house in West Sussex that was almost self-built by its penurious owner, Easterney Smith, who appeared on Stout and Litchfield's doorstep clutching the *House and Garden* feature on Somerton Erleigh, which he had held on to during years in the Royal Navy.

From the mid-1970s and throughout the 1980s, Stout and Litchfield were preoccupied by housing for local authorities and housing associations. This they combined with teaching at Thames Polytechnic, now the University of Greenwich, 'a less dedicated lot than the students at the AA', they recalled. The late 1970s saw them building for the London Borough of Lambeth at Myatt's Fields, a two-storey scheme of 82 units that included 43 sheltered flats and a club room for elderly people, The Cloisters, where Stout and Litchfield were assisted by David Burn, Martin Hunt and Lloyd Stratton. Tucked into a backland site on a new road, Melbourne Mews, the development used London stock brick at the insistence of Lambeth's director of development, Ted Hollamby.

Much of their later work was concentrated on the Isle of Dogs. In 1969 Michael and Jenny Barraclough, he a doctor, she a television producer, were living on Narrow Street in Limehouse when they spotted a site available directly across the river from Greenwich Hospital. They then met Roy Stout at a party on New Year's Eve 1969-70. The original intention was that Barraclough would make a development agreement for the whole site, which included the use of Stout and Litchfield as architects, then sell the 16'6" wide plots for private houses. He began this, and although the local authority limited this private development to one acre there could have been up to twenty plots, but it proved extremely difficult to find a developer in the years before the Docklands Development Corporation. Eventually Stanley Bragg of Colchester stepped in. An agreement was made whereby Stout and Litchfield would design flats and Bragg would build them, until the market collapsed in 1973-4. Most of the site was finally developed as flats and maisonettes by Levitt Bernstein for Circle 33 Housing Trust in 1979-83, leaving Stout and Litchfield to design a terrace of just four houses for Dr Barraclough, who was

Figure II. Dr Barraclough's Houses, Isle of Dogs, 1975-9 (author)

interested in building and acted as his own contracts manager. Building began with his own house in 1975 and those for his clients followed; they are constructed of white flint lime bricks (which do not stay as clean as true Midhurst bricks) but again there are criss-cross monopitch roofs of Westmorland slate, here incorporating clerestory glazing. The terraced houses were built directly off the river wall, physically as well as visually; their stepped elevations have tiers of balconies and the upper floors are set within the roofs.[17] Thus the simple pavilion form that began in the Cotswolds evolved into a London terrace. Another happy outcome for Stout and Litchfield was that they got paid twice: once for the Bragg scheme and again for that part eventually built.

Unlike the Barraclough houses, the scheme nearby at Maconochie's Wharf was a scheme of self-built housing, initiated by Dr Barraclough and Jill Palios. It claimed to be the largest single self-built development in the United Kingdom, comprising 89 homes constructed in three phases between 1985 and 1990 to designs largely by Roy Stout. He faced a very disparate group of would-be homeowners, ranging from dockers to newspaper people, for whom he had to produce an overall design but with variations that allowed individual expression. All wanted a house rather than a flat. Their number comprised, however, an unusually large proportion of building tradesmen, so that conventional brick construction was preferred to a prefabricated or timber solution such as that developed by Walter Segal for less-experienced self-builders. Stout described his role as 'being parental', treating each builder as an individual client. The scheme evolved from an early horseshoe arrangement, which would have given each house a view of the river somewhat like the initial Barraclough scheme, into simpler terraces that maximised the available land. Though lacking the obvious details found in the Barraclough houses, there are still typical Stout and Litchfield features; that there were not more was due to the need for simplicity and the demands of the London Docklands Development Corporation.

The stepped roof profile was simplified into gables of various sizes, with balconies or bay windows offering variety round the scheme, save where the LDDC insisted that the terraces facing the river have a uniform design – indicative of the returning formality of planning in the 1980s. Stout again selected white sand-lime brick, which was successfully used on the first houses, but the LDDC required that London stocks be used for the phases facing West Ferry Road and adjoining the historic site of Burrell's Wharf.[18]

Figure 12. Maconochie's Wharf, Isle of Dogs, 1985-90 (author)

Stout and Litchfield evolved their distinctive style with remarkable consistency and logic over some twenty years in a series of houses of all sizes and set in both very rural and intensely urban locations. The descent of the Kingston house in the late 1970s from that at Shipton is evident, while both respond very carefully to their contrasting settings. Characteristics of Stout and Litchfield's style include the articulation of rooms as visibly separate volumes and their arrangement round a central main living space, while the use of a rogue angle in plan leads to variations in the proportions of the roof (usually left exposed below). There is a strong three-dimensional geometry combined with the use of natural – and in their best work very local – materials.

Stout and Litchfield assembled an exhibition in January-February 1984 for the Warwick Arts Trust in Pimlico, *Continuity in Architecture*, a title that perfectly sums up their own work. It also looked at the humane modernism of Edward Cullinan, Richard MacCormac and others who similarly featured broken massing and rooflines as well as natural materials in their work. The show, which later toured to Bristol's Arnolfini Gallery and elsewhere, highlighted modern buildings that respected the scale and materials of their setting, their style evolving out of an understanding of local traditions without resorting to pastiche.[19] A debate led by Peter Davey and Gillian Darley discussed the exhibition in terms of 'Romantic Pragmatism' to which they had dedicated an issue of *Architectural Review* the previous year, highlighting the 'unmapped area' between structural rationalism and neo-vernacular where much of the best architecture of the period lay and commending the work of Cullinan, MacCormac, Robert Maguire, Peter Aldington (by then Aldington, Craig & Collinge), Ralph Erskine, and even Philip Dowson.[20] All produced work that is expressive of its structure, using traditional materials in a modern way, with a great sensitivity to the needs of their clients. Stout and Litchfield, so much less heralded, belong firmly in this genre too, and the house at Shipton can be admired as one of its begetters.

Acknowledgements:
I would like to thank
Roy Stout and the
late Patrick Litchfield,
Milton Grundy, David
and Suzanne Burn,
James O. Davies,
Ignacio Martos,
Stephanie Morgan,
Mr and Mrs Pretor
Penny and Adam Stout

1. Roy Stout and Patrick Litchfield in conversation, at Patrick Litchfield's flat in Clarendon Street, 9 October 2001. Stout presented a copy of the interview to the RIBA British Architectural Library, where it is lodged in the biography file for Stout and Litchfield.

2. Mark Goldie, *Corbusier Comes to Cambridge, Post-War Architecture and the Competition to build Churchill College*, Cambridge, Churchill College, revised edition 2012.

3. Hilary Gelson, 'Partners in Design', *The Times*, no.58219, 8 July 1971, p.10.

4. 'Single-Storey Cottage in Sussex', *Architectural Design*, vol.25, no.6, June 1955, pp.194-7; *House and Garden*, vol.10, no.6 (78), June 1955, pp.52-3.

5. 'Pavilion House and Japanese Gardens', Richard Einzig, *Classic Modern Houses in Europe*, London, Architectural Press, 1981, p.140.

6. *Architectural Review*, vol.137, no.816, February 1965, pp.144-6; *House and Garden*, vol.22, no.3 (217), March 1967, pp.52-4; Penelope Whiting, *New Single-Storey Houses*, London, Architectural Press, 1966, pp.26-32.

7. *The Times*, op.cit; information from Simon van Heyningen.

8. *Building Design*, no.126, 10 November 1972, p.18, in a review of Joyce Lowrie's *Town House Conversions*.

9. 'How Two Architects got Two Homes out of One Run Down Mansion', *House and Garden*, vol.27, no.4 (269), May 1972, pp.90-3.

10. Whiting, *op.cit.*, pp.33-7; *Architect and Building News*, vol.231, no.2, 11 January 1967, pp.65-6; Robert Harling, ed., *The House and Garden Book of Holiday and Weekend Houses*, Condé Nast, 1968, pp.16-19.

11. 'Surrey Suburban', *Architectural Review*, vol.144, no.858, August 1968, p.108.

12. *Architectural Review*, ibid., pp.87-9; LB Camden Planning Applications on-line searches, 60 Regent's Park Road (3063); 47 Kingstown Street (9003411).

13. *Architectural Review*, vol.153, no.913, March 1973, pp.201-4.

14. *Architectural Review*, vol.150, no.894, August 1971, pp.84-6; *House and Garden*, vol.26, no.9 (264), November 1971, pp.87-9.

15. *Architectural Review*, vol.158, no.941, July 1975, pp.27-40; *House and Garden*, vol.30, no.8 (303), October 1975, pp.109-11; *A+U*, no.82, September 1977, pp.123-5.

16. Martin Richardson, 'Four Houses', *Architectural Review*, vol.162, no.966, August 1977, pp.84-6; *A+U*, no.9 (96), September 1978, pp.127-32.

17. Maurice Cooper, 'On the Waterfront', *Building Design*, no.470, 2 November 1979, pp.20-1.

18. 'Homes of their Own', *Architects' Journal*, vol.190, no.16, 18 October 1989, pp.50-65.

19. *Concrete Quarterly*, no.140, January- March 1984, pp.15-22.

20. Gillian Darley and Peter Davey, 'Sense and Sensibility', *Architectural Review*, vol.174, no.1039, pp.23-5.

Rachel Williams

12 Brothers in Arts: Tim and Bob Organ, Artist Constructor

Artist Constructor was a design-and-build company working in south-west England founded in 1968-9 by Tim Organ. Tim had a background in construction management, having joined the Bristol-based building firm John Knox ten years previously. He had found the disjointed nature of the industry frustrating, however, and he and his colleague John Pontin had used their combined Christmas bonuses to form a new company, JT (John-Tim) Construction, in 1960 with Tim's bedroom as a makeshift office. They pursued an integrated approach to building, undertaking both the design of the structures and their construction, and operated under a socialist ethos with profit sharing and sick-pay schemes. Their approach proved efficient and expedient; the company grew quickly, doubling its turnover in each of its first few years of operation. Despite this great success, the predominantly functional storage or industrial buildings that came to JT allowed little scope for Tim's interest in design. Thus in 1969, with a sharpened pencil and focussed eye, and an intention to create buildings where good design and artistic value were of equal importance to function, Tim left to concentrate on a new venture with his brother.

Tim's brother Bob Organ (b.1933) was a painter trained at the Slade School, who had spent the 1960s living in Flushing and teaching at Falmouth School of Art. When he resigned in 1970 and transformed himself into an architectural designer, it was not such a stark switch as it might sound, for Bob had harboured this interest for many years, fostered in part by Tim, with whom he had visited Finland in the mid-1960s to admire the new housing being produced by architects such as Alvar Aalto. Although neither Tim nor Bob were formally trained in architecture, a talent for design was an evident family trait, which combined with Tim's astute business sense and practical abilities proved a successful mix. The company offices they designed for Artist Constructor at Wrington, North Somerset (demolished), typified both their style and Tim's forethought: the land was bought with permission for housing, and the intention was that the offices could be converted later. Bob preferred to work from home, at a distance from the mechanics of the business and the construction process, waiting until completion to see the end result. He continued to teach regularly throughout the 1970s at the Architectural Association and the architecture department at Bristol University, and occasionally lectured to the Royal Institute of British Architects and the Society for the Preservation of Ancient Buildings, always on the subject of aesthetics, while also displaying a passionate interest in architectural conservation.

Owing perhaps to his lack of formal training, Tim was a great believer in the exchange of ideas outside one's specialism, valuing contributions from all staff members equally. For practical purposes, the young, often newly-qualified architects recruited to the practice acted as interpreters of Bob's drawings of sculptural forms and masses, translating artistic visions into working drawings and specifications. Among these assistants were Jeremy Gould, Colin Harvey and Niall Phillips, who enthused over Bob's astonishing ability to conjure and depict three-dimensional spaces with no reference to plans, and to produce beautifully sensitive and illustrative representations from his imagination. They recalled halcyon days spent working with Bob in his house in Chard, eating and drinking, talking and laughing, enjoying varying levels of productivity. Gould worked with the firm early in his career, in 1974-5, and valued the practical, hands-on experience that the building aspect of the firm offered. The company philosophy was based on a firm commitment to the artistic vision, demonstrated by the firm's inability to compromise on their designs. As a result, frequent battles were fought with local authority planning departments, resulting in expensive delays and poor relationships.

Controlling both the design and construction of projects meant a greater flexibility in specifications and site work than the conventional division between the two, while better communication and quicker reactions led to a general increase in efficiency. It was this that allowed Tim to offer competitive prices and to take on a multitude of projects. Colin Harvey, later cofounder of the Bristol based conservation-architects

Figure 2. No. I Post Office Lane, Flax Bourton, 1972-4 (John East)

Architecton, briefly worked at Artist Constructor in 1972 and described it as design and build at its rawest. Details could be drawn up in the morning to be built in the afternoon. Niall Phillips, who undertook work experience at the firm, describes the construction side as somewhat secondary to design, which was the principal concern. It was only through this exceptional interpretation of 'design and build', usually a byword for mediocrity, that such extraordinary buildings could be executed within the limits of Somerset builders' technology in the 1970s. Tim's salesmanship and industriousness meant the offices were continually busy, with commissioned projects and speculative developments. Alongside the more creative projects that are the subject of this study, there was a background of more everyday work, adapting and extending existing buildings, and restoring and renovating historic structures.

Building and landscape

Designing the building to suit the plot, the locality and the landscape was of paramount importance. While certain features and motifs recur, the composition of each building was specific to its site and intended to complement and enhance it. Bob spent a long time at the prospective building sites, carefully considering the topography, flora and wider landscape, which were to be directly influential on the positioning, form and design of the houses. At Flax Bourton, a small village in north Somerset, five houses were built as a speculation between 1972 and 1974. The site was a former orchard, and the houses were designed with long narrow ranges to retain long avenues of espalier apple trees and benefit from their cast shadows. Bob believed in looking and drawing not once but twice, seeing this as the only way a site could be fully understood and an appropriate

Figure 3. New Place,
Ubley, 1970,
front elevation
(Historic England,
James O. Davies)

Figure 4. Victual's
Grove, St Briavels, 1969
(John East)

building be designed for it. From a wheat field on the edge of the village of Flax Bourton, one sees the sculptural white forms peeking out over walls and trees, a union between building and place achieved not through the imitation of natural form but through contrast. Angular masses with strong vertical emphases are joined by long and low horizontals, the antithesis of the natural surroundings yet beautifully harmonious with them.

The vistas from buildings were an equal consideration, putting the house and its landscape in a reciprocal relationship. At Oakhill in the Mendips is Somerfosse, a single house built in c.1973 that nestles, sheltered and protected, below a steeply rising rock face and enjoying views south across a valley. The same is true for Victual's Grove near St Briavels in the Forest of Dean, 1969, where the single house originally enjoyed views from the full-height living-room windows down and across the Wye Valley, although the outlook is now densely wooded.

Community and Privacy

Serge Chermayeff and Christopher Alexander's book, *Community and Privacy*, 1964, with its concern for the distinction between the public and private realms, adequate provision of privacy between neighbours and within the home, was an influence on the planning of interiors and the layout of groups of houses.

The development of four houses at Ubley, north Somerset, was the first of Artist Constructor's speculative ventures, dating from 1970. The plot had been occupied by piggeries, and it was bought from the retired pig-keeper Emmy Fears on the condition that they built her a house. She was very pleased with the resultant dwelling, one of four on the site, though she would have preferred an outward-facing kitchen in order to observe the comings and goings of the locals – a suggestion that was duly considered in later buildings. A deep bank provides a buffer for the houses from the main road, with a communal driveway providing access, a semi-private area without formal divisions that encourages informal interaction and a useful level of surveillance between the neighbours. The front elevations are a host of white rendered jagged planes and angles, with fenestration limited to small punctured squares or rows of slit windows. Monopitch roofs generally slope towards the rears of the houses, but an occasional frontward-facing pitch, covered in terracotta pantiles, gives depth and interest. Intriguing, high-walled white alleyways lead to the private back gardens between the houses. The influence of Peter Aldington's group of houses at Turn End in Buckinghamshire (1964-8) is apparent in the use of pantiles, monopitches, weatherboarding and white walls. The development was undertaken in collaboration with Peter Smith and Associates, and Tim recalls the interest the development aroused at the time, with locals dubbing it the Arab Quarter. Incidentally, Artist Constructor was invited in 1971 by Aldington and Craig to collaborate as builders for an abortive housing scheme at Iwerne Minster, Dorset.

The five houses at Flax Bourton are similar to the Ubley scheme, with their semi-private approach, this time into a cul-de-sac, on which the houses are sited on generous plots. Their public-facing elevations are almost fortress-like, with towering vertical planes, recessed openings and spy-windows, in complete contrast to the private, garden elevations with their floor-to-ceiling glass.

Another group of three houses was built in the garden of a former vicarage at Backwell, north Somerset, in 1972. Here the separation from the public domain is handled rather differently, and instead of the façades towering they are sunken in response to their slightly awkwardly position below road level. The effect, however, is the same – from the road side you must pass down steep stairs to reach the ground level and it is this drop that creates the physical and psychological barrier between public and private spaces. The houses, which are largely single-storied, are formed from a system of octagonal cells connected by top-lit corridors. Passers-by look down on an intriguing network of geometric roofs but the houses retain their privacy with limited

**Figure 5. (previous page)
New Place, Ubley,
rear elevation
(Historic England,
James O. Davies)**

**Figure 6. No 5 Post
Office Lane, Flax
Bourton, rear elevation
(Historic England,
James O. Davies)**

areas of window. Their position on the side of the hill provides views towards the west, so that advancing rain clouds from the Severn Estuary can be spotted well in time to get the washing in.

At Somerfosse and Victual's Grove, the stand-alone houses in private plots avoid overlooking from neighbours, but even at the more secluded Victual's Grove, the elevations facing onto the driveway have only narrow slit windows from the bedroom range, while a small square peep-hole looks directly out onto the front door from the dining room. As a functional and utilitarian space, the kitchen receives different treatment with a kitchen window above the sink overlooking the driveway.

With the groups of houses, care is taken to ensure that it is impossible to see into any house from another, and the outdoor sitting spaces are similarly protected. At Ubley the houses stand tightly together, so much so that one could mistake them for a single building. They have a common plan form in the shape of a shallow V, each tightly interlinking with its neighbours though retaining privacy in the gardens to the rear by providing enclosure in the cup of the V. At Flax Bourton the plots are larger and much further apart. The houses are taller, but views into each other's gardens were avoided by utilising the natural screening offered by the existing apple trees, in addition to the well-considered positioning of windows to the upper floors.

Functional zoning, or the creation of distinct areas for different functions and uses, in the internal layout is apparent in all of the houses. Buffer zones were inserted between private living and sleeping spaces and communal spaces, adult and child domains were clearly defined and separated, utilitarian spaces were removed from areas for leisure, and rooms used for office working were removed entirely, at Ubley occupying a separate 'pod' in the garden.

The houses at Ubley, Victual's Grove and Somerfosse share a loose linear plan form, with separate wings dedicated to occupation by day and night. Functional and utilitarian

Figure 7a and b.
Bob's sketches for the
scheme at Backwell, 1972
(Tim Organ's
personal archive)

rooms at the junction between these zones provide an acoustic buffer between private and communal rooms. At Ubley the communal living spaces occupy a single storey situated on the east, exploiting the southwest aspect, with a single or double storey of bedrooms to the west. Again, utility and service rooms are positioned centrally, separated and to the north, and often lead to walled gardens or courtyards, covered walkways and annexed offices and garages. There is frequently a garden room to the far west, with external access only. At Flax Bourton the plan radiates outwards and upwards from a central entrance hall and stairway. There is a strong feeling of openness to the communal areas and rooms, with flexible routes for circulation provided by multiple entrances between rooms. By contrast, the master bedrooms are reached by a dedicated staircase, providing an unambiguously private area. Private bathrooms and balconies lead off the bedrooms, with skylights giving views out when in bed or bath. Victual's Grove comprises a single storey which changes level with the slope of the land. The front entrance leads into a large foyer from which the utility and service rooms are accessed; bedrooms are in a wing up a short set of stairs on one side, and communal rooms are set down in the other. Like Flax Bourton, circulation routes through the communal rooms are flexible; the living room can be entered from either side of the dining room, providing a complete route without doors around the hearth at the heart of the house.

The connection between interior and exterior spaces is maximised and efforts are made to bring the outside in by minimising solid divisions and creating multiple points of access; at Victual's Grove, for instance, every bedroom has a door out to the garden, a 'rule' laid down by Chermayeff in order that children need not interfere with the adult and family domains. The large glazed windows to the garden elevations make the garden an integral part of the houses, and at Ubley and Somerfosse the V-shaped plan form and linear arrangement of the rooms mean that the gardens are embraced. At Ubley deep awnings were provided to offer shelter, though many of these have been glazed in to add to the internal accommodation. These are largely single-aspect houses with south-facing principal elevations, and as the sun moves across the sky so different parts of the houses come to life.

A striking characteristic of the interiors is how very light and airy they are – the positioning of subtle strip windows at ceiling height, the huge swathes of glass on rear elevations, and the presence of picture windows and puncture holes encourage light penetration from all sorts of unexpected angles. On entering the houses at Ubley one is struck by the very lofty living area, and the external monopitch is expressed within, with exposed beams so the skeleton of the structure boldly displayed.

Geometric Formations
A theme evident in many Artist Constructor houses is that of modular formation. The octagon and the 45-degree angle recur in the plan forms of the houses, creating interiors of similar character yet differing in their ordering, orientation and scale. The houses at Backwell are a clear example of this; they are planned on a system of octagonal cells, interlinked or adjoined by top-lit connecting corridors. The central one of the group of three, Folleigh, is the least altered and retains its original plan form. One enters through a gap beneath an octagonal tower, stacked between another two octagons like children's building blocks – though far more sophisticated. Geometric concrete shapes and glass make up the roofs of the adjoining corridors, creating both light spaces and contrasts filled with ever-changing blocks of shadow. The octagonal rooms take their light from ceiling level strips of window when overlooked, or full-height glazing when not. To maximise the light in the octagonal dining room the present owners have covered the walls in mirrored mosaic, a play on the geometry with reflection; it is a really fun room.

At Victual's Grove the kitchen is housed in an octagonal pod formed from pillars with a shallow pyramidal roof. Between the pillars glazing wraps vertically and skywards

to meet recessed panels beneath the roof, resulting in a wonderfully light room
throughout the day. In the centre is a rotating octagonal unit with cupboard space
beneath a hob and octagonal extractor hood overhead. An octagonal splay-footed
chimney hood hangs between the dining and living room, providing a two-way fireplace;
of bare concrete, it is a robust, angular and unashamedly brutalist form, proudly
celebrating its material and function with a well-matched shape that continues the
geometric theme. There is a scaled-down, single-hearthed version of the same fireplace at
the far end of the house. At Somerfosse a rectangular, bare, hanging concrete chimney
hood loosely divides the living and dining areas and provides a hearth on either side.

Made to Measure

Fittings within the houses were well adapted to the requirements of family living and
bespoke furnishings were sometimes made to order. The marketing material for Flax
Bourton states that the company would be happy to discuss variations that would enable
the houses to 'reflect the individual living patterns of the occupants'. Cupboards were
built-in as standard and were sometimes hidden within pillars and walls. At Victual's
Grove, a site which Tim acquired when he foresaw the potential for commuting to Bristol
following the opening of the Severn Bridge, his client, the head of a tool hire company,
was an avid collector of shirts and a wardrobe was built to hold 300!

Experiments were conducted with in-built speaker systems, and both under-floor
and air heating systems – that at Somerfosse continues to operate effectively. Interior
design was undertaken by request, and for one client even the cutlery was provided.
Many of the fittings were made up on site, an ad hoc approach that is remarkably
successful; simple door handles from timber blocks fulfil their function un-fussily and
effectively. Concrete shower trays were spoken about, but none has so far been traced.

The shirt-collector of Victual's Grove also wanted a swimming pool and the result
must have been phenomenal. A round building was erected to the rear of the house,
accessible directly from the patio to the master bedroom. There were full-height windows
looking down and across the beautifully forested Wye valley, and two pools of different
size and temperatures; all were enclosed beneath a glazed geodesic dome. This indulgent
playfulness is fascinating and endearing. Little of it now remains, but the reinstatement
of the pool is a far-off dream for the current owners.

Figure 10. Victual's
Grove, the living
room with hanging
chimney piece
(Historic England,
James O. Davies)

Style

The houses can be separated into two broad groups: those which are rendered
geometric masses, as at Flax Bourton, Backwell and Ubley, and buildings of bare and
exposed materials like Somerfosse and Victual's Grove. At Flax Bourton and Backwell
the emphasis is on the form of the buildings: both groups are sculptural compositions
in a landscape, and at Flax Bourton, particularly, this is the most striking element.
The buildings were originally painted in a palette of cold and warm pastel shades
carefully chosen by Bob and intended to complement each other as well as their
landscape. All are now white, and though not the designer's intention this new
uniformity of colour unites the group and places emphasis on form over surface.

The bare lignacite block elevations at Somerfosse and Victual's Grove have no
coatings or paint. After forty years the blocks have mellowed to an earthen colour with
blending golden lichens on sheltered elevations, contrasting with darkened metallic
weathered elevations. The pale grey exposed blocks provide the interior wall surfaces
and their coursing continues the geometric theme. Externally, Victual's Grove has a
castle-like quality and after a long approach through densely forested landscape,
encounter with this bare grey brute formed of substantial concrete-block with towers
and stacks resembling buttresses and crenellation, feels entirely appropriate. Timber
frames the windows and forms roof structures, although much has been replaced as
building material technology and expectations of thermal performance have
progressed.

Conflict

Battles for planning permission featured throughout the life of the company and
contributed to its demise. It was a conflict that the brothers played upon; in order to
teach his Architectural Association students about the planning process Bob had them
submit multiple applications for schemes for a plot of land the brothers owned in north
Somerset. One hopes the planning department understood the joke, though perhaps it
was not amused at having to process the numerous applications. Both brothers were
unafraid to gripe at the lack of formal education in design, architectural history, art or
aesthetics necessary to become a decision maker in the planning process. A delightfully
mischievous rebuttal from Bob when defending the Backwell scheme after the planner

questioned 'who builds octagons?' was to ask him to look up to the octagonal stair tower of the overlooking medieval church.

Shorland House is a block of flats in the affluent Clifton area of Bristol, and was the last project undertaken by the firm, completed in 1975. A battle with the planning authority delayed and upset the development to such an extent that the financial implications were beyond recovery. Although a sad end to the story, the building is a triumph thanks to the commitment to the design that the brothers fought for, and eventually secured. It is a four-storey building with an attic and basement car parking, with four flats to each floor. The symmetrical front and rear facades are strong compositions, with features that compliment the surrounding Victorian villas and the exposed concrete frame with ribs and chamfers is a progression from the Bath stone string courses and dressings of its older neighbours, with bows to the front and bays to the rear similarly deriving from the local vernacular. The brick infill of the frame was a major cause of conflict with the planners, who wanted a pinkish snecked stone cladding as a pastiche of the local Pennant limestone. This wholly inappropriate gesture was thankfully resisted. Although the block is much larger than its neighbours, it is neither overwhelming nor out of place, an effect achieved through appropriate proportions and massing in the design. A rhythm is created in the elevation through a rising and falling parapet and areas of solid and void. Flats at first floor level have balcony gardens on either side of the building and to the rear there is a communal garden with access from all floors via a central pre-cast concrete external stairwell, partially enclosed by matchboarding.

A 45-degree octagonal angle is prevalent; the front steps are bounded by low walls which zigzag in then out to meet the front door. The building has a passage on each floor providing a route between the front and rear, and access to each of the flats. Doors are angled at 45 degrees, and the rooms behind continue diagonally, much like a butterfly plan, contained within square walls. Internal panelled doors were scored and stained, continuing the geometric theme with dark trapeziums and chevrons. A communal stair rises at the front of the building in a canted bay; a pre-cast concrete dog-leg suspended slightly away from the stairwell walls and windows allows the circulation of air and penetration of light from the full height glazing. The windows are mullioned and transomed, and these divisions, combined with the diagonal angles of the stair and the banister, and the verticals and horizontals of the open string steps, create a strong geometric composition playing with light and shade.

The flats are spacious, and typically have built in cupboards, kitchens, audio and heating systems, not all of which have been modernised. Although it is the least altered of Artist Constructor's buildings, a testament to its fitness for purpose and functionality, Tim regrets that stronger covenants could not have been imposed to limit changes. To agonise over the details of a design, and to create a form which is such a considered and complete composition that is then extended and altered by subsequent owners is a torment for artist and constructor alike, a factor which eventually caused Bob to retreat to his first art form.

Conclusion

The spirit and vigour of the firm was at odds with the general climate of the 1970s, which was witnessing a crisis in the architectural profession. The *trente glorieuses* were coming to their end, the building boom of the 1960s had wound down, social housing was proving antisocial and money was running out. There is resonance with the present times of economic downturn, great inflation, an oil crisis and unjust war, and dreadful weather. Architecture, as the most visible of the arts, was seen as having the potential to make the world a better place; Artist Constructor embraced this, creating high-quality, progressive and exciting buildings in sleepy West Country villages.

The closure of the company in 1975 is not the end of the story. Tim soon began another: Form and Structure, and continued working in collaboration with Bob and

Within the image:
section of dining hall, with cloakrooms below.
elevation of staff room, which has a tiled or slated roof & coloured lime washed block walls
slate tiled roofs
clay tiled roofs, coloured lime washed block walls
west elevatio

Bristol children's help society
Barton camp, new buildings.

Robert Organ.
Form & Structure ltd.

Figure 12. Bob's drawing for Barton Children's Help Society, 1979 (Tim Organ's personal archive)

many of those involved with Artist Constructor. In the late 1970s he undertook some very interesting large-scale building projects, including a riding school for the disabled near Bristol and a children's activity camp at Barton, North Somerset, using unskilled labour and day-release prisoners, and creating training opportunities via the Manpower Services Commission. Tim now works alongside his son Sam in their company CO² Architects, a firm with a focus on sustainability and environmental considerations. These days Tim tends to leave dealings with planners to Sam. Architecton was formed in 1974 by Colin Harvey and Paul Richold, and continues to thrive; work was recently carried out on the Grade I listed Godolphin House in Cornwall, which links back to Bob's interest in conservation and his tutelage at the Architectural Association of John Schofield, the former architect owner of the house, with whom Bob formed the Cornish Buildings Group in 1969. Jeremy and Caroline Gould began their own private practice, and Niall Phillips is Head of Design with Purcell. JT Construction also went on to do interesting work, building Whichloe Macfarlane's High Kingsdown Estate, Bristol, completed in 1974. By the end of the 1970s Bob was sufficiently well-known for the RIBA to accept him as an architectural partner without recognised qualifications. Following the breakdown of Artist Constructor his disillusionment with the industry drove him back towards painting, where control was complete, though he continued design to an extent, working with Architecton and Form Structure. His son Tom inherited his father's interest in conservation, running his own company, Arte Conservation, and specialising in stone. An unexpected and coincidental encounter with Tom in a pub in Totterdown, when he overheard Jeremy Gould's name in conversation, was an example of the strange muddling of art and life.

The pursuit of excellence in terms of form and function is admirable; the idea that good design would make home life easier, cleaner, safer, and more enjoyable, and would allow more fun and comfortable living is such a marvellous ambition, and is achieved. The owners of the buildings have records of long tenure, and testify to the enjoyment gained from their homes.

There are only two useful articles on Artist Constructor: Douglas Frank, 'Houses and Conversions by Artist Constructor', *Architects' Journal*, vol.155, no.15, 12 April 1972, pp.762-6; Bob Organ, 'Desolation by Design', *The Listener*, no.2412, 26 June 1975, p.835